P9-ASE-653

POTATO

Also by John Reader

Pyramids of Life
Missing Links: The Hunt for Earliest Man
Kilimanjaro
The Rise of Life
Man on Earth
Mount Kenya
Africa: A Biography of the Continent
Cities

POTATO

A HISTORY OF THE PROPITIOUS ESCULENT

————

JOHN READER

Yale University Press
New Haven and London

Published 2009 in the United States by Yale University Press
Published 2008 in Great Britain by William Heinemann

Typeset in Bembo by Palimpsest Book Production Limited,
Grangemouth, Stirlingshire
Printed in the United States of America

Library of Congress Control Number: 2008937284
ISBN 978-0-300-14109-2 (hardcover: alk. paper)

A catalogue record for this book is available from the British Library.

This paper meets the requirements of ANSI/NISO z39.48-1992 (Permanence of
Paper). It contains 30 percent postconsumer waste (PCW) and is certified by
the Forest Stewardship Council (FSC).

10 9 8 7 6 5 4 3 2 1

For Brigitte

Contents

Introduction

I used to take potatoes for granted. My earliest memories of them are as an unassuming item of food that was plentiful enough to eat daily and might occasionally bulk up a meal whose major attraction was in short supply: no more, they'd say, you can fill up on potatoes.

A memorable schedule of consumption was established in childhood. Roast with the joint on Sundays; boiled with slices of cold meat on Mondays; mashed and baked as topping for the cottage pie (or shepherd's pie if Sunday's roast had been lamb or mutton, rather than beef) that finished off the joint on Wednesdays. Memory fails me as to what Thursday might have brought – boiled perhaps, with a couple of rashers and an egg – but Friday was definitely when potatoes were best served as chips alongside a nice piece of fried fish – fish and chips from the shop down the road, anointed at the counter with shakings of salt and malt vinegar and tastiest when eaten straight from the paper wrapping; the treat of the week, no cutlery, no plates (and no washing up). Saturday was frugal, so far as I recall; baked beans on toast, perhaps, or Welsh rarebit, as though to ensure there would be room for Sunday's blow-out.

Even an eighteen-month stay in Connemara in the early 1960s, on Ireland's western shores where potatoes were the staple crop, failed to raise their status in my estimation. I knew about the Irish potato famine of the 1840s, of course, but that was hardly commendation. I was mildly astonished at the quantity of boiled potatoes that a neighbour, Cornelius, could consume at a single sitting, but concluded that was a matter of economy not choice, and when another neighbour, John Coyne, told me that a man could live for ever on potatoes and nothing else I attributed his opinion to ignorance. Everyone knew that potatoes were unhealthy and fattening – and John was a little on the plump side.

Every Connemara household I knew planted a field of potatoes in 1964, but when I returned in 2004 it was only those who really enjoyed gardening that bothered – and they were few. The rest bought such potatoes as they needed from the supermarket and grew flowers and salad, or kept bees (some even had lawns), where previous generations had devoted so much time and energy to growing potatoes. The changes were striking, and clearly driven by economic factors. Connemara was much better off – thirty years of benefits from the European Union had raised living standards throughout Ireland, but most especially in previously impoverished rural areas. People had money to spend, and although fresh potatoes might feature in their weekly shop, a taste for the processed form was evident too – crisps, frozen chips and in ready-meals that the microwave would put on the table in minutes.

The potato as an indicator of social status was a central theme of Redcliffe N. Salaman's book *The History and Social Influence of the Potato*, published in 1949. The title alone was enough to excite the curiosity of anyone browsing through library shelves, but the publication of a revised and updated edition in 1984 was fortuitous indeed, for it coincided with my researches for a book on the extent to which culture and social systems are influenced by environment and food production systems – human ecology.

With Salaman's book never far away, research for a chapter on the potato-growers produced a great deal of fascinating information – on the potato's unique biological properties; on its role in the early days of botanical science, and its contribution to the economic history and welfare of people for whom it became a staple food. Far from being an unassuming item of food that Europeans had been eating since time immemorial (as I, like many, had once supposed), the potato is a native of South America, where it had been domesticated by the pre-Inca people of the Andes about 8,000 years ago. It was brought to Europe among other spoils of the Spanish Conquest at the end of the sixteenth century and thereafter spread fitfully, only becoming fully established as a staple food of Europe's rural and working families during the nineteenth century. It had encountered a good deal of suspicion at first. When an early edition of the *Encyclopædia Britannica* described the role of the potato in Irish history as that of a 'demoralising esculent' (esculent being a formal term for any edible plant) most readers would have probably agreed. But approval mounted rapidly as the industrial revolution gained pace. Mrs Beeton wrote of the potato as a 'valuable esculent' in her *Book of Household Management* (1861), noting that 'from no other crop . . . does the public derive so much benefit'. Meanwhile, adventurers, missionaries and colonial agencies were introducing it to Africa, India, China, Australia and New Zealand. Today, the potato is eaten and appreciated the world over – a most propitious esculent.

However, tucked away towards the end of his 685-page book, Salaman had declared that 'The potato can, and generally does, play a twofold part: that of a nutritious food, and that of a weapon ready forged for the exploitation of a weaker group in a mixed society.' I don't recall anyone blaming the potato directly for the exploitation that plagued Britain's class-ridden society, but the sentiment chimed with my memories of post-war family conversations at which the Labour government was applauded for getting 'them' out of power and making far-reaching commitments to improving the lives of working people. And the material I was assembling from other sources also tended to confirm Salaman's contentions, as well as correcting the misconceptions about its nutritional value I had taken to Connemara, and defining an ecological context for the course of Irish and European history in the seventeenth to nineteenth centuries. But there was to be more.

In 1999, the historian William H. McNeill published a paper in the journal *Social Research* entitled 'How the Potato Changed the World's History'. William H. McNeill is a highly respected historian; his most influential work, *The Rise of the West* (1963), had a major impact on historical theory, in that it examined world history in terms of the effect different civilisations had on one another, rather than treating them as discrete, independent entities. Similarly, his *Plagues and Peoples* (1976) was an important early contribution to the emergence of environmental history as a discipline.

When an historian of McNeill's standing declares, without equivocation, that the potato changed world history, you can be sure it is not something that should be taken for granted. The potato deserves the fullest attention. And that, in short, has been the motivation for this book.

Acknowledgements

Bringing together the information that tells the story of the potato in world history has been an exercise that relied very much upon the efforts of others, and therefore one that leaves an author humbled, indebted, and deeply grateful. First there were the scientists and historians whose publications are listed in the notes and bibliography, then the institutions which facilitated their research and my enquiries, and then the libraries which have made their published results so readily available. Along the way, of course, there were encounters with farmers, scientists, historians, managers, administrators and librarians – all generously welcoming with time, help and information. Their contributions have been accumulative, and therefore not always independently evident in the narrative, but always important to the framework of the project. I offer thanks to all.

In addition, the late Jack Hawkes and Richard Lester merit special thanks for their encouragement and hospitality at a crucial stage of my research, and I am similarly indebted to Stef de Haan for access to his on-going research in the Huancavelica region of the Peruvian Andes, and to the Ramos family of Villa Hermosa for the insights I gained from them during the potato harvest.

In Connemara, the families that cheerfully endured eighteen months of my photojournalistic intrusions in the early 1960s are always remembered with special affection and gratitude – in this instance most especially for the experiences I have drawn upon in respect of the potato.

The International Potato Center (CIP – Centro Internacional de la Papa) was generous with hospitality and facilities, both at its Lima headquarters and at the Huancayo research station. Scientists at the Scottish Crops Research Institute (SCRI), where the Commonwealth Potato Collection is maintained, were similarly helpful with my quest for basic understanding on a number of topics. Libraries at CIP and the SCRI gave me access to uncommon and specialist publications, and the Lindley Library of the Royal Horticultural Society was an indispensible resource. As I have always found, the usefulness of these and other libraries was greatly enhanced by the helpful efficiency of dedicated librarians – let's raise a cheer of gratitude for librarians everywhere.

Following the chronological order in which their names appear in my notebooks, I am particularly indebted to: Christine Graves, Maria Elena Lanatta, Paul Stapleton, Martin at the guest house, Cecilia Ferreyra, Hugo Li Pin, Carlos Ochoa, Keith Fuglie, William Roca, Merideth Bonierbale, Juan Landeo, Marc Ghislain, Enrique Chujoy, Sylvie Priou, Alberto Salas, Gordon Prain, Oscar Ortiz, Hubert Zandstra, Pamela Anderson, Andre de Vaux, Ana Panta, Maria Scurrah, Roberto Quiroz, Elias Mujica, Sarath Ilangantileke, Yi Wang, Carlos Arbizu, Greg Forbes, Victor Otazu, Yi Jung Yoon, Seo Hyo Won, Oscar Hualpa, Luis Salazar, Maria-Ines Rios, Brian W. Ogilvie, Harold J. Cook, Stef's assistants: Anna, Marlene & Armando, Michelangelo Samaniego, Edward & Phillada Collins, Bob Holman, Sarah Stephens, Peter Gregory, John Bradshaw, Gavin Ramsey, Finlay Dale, Dave Cooke, Paul Birch, Brian Fenton, Hugh Jones and Robert Rhoades – my thanks to all.

Ravi Mirchandani and Pat Kavanagh made the arrangements that set the project securely on course from concept to publication, and its progress has been overseen by Jason Arthur, Caroline Knight, Gail Lynch, Alban Miles and Mark Handsley. An old friend, Chris Lovell created the endpapers map with a flourish of his exceptional talents – Thank you.

List of Plates

Part One
South America

Chapter One

To Mars from the Andes

When astronauts venture beyond the Earth's orbit to colonise Mars, potatoes, freshly harvested, will be a regular feature of their meals.[1] The round trip will be a three-year enterprise and since carrying a sufficient weight of ready-made meals is impractical, the crew will grow their own vegetables, courtesy of a Bioregenerative Life Support System that the US National Aeronautic and Space Administration has been developing since the 1980s.[2] The BLSS is a self-sustaining system that recycles the output of one generation of crops into the production of the next; it will offer astronauts a veritable 'salad bar' of fresh produce, including radishes, onions, lettuce, tomatoes, peppers and strawberries,[3] but when it comes to providing dietary mainstays – both in space and on Mars – the potato will be especially prominent. Neither cereals nor pulses can match its generosity: the potato is the best all-round bundle of nutrition known.

And food is not all that the potato will give humanity's planetary explorers. In space a sustainable oxygen supply is also essential, and here the photosynthetic process in which plants absorb carbon dioxide and emit oxygen as they grow makes the potato invaluable. The conjunction is fortuitous indeed: in the enclosed environment of a spacecraft, a stand of potatoes large enough to provide as much as each person needs per day will also supply all the oxygen they must have and remove all the carbon dioxide they exhale.[4]

For those who know about potatoes, NASA's demonstration of the plant's potential for keeping people alive and healthy in space and on Mars is simply another example of the plant's exceptional usefulness and adaptability. That these commonplace and down-to-earth tubers should be a vital component of humanity's venture into space is a sublime vindication of their worth. Trillions of dollars, billions of man-hours and the success of humanity's most ambitious and complex enterprise will ultimately depend upon the astronauts' ability to grow potatoes.

If the future of the potato stretches to Mars, its origins are firmly rooted in the Andes. The ancestral species grow wild there – hundreds of scraggly, undistinguished plants whose value as food is far from obvious. The foliage cannot be eaten because it is packed with poisonous glyco-alkaloids; the tubers of most species are poisonous too, and small, so that it is difficult to imagine what might have initially encouraged people to experiment with them. Yet experiment they must have done, and archaeological evidence indicates that the process that ultimately produced edible cultivated potatoes began more than 8,000 years ago.[5] Since then Andean farmers have raised hundreds of edible varieties – in fact, they have given over 1,000 names to the different potatoes they grow regularly, each known for its particular degree of productivity, palatability, temperature tolerance, disease and pest resistance, and storage quality. Many of the names are synonyms, but it is generally agreed that at least 400 distinct varieties of potato are grown in the Andes.

They fall into three broad groups, each suited to grow best at different altitudes on the ascending slopes. Between 3,000 and 3,500 metres, where rainfall and temperature are congenial, the varieties called *papa maway* produce good crops; between 3,500 and 4,000 metres the more hardy *papa puna* are grown; and above 4,000 metres only the frost-resistant *papa ruki* will thrive.

No one household grows all 400 varieties of potato, but each will customarily plant from among a local selection of thirty, forty or fifty varieties, and the selection itself varies with personal preference. Every farmer has firm opinions concerning which can be expected to produce the highest yields under specific conditions, which are most resistant to frost and disease, which keep longest, which are easiest to cook and which are most palatable; every member of his family probably could take twenty-five varieties at random from the store, and readily give the names and characteristics of each. This is not quite as difficult as its sounds, for the native potatoes (as they are generally known) bear only a slight resemblance to the ones we know. They come in a wide variety of shapes and colours. Long and thin, short and fat; conical, round, kidney-shaped, coiled – even concertina-shaped. Colours range from white to black, with all shades of red, yellow and blue in between;

in a variety of patterns: spotted, striped, splashed, spectacled and stippled.

As agronomists and anthropologists have confirmed, human life and survival in the high Andes are intimately bound to the potato.[6]

Where the road from Huancayo, high in the Peruvian Andes, made a hairpin bend and began its descent into the valley and the town of Huancavelica, road improvement work was under way. A track led away from the noise, up and across a meadow the sheep kept close-cropped, past a patch of oats, ripening and shoulder-high; over low stone walls that seemed to have come about as somewhere to put boulders cleared from the land, rather than as divisive features – up towards the scattering of fields and dwellings that goes by the name of Villa Hermosa. The slope was steep, and breathing was laboured for those unaccustomed to such exertion at more than 3,500 metres above sea level, but Marlene kept up a steady conversation with Armando Ramos, softly, in the Quechua language, catching up with news about his family and events locally, she said. It was late May, time to harvest potatoes, and Marlene had come to record details of the crop for a study on the role of the potato in low-income communities that was being conducted under the auspices of the Centro Internacional de Papa (the International Potato Center, most widely known by its acronym – CIP), an independent internationally funded scientific research organisation founded in 1971 with a mandate to increase food security and reduce poverty in the developing world, which has its headquarters in Lima, and a large research and field station in Huancayo. Identifying and preserving the genetic resources of the potato in its Andean homeland was another aspect of CIP's research programme to which the study was contributing.

Armando led the way to his compound – three buildings set horseshoe-fashion around an open yard. To the right, a low adobe hut thatched with straw; ahead, a larger mud-brick building with a pantile roof; and to the left, a double-storey house of similar construction but roofed with corrugated iron. Did the progression of roofs around the courtyard represent the improving fortunes of the family, one wondered. No, the 29-year-old Armando replied, the double-storey house was built as a necessity to provide additional accommodation when he got married a few years before. The others were already there; the pantiled one a store and the thatched adobe hut a kitchen, into which he now led us.

The hut had no windows, and with the only light coming through the door, the far interior was dimly illuminated. Aidé, Armando's

22-year-old wife, was seated at the fireplace that filled the far end, nursing the youngest of their three children. Her face caught the light, shining like copper, while her black hair and clothing merged into the sombre darkness of the walls and shadows behind her. We sat on the benches strewn with sacks and sheepskins that lined two walls of the hut; Armando took his baby daughter while Aidé served out mugs of a meat stew, and handed round a bowl of boiled potatoes – native potatoes, a novelty to the visitors, with their assorted shapes, deep eyes and variety of colours, but uniformly tasty once unpractised fingers had managed to remove the skins.

The harvest was late throughout the region that year, Armando explained, his potato fields were not ready yet, but one his father had planted out a few weeks earlier than most was ready – and he was expecting us. We walked a few minutes along the contour of the hill, past the pits where clay had been mixed with straw to make the mud-bricks for Armando's house, past a horse grazing on a field of oat stubble, and whinnying to get at the sheaves of grain which stood, temptingly, just beyond the length of its tether, past the spring and small pool of beautifully clear water that supplied the Ramos households, and on to the field where sixty-year-old Juan Ramos, his wife Sofia (aged fifty-nine), and several of their children and grandchildren were harvesting potatoes.

Juan had planted between fifty and sixty varieties in a field behind his house early the previous November. Unseasonable frosts had damaged the plants in the early stages of growth, but they had recovered. This was because the mixture of varieties included some that were strong enough to withstand the frost, Juan explained, and also tall enough to lean over and protect their weaker brothers. The field was small; twenty ridged rows, each perhaps 20 metres long, but at the region's average rate of 5–6 tonnes per hectare, Juan and his family helpers could expect to harvest about 2 tonnes of potatoes that day. Not that they spoke in terms of areas, weights and average yields. Their appreciation of the crop was more direct. Juan was pleased with the tubers their *ayachos* (a short-handled mattock with a leaf-shaped blade that is wielded like a pick-axe) were uncovering. The crop could have been much worse. Neighbours over the hill were harvesting tubers the size of sheep droppings, he said with a sly laugh. But look at these: big as a bull's *cojones*!

Juan told us the local Quechua names of the twelve different varieties that he had dug from just 5 metres of ridge – all related in some way to the colour or shape of the tuber. Among them *Waka qallu* – cow's tongue; *Quwi sullu* – guinea pig fetus; *Puka pepino* – red cucumber; and *Papa Ilunchuy waqachi* – the potato that makes the new bride weep because it is so difficult to peel. He cut open some tubers to show us the red and purple flesh that distinguished some varieties but it was his hands, in contrast with the fresh-cut potatoes, that left the strongest impression – working hands, with thick distorted fingernails and encrusted skin, such as Vincent Van Gogh would have known when he painted *The Potato Eaters* in 1885.

Papa Ilunchuy waqachi is a severe test for any girl wanting to impress her prospective mother-in-law, though conditions are testing for anyone trying to scratch a living from the Andean highlands – or from any of Peru's rural environments, for that matter. Peru has one of the most difficult and demanding landscapes in the world. For a start, only 3 per cent of its land surface is suitable for growing food crops, compared with 21 per cent in the United States and over 30 per cent in Europe. And the problems of inadequate arable land are intensified in Peru by the extremes of its three distinct geographical regions: the arid coastal plain, the snow-capped Andean chain and the lush tropical forest.

Indeed, Peru is a land of extremes and paradox. Rainfall is almost non-existent on the coast, overabundant in the tropical forest and highly variable in the mountains. Paradoxically, the arid coastal plain is the country's most productive agricultural region, since the narrow desert strip (90 kilometres wide and 1,800 kilometres long) is cut through by some fifty rivers that drain the Andes into the Pacific Ocean. Over a million litres per second rush off the western slopes of the Andean chain. The river valleys lie like green snakes across the drab grey desert, with irrigation canals carrying their waters to farms and extensive plantations of sugar and cotton. Thus the region with least rainfall contributes far more to national production than the lush tropical forest – which gets most. In terms of productivity (as well as geography) the Andean highlands fall between these two extremes, but are especially important as they contain virtually all the country's rain-fed agricultural land and are a vital source of food crops – including, of course, potatoes.

Ten million people (36 per cent of Peru's population) live in the Andes at altitudes of 3,000 metres and above. The majority are the Quechua descendants of the hunters and gatherers who first established a human presence in the mountains, 12,000 years ago. It was they who first domesticated the potato, they who created the Inca empire, and were cruelly reduced to less than 10 per cent of their number by the

Spanish conquest and the diseases it introduced. Their descendants are a resilient stock who came through that genetic bottleneck with a stoic and unhurried capacity for survival that persists to this day.

The towns are in the valleys, but the valleys containing major centres such as Cuzco, Ayacucho, Huancayo and Huancavelica are already more than 3,000 metres above sea level, while the majority of the population lives in farming communities at even higher elevations on the slopes and plateaux above. Theirs is an exceptionally demanding environment, where solar radiation is intense but temperatures generally low. Snow and forsts are seasonally frequent, but rainfall erratic, and, most limiting of all from a human point of view, oxygen pressure is far lower than at sea level. New arrivals always feel distressingly short of breath, and many are stricken with severe headaches and nausea. They tire easily, sleep badly and may experience disconcerting bouts of mental disorientation. Their bodies adapt after a while, but never completely. Even years of living at altitude will not enable migrants to match the work capacity of the Quechua who were born and raised there.

On Juan's field, the harvesting continued. Three, four, five hefty blows of the *ayacho* broke the crust of soil, the dried haulm was lifted and shaken free, the potatoes detached and set in a neat pile on the cleared ridge. Then on to the next. Juan and his nephew were wielding the *ayachos*, his wife and Armando were gathering the potatoes and cousin Estelle was following up behind with a plastic sheet onto which she collected about 15 kilos of tubers before neatly gathering in the corners and transforming the sheet into a sling that served to carry them to the pile beside the field. Back and forth she went, the *ayachos* thudding into the dry hard soil; they stopped for a swig of water now and then, but there was little conversation; Juan occasionally refreshed the wad of coca leaves he chewed from dawn to dusk. Estelle's four-year-old son had been chasing chickens in the yard, then he came to his mother and promptly fell asleep on the harvested ground, sprawled face up in the open sun until his mother, sweating and breathing hard, fetched a jacket to lay over his face. In one hour she collected and carried 150 kilos of potatoes from the field.

Meanwhile, the bulldozers and earthmovers working on the road a few hundred metres below had cut and shifted many tonnes from the hairpin bend they were widening. Throughout the morning the syncopating thud of the *ayachos* was backed by the hum and squeals of machinery. Like a piece of modern music, one might say, but more an eloquent reminder of how little can be achieved by human labour in the modern world. Worthy, yes, but arduous and so very slow. Most of these lands were brought into cultivation before even draught animals and the wheel were introduced to the Andes, and the topography puts a lot of agricultural land beyond the use of machinery anyway. A tractor could never reach the high and steep-sloping fields, and oxen could never plough them – even for those who could afford to buy and maintain such things.

Human muscle power created the thousands upon thousands of neat ridged rectangles that are scattered throughout the high Andes – muscle assisted only by the *taclla*, a spade-like foot plough with a narrow blade and a handle set low on the shaft to ease the job of lifting and turning the heavy soil. The Inca are said to have invented the *taclla* as a means of increasing agricultural productivity as their empire expanded in the fifteenth and early sixteenth centuries. Along with the *taclla* the Inca introduced a new order to the Andes, one which harnessed a substantial fraction of all available muscle power to the service of the state and established an ominous precedent. Pre-existing traditional customs which obliged families and villagers to work cooperatively among themselves, giving and receiving labour as required, were formalised into mandatory public service known as *mita* – from the Quechua *mit'a*, which means a turn or a season.

The Inca *mita* required every man and woman to contribute a proportion of their annual labour output to the state and was arranged so that at any given time around one-seventh of a community was doing its turn. They cut roads through the mountains, mined gold and silver, harvested state crops, sheared its livestock, wove its cloth and fought its battles. The staggering achievements of the Inca state – an empire which extended from Columbia to Chile; up to 10 million subjects (40 per cent of the entire population of north and south America at that time); over 40,000 kilometres of paved road; massive irrigation and terracing projects – were a product of the *mita*.

There is much to admire in the achievements of the Inca. Their legacy is visible at Macchu Picchu and other sites, and in the gold and silver craftworks that escaped the attention of Spanish plunderers. But their *mita* system of extracting labour from the general population bestowed an oppressive burden on future generations. It lingered on as a tradition of forced labour – even to recent times. Juan Ramos speaks angrily of work on the hacienda which until the land reforms of the 1970s encompassed the fields that are now his. Juan was born on the Sanchez hacienda, as were his father and grandfather. The owners treated us like slaves, he says. No wages, just the space to build a house and the use of some land – good land, he admits, but they were never given enough time to make full use of it.

'We worked like slaves on the hacienda,' he said, and one refrained from mentioning that he worked like a slave now too. Standing there, thin and drawn, half the day gone and not half the crop in yet. His demeanour was an expression of deep unquestioning resilience: the work had to be done. Was it so much worse for all the generations before him? I asked. He gestured dismissively down the valley towards Huancavelica – a town founded on the rich deposits of mercury ore that were discovered close by in the sixteenth century. 'It was much worse working down there in the old days,' he said, 'much, much worse.'

In 1532 the Inca offered the Spanish conquistador Francisco Pizarro and his compatriots a roomful of gold and silver in return for the life of their divine Sun King, Atahuallpa. Good to their word, they delivered 11 tonnes of exquisitely crafted artefacts, which were promptly melted down and shipped back to Spain, where the sudden influx of so much wealth caused serious perturbations in Europe's monetary systems. In Peru meanwhile, Pizarro had decided that Atahuallpa should be executed anyway and the Spanish searched for yet more wealth, and especially for the mines from which it had been extracted.

In 1545, the massive amounts of silver ore which a volcano had left standing to a height of 800 metres as its flanks were eroded away at Potosí, almost 1,000 kilometres south-east of Cuzco, came to the Spaniards' attention. Potosí became a boom town. In 1592 alone, its mines produced over 400 tonnes of refined silver, and although annual outputs never reached that level again, an average of nearly 100 tonnes of silver was shipped from Potosí every year from 1600 to 1800.

Mercury was an essential ingredient of the refining process that enabled Potosí to sustain such levels of production. The scarlet to brick-red mercury ore, or cinnabar, was known to have been used as a cosmetic by the Inca, but it was not until 1563 that the source at Huancavelica was discovered. The site was more than 1,300 kilometres from Potosí, but still a lot closer than the European mines which had been the only available source hitherto. Now Huancavelica also became a boom town: 'unique and irreplaceable . . . this rich jewel, precious beyond compare in all the world'. Together, Potosí and Huancavelica were described as the 'two poles which support [Peru] and the kingdom of Spain'.[7]

With its mercury facilitating the production of silver at Potosí, Huancavelica was acknowledged to be an essential factor in Spain's economic life, the keystone of Spanish prosperity – both in Peru and in Europe. Mercury was indispensable, an administrator wrote, 'como el agua que fecunda los campos' – like the water that irrigates the fields. The town soon began to acquire the manifestations of its importance. Towards the close of the eighteenth century Huancavelica had a population of some 5,000 people, of whom only 560 were Spanish or mixed-blood; the remainder were Quechua Indians – a relatively small population, but with enough revenue from the mercury mine to support nine churches, three convents, a hospital, an elementary school, twenty-one priests and eighteen members of the Dominican, Franciscan and Augustinian orders (the Jesuits were there too, running a college and primary school, until they were expelled from the Spanish empire in 1767).

But, as might be expected, the dominant note in this rich isolated mining town, sited in a narrow valley more than 3,000 metres above sea level, was more secular than religious. Its elite lived well. Most of their food, including delicacies such as fish and fresh fruit of all kinds, was brought up on llama caravans from lower valleys and the coast. The elite spent a small fortune on *aguardiente* (a fierce brandy made by one of the religious orders) each year, while paying Indians a pittance to hack the source of their extravagance from the mine. Gambling was a popular pastime, sexual promiscuity was widespread and musicians were always on hand to accompany the *chachúa*, a dance which a contemporary described as 'surpassingly lascivious'. In short, a spendthrift, rowdy, licentious atmosphere permeated almost every aspect of society and conditioned the operation of the mine and the administration of local government.[8]

The mine itself was situated some five kilometres south of Huancavelica and 350 metres above it. The ore was carried from the mine to the furnaces at the edge of town on the backs of several thousand alpacas and llamas – the only part of the operation that was not performed by Indians. Conditions in the mine were little short of lethal. Miners followed the richest seams, sometimes leaving spacious chambers behind them, sometimes leaving only cramped tunnels that workers could barely squeeze through. Yet ore carriers had to struggle past all the obstacles and up countless rickety ladders to get the ore to the surface – a task so arduous that only the richest lumps of ore were carried up, and the rest left to clutter the galleries and make access even more difficult. Candles and torches lit the miners' way, but also filled the galleries and pits with smoke, which combined with sulphur in the rock to give off 'an intolerable foul stench'. Fumes and the perspiration of 'so many people enclosed together working continuously and without end and from the excrement and filth' resulted in 'a great infection and corruption of the air, very prejudicial and injurious to human health', says a contemporary report. But worst of all, poor ventilation and the excessive heat of the galleries caused mercury in the ore to volatilize, making the atmosphere of the mine a veritable 'culture of mercury intoxication'. The richer the ore, the more dangerous the atmosphere.

Miners inhaled a dose of mercury poisoning with every breath. They absorbed it through every pore, and since they were obliged to stay at the mine for six days of the week, they had little opportunity to wash away the contamination. And on their day away from the mine they inevitably polluted their living quarters and contaminated every acquaintance.

Sooner or later, even the strongest miners succumbed to mercury poisoning. The 'Huancavelica sickness', as it became known, began as a cough then 'settled in the bones'. It entered their very marrow, a superintendent wrote, and made its victims tremble in every limb. Many turned to alcohol for relief of their mental and physical depressions and restlessness; they suffered powerful tremors that made walking, eating and drinking difficult. In fact, many mercury-afflicted miners trembled so badly that they had to be fed as though they were infants. Six months was said to be the longest a miner could work at Huancavelica without succumbing to mercury poisoning, and four years the longest they could survive with it. When workers coughed up mouthfuls of blood and mercury, doctors opened their veins in the hope that copious bleeding might restore the balance of the bodily humours; but such debilitating treatment could only usher the sufferers closer to death's door.

With fatalistic resignation, Huancavelica miners customarily made a small donation to the Franciscans each week in return for the promise of a shroud and a Christian burial. It seems hardly credible, but an official reported in 1604 that, when reopened, the graves of dead miners contained puddles of mercury which had leached from the decomposing bodies.[9]

The Spanish authorities were fully aware of the death sentence that the Huancavelica mine imposed on most of its workers, but also conscious that the failure to supply enough mercury would limit silver production at Potosí and thus cripple the economies of Peru and Spain. Attempts were made to improve conditions, but it was always the importance of maintaining output that was given priority. Racial prejudice made Indian lives an acceptable price to pay for the security of mercury and silver production. A typical mine owner, Pedro Camargo, gave his opinion of the Indians in a letter he addressed to the king of Spain in March 1595:

> They are barbarous people and without knowledge of God; in their lands they are only occupied in idolatries and drunkenness and other vices of great filthiness . . . These people going to work in the mines first seems to me a service to God . . . and for the good of the natural Indians themselves. Because in the mines they teach them doctrine and make them hear mass and they deal with Spaniards . . . losing their barbarity.[10]

Such prejudice extended even to the point of suggesting that working in the mines exercised a positively civilising influence on the Indians. With more ingenuity than understanding, one commentator even sought to justify the practice of commuting a death sentence to labour in the mines on the grounds that it indicated not that mine labour was substantially equivalent to a death sentence, but that the benevolence of the government even permitted capital offenders to share the regenerating benefits of mine labour.[11]

But sophistry fooled no one. Huancavelica was deservedly known as 'the mine of death . . . a public slaughterhouse'. Only the *mita*, forced labour, could have kept it working.

In the 1570s, the King's viceroy, Francisco de Toledo, had adapted the traditional Inca *mita* more closely to the needs of Spain's mercury and silver production, ordering that the surrounding provinces should keep the mines supplied with a rotating labour force. As a concession to the dangers of mercury mining, the Huancavelica contingents would work two-month stints (as compared with twelve months at Potosí), Toledo declared. In point of fact, this was more disruptive than helpful, since it meant that a mercury miner's turn came round several times a year, whereas at Potosí an individual could expect to be called only every seventh year.

At first Toledo had ordered that 900 *mitayos* should be available for work in the Huancavelica mine at any one time, but later was obliged to raise the figure to over 3,000. The numbers fell in subsequent decades, as deaths and a determination to avoid the *mita* reduced the pool from which labour could be extracted. In 1630 a visiting dignitary, the Count of Cinchón, reported:

> they take these miserable Indians by force against their will from their houses and take them in iron collars and chains more than 100 leagues to put them in this risk, . . . and from this has resulted their mothers maiming and crippling their sons to preserve them.

It is no fault of the potato that it provides a filling, wholesome and nourishing meal, but it doubtless helped to perpetuate the Spanish exploitation of Peru's indigenous population. Sadly, the innocent potato has facilitated exploitation wherever it has been introduced and cultivated. Potatoes fed the miners at Huancavelica and Potosí. Spanish settlers grew rich supplying potatoes to the mines,[12] and by an ironic turn of fate also saved numerous Indians from having to work there. This was because settlers sought more land and labour as the expansion of the mining industry increased the demand for potatoes. For Indians threatened with *mita* service in the mine, giving up land and joining the labour force of an expanding hacienda was a price worth paying. It bought security. At a hacienda owner's behest, *mita* obligations could be commuted to a cash payment[13] – which the labourers would have to work off. It was the lesser of two evils, but in effect exchanged the life-threatening obligations of the *mita* for a lifelong commitment to the hacienda.

It was on the arid uplands above the valleys that haciendas multiplied, on land best suited for livestock and potatoes such as Juan and his family occupy above Huancavelica. The hacienda boundaries were usually quite extensive, but only a small proportion of the land was actually used at any given time for growing crops; long periods of fallow were the norm. The labouring households were given a subsistence plot, the right to pasture their own animals on hacienda lands, and a limited number of items such as clothes, coca and so on. In exchange they worked on the hacienda as required.[14]

The families lived in low, windowless, thatched adobe cottages such as Armando now uses as a kitchen. The head of each household was assigned a portion of the hacienda's livestock to care for on his sector of pasture, which he must satisfactorily account for every six or twelve months. And aside from this year-round work of herding, he and eligible family members had to work on shearing the hacienda's sheep and slaughtering its mutton and beef animals – two major annual tasks that might last up to a month each. Then there was the agricultural work: ploughing, sowing, weeding and harvesting the hacienda's potato and cereal crops, as well as tending the owner's kitchen gardens, and providing fodder for the dairy cattle and pack animals. They were also obliged to transport hacienda produce to market and collect stores – using their own llamas or mules and without any recompense for loss or damage – and all adult family members had to work as general-purpose servants in the owner's residence for up to one month per year.[15] Only after these obligations had been fulfilled could they attend to their own needs.

Labour relationships on the haciendas were unregulated. There were no written contracts, and this inherent vagueness concerning the work that a labourer could be called upon to do, and for how long, left plenty of room for conflicting interpretation. Dispute and bad feeling were endemic, and while there must have been some instances of genial and mutually supportive relationships between workers and hacienda owners, the overwhelming impression is one that supports Juan's assessment: the workers were treated like slaves.

Thus the *mita* system of forced labour upon which the Inca had built an empire persisted in the mercury and silver mines and was transposed to the haciendas, where it survived through three centuries of Spanish rule to Peru's achievement of independence in July 1821. And did not end there. By then a home-grown (and often mixed-blood) elite had inherited the estates. Quechua was the first language for many of them. They were Peruvian, but with Spanish names implying some right to live and behave as aristocracy. They expected to be addressed as 'Don', and saw no need or reason to change the longstanding modes of operation on the estates – least of all, arrangements for the acquisition and deployment of labour.

The haciendas were by now the mainstay of Peru's agricultural production – their viability dependent upon a relic form of forced labour and the unacknowledged value of Peru's gift to the world: the potato. Potatoes were the staple food of workers on haciendas in the high Andes.

Like the feudal estates of medieval Europe, the haciendas supported the extravagant lifestyles of a select and relatively small section of the population. But unlike the European examples, social and economic factors in Peru were slow to dismantle them. The oppressive arrangements persisted well into the twentieth century – reinforced by the wealth that many owners accumulated during the First World War, when the demand for wool (to make uniforms) made Peru's production very valuable indeed. But economic viability slumped steadily thereafter, and the owners' enthusiasm for agriculture with it. The haciendas carried on, but largely as before; producing no more than they had ever done, and therefore ensuring that agricultural production fell increasingly short of the country's growing needs. The owners were rich in land, but incomes fell while costs were rising. The government had set a minimum wage; it was low but few haciendas paid it. Indeed, an agronomist reported that if the workers on haciendas in the Andes were paid even the legal minimum wage no hacienda would make a profit, and a living wage would drive most into bankruptcy. Only the Indians' forced labour kept them going, he concluded.[16]

The adjustments that finally broke the hacienda owners' feudal stranglehold on agriculture and farm labour came in a programme of agrarian reform enacted by the government between 1969 and 1977. Under these plans, the ownership of all estates of more than 30 hectares in the highlands (and 50 hectares on the coast) was transferred to their labour force in the form of production cooperatives. The former owners were financially compensated – but on the basis of their previous tax returns, which neatly ensured that valuations were as low as they could be.[17]

Juan spoke harshly as he recalled the events of that time. The landowners attempted to avoid the takeover, he said, by trying to have their estates divided up into units of less than 30 hectares, but a nation-wide outcry forestalled them. The disposal of livestock and equipment could not be stopped, however. 'Those *hacienderos* would have taken the soil from the ground if they could,' he said, 'and left us just rocks.'

He gestured to fields dug on the ridge above us, and on high slopes across the valley, ten kilometres away; he pointed to a string of farms on the road down to Huancavelica, and to his own land facing the limestone outcrop they call Urahuaca. He named the communities we could see: Attaya, Antaccocha, Harawasa, Chacariya – all these and several more had been part of the hacienda owned by the Sanchez family; now they are grouped in an autonomous farmer community that takes the name of the former hacienda: Villa Hermosa.

The highest land is used communally for pasture and potatoes, with individual householders planting and fallowing the land in a sequence of rotations that all have agreed upon. No one can do just as they like on the common land; that privilege applies only to land at lower elevations, which is privately owned. The boundaries between individual holdings are precisely known but very rarely registered in any legal manner[18] – villagers are confident they can resolve any disputes that arise among themselves, without recourse to documents and legal expertise.

Each community has a president, who is elected for a two-year term and presides over the democratic process by which village affairs are conducted. Issues that cannot be mutually agreed are put to the vote. But the presidency is not a job for which farmers seek nomination; it is time-consuming, and a duty the man who receives most votes must fulfil – whether he wants the post or not. And if two years of authoritative status should happen to leave a man feeling superior and deserving of even a little additional respect from his fellow villagers – he may be sure they will hatch plans to bring him down a peg or two.

After centuries of oppression under first the Inca *mita*, the mines, and then the Spanish and Peruvian hacienda owners, modern generations farming the high Andes will not allow one of their own kind to develop airs of superiority. Each community of villages is quite literally a law unto itself, the government having granted them the right to charge, convict and even hang people on the strength of eyewitness or other irrefutable evidence. Juan's community hanged two men in 2001, he said, or it may have been 2000. He was unsure of the year, but in no doubt of the crime: extortion. The men had been forcing villagers to pay excess charges – for years.

The crime, though deplorable, hardly seemed worthy of a death penalty. And if men were hanged for extortion, what would happen to the individual who raped a girl two nights ago? If he had been caught at the scene they would have beaten him to death, there and then, Juan said. Rough justice, but too late for that now. So he would be banished – thrown out of the village, and would probably have to travel far before he found people who did not know or care what he had done. A better fate than hanging, certainly, but a bleak prospect in a social environment that was predisposed to suspicion, where strangers were likely to be suspected of malevolent intent.

Villa Hermosa was one of over 500 farmer communities that now owned the former haciendas and controlled agricultural production in the Huancavelica Department. In total, those 500 communities consisted of over 86,000 farming household units with an average of five people in each. Fully 97 per cent of the economically active population depended on agriculture and livestock as the primary means of supporting themselves and their families, even though almost two-thirds of them had access to less than three hectares of agricultural land. Stark statistics, which explain why Huancavelica was described as the poorest of Peru's twenty-four departments. More than 70 per cent of the total population was considered to be 'extremely poor' by World Bank standards. Chronic malnutrition affected 52 per cent of children in rural areas, where average infant mortality rose to 112 per thousand in 2006 – nearly four times the national average (32.5 per thousand) and only marginally better than that of traumatised Sierra Leone (145.24 per thousand).[19]

The fundamental reason for such poverty and malnutrition was that the department's independent and self-supporting farmers were literally scratching a living from one of the harshest environments that humanity has colonised. Only a fraction of the land they utilised was less than 3,000 metres above sea level (more than twice the height of Ben Nevis, Britain's highest mountain), and much of it rises to 4,500 metres (higher than any peak in the Rocky Mountains). Whether anyone would actually choose, voluntarily, to inhabit the Andean highlands if other options were available is a moot point. The prime motivating factors seem to have been coercion and lack of an alternative – though one should not forget that the region had its attractions: pasture and potatoes.

Juan Ramos was born on the Sanchez hacienda in 1946. He grew up on potatoes without formal education, working like a slave, as he said, but mindful of the harder times that his parents and grandparents had endured and confident that improvements would come in his lifetime. In the upper echelons of society, economists and politicians had been saying that the existing system was unsustainable and destined for ignominious collapse if radical reforms were not introduced. But the lowliest workers on the haciendas had known that too – not because they had been aware of the system's economic and political short-comings, but from their fatalistic awareness of the inevitable: things could hardly get worse; so now they might get better.

'Yes,' Juan said, 'life was easier now than when he had been growing up.' Much easier than in his parents' and grandparents' day. And the future? He feared for his children and grandchildren. 'There's no spare land,' he said. Where in the recent past there had been enough for him to leave a field uncultivated, fallow, for seven or eight years before planting potatoes on it again, the field he and his family were harvesting had been fallow for only three years. And from the top of the lime-stone outcrop you could see the problem: the homesteads of six families were spaced among the patchwork of tilled fields and pasture which had once been expected to support just one household. 'What else could we do?' Juan asked. 'My brothers and I needed land and a house when we married, so our father gave us some of his; and I've done the same for my son, Armando. But he will have to do something else for his children.'

Like the American Declaration of Independence, the Declaration of Human Rights and Duties adopted by the Organisation of American States in April 1948 (six months before the United Nations adopted the Universal Declaration of Human Rights) enshrines the attainment of happiness as an essential right of every individual.[20] Peru is a signatory, but Juan was puzzled when asked how much happiness had been attained in his lifetime. Happiness? What makes people happy? 'Healthy animals,' he said cautiously, 'and a good potato harvest.' And then added: 'Money! And best of all, a job. Yes, a job would make us happy. The farm is not enough anymore, but with a job we'd have money and could buy our potatoes.'

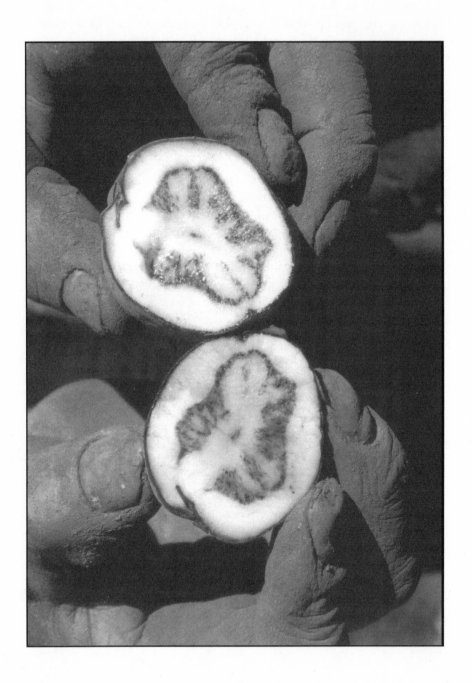

Chapter Two

What exactly is a potato?

A potato is mostly water (79 per cent), but the remainder is an exceptional all-round package of food, with a ratio of carbohydrate to protein content which ensures that anyone eating enough potatoes to satisfy their energy requirement will automatically ingest sufficient protein as well. And apart from carbohydrate and protein, the potato contains significant quantities of essential vitamins and minerals. Just 100 gm of potato provides nearly half the minimum daily requirement of vitamin C, for instance (it is said that when men were dying of scurvy during the Klondike gold rush, potatoes sold for their weight in gold[1]). Potatoes are also rich in the B complex vitamins and have useful quantities of calcium, iron, phosphorous and potassium. Their sodium content is low, but potash and alkaline salts content is high, which qualifies the potato for salt-free diets (and helps to control acidity).

The protein content of a potato is low compared with grains, but of high quality, rich in the essential amino acids that the body cannot assemble from other ingredients but must ingest, ready-made. Furthermore, the 'biological value' of potato protein (an index of the nitrogen absorbed and retained by the body for growth and maintenance) is 73, second only to that of eggs at 96; just ahead of soya beans at 72, but far superior to maize at 54 and wheat at 53.

The potato's carbohydrate is mostly starch, which has an undeservedly bad reputation but is actually a far more healthy source of calories than the sugars and fats so prevalent in modern diets. Contrary to popular belief, the potato's carbohydrate is not fattening (the fat that chips, french fries and crisps retain from cooking is the culprit). Also, the body assimilates the carbohydrate in a potato slowly, so that it provides a steady stream of energy – rather than the 'rush' that sugars and fats give.

Furthermore, the potato is an exceptionally productive plant – far more of its total biomass can be eaten than is the case with other food crops. Among cereals, for instance, the edible grain amounts to only about one-third of the mature plant's weight, while edible tubers comprise more than three-quarters of a potato plant. This means that potatoes produce more energy per day on a given area than any other crop and are, therefore, a most efficient means of converting plant, land, water and labour resources into a nutritious and palatable food.

But the most valuable asset of the potato is undoubtedly the balanced nutrition it provides. In controlled experiments[2] people have sustained active lives for months on a diet consisting only of potatoes (plus a little margarine), maintaining perfect health throughout and without losing (or gaining) weight. Admittedly, this has obliged the participants to eat between two and three kilos of potatoes per day – which is not something that inhabitants of the developed world would contemplate with much enthusiasm – but there have been plenty of occasions when the potato's outstanding nutritional value has been a life-saver.

And the sweet potato? A shared name invites the assumption that the potato and the sweet potato are closely related, with one perhaps a little more delectable than the other. In fact, they are not even distantly related.

The potato, *Solanum tuberosum,* belongs to the *Solanaceae,* which is one of the most familiar and diverse families of flowering plant, with some 90 genera and 3,000 to 4,000 species – some of which are found in every part of the world except Antarctica. Such exceptional morpho-logical and chemical diversity and worldwide distribution has made the *Solanaceae* one of the most economically important groups of plants. Apart from the potato, it includes tomatoes, aubergines, chilli peppers, tobacco and numerous ornamentals – such as the petunia. At the same time, a number of species are known for their alkaloid content and have been used throughout history as medicines, poisons, or psychotropic drugs; examples include tobacco, jimson weed, henbane, and belladonna.

The sweet potato, *Ipomoea batatas,* belongs to the same family as morning glory – the *Convolvulaceae.* Columbus and his followers found the sweet potato established as a staple food throughout the Caribbean, where it was known as batatas and was brought to Europe in the early 1490s under that name. When the true potato crossed the Atlantic seventy or eighty years later it came with its original Andean name, papa. Since both papa and batatas grew underground and looked similar, their names inevitably became confused – especially at a time when written language and printing technology were not distinguished by accuracy or consistent spelling. The literature of the day contains references to batatas and patatas; and a book of 1514 describes the botato growing wild in Darien.[3]

But although the two are so totally different in nature, in cultivation they share one significant feature: both are propagated vegetatively. That is to say, growers do not plant seeds, but pieces of the plant itself. In the case of the sweet potato it is pieces of stem (or vine) that go in the ground, complete with the nodes (growing points) from which the plant will produce another generation of leaves, stems and roots. In the case of the potato it is tubers, which, odd though it may seem, are also pieces of stem.

Take a close look at a potato; look deep into its eyes. Each eye has a number of tiny buds at its centre, and an arching eyebrow above. The eyebrows are all the same way up for, like any stem, the potato has a distinct top and bottom. The eyebrow is actually a form of leaf, or the mark where a scale leaf was borne and then fell off, and the buds are the nodes from which the potato's main stems and roots will sprout when the tuber is planted. In short, a potato is a grotesquely swollen piece of stem and buds, broken off from a part of the plant's underground stems (known technically as stolons). That is why it is classified botanically as a tuber, and not a root like the sweet potato.

So, the propitious esculent that we boil, fry, roast, bake and eat with hardly a thought is not a seed, a root or a fruit but a piece of stem – grown fat underground. From the potato's point of view the most important function of the engrossed piece of stem is as a reserve means of reproduction. The buds on its tubers will sprout and produce new plants in due course whether or not the plant above ground has managed to flower and set seed; and each plant will be an exact copy of the parent, with none of the mutation resulting from the reshuffling of genes that occurs when plants reproduce sexually. In short, tubers are clones. Furthermore, they remain alive and viable for months underground, while roots (such as sweet potatoes) rot much more quickly.

For the greater part of the potato's evolutionary history, however, flower and seed have been its principal means of reproduction. Only since people began cultivating its wild ancestors has the potato been obliged to rely so much on its tubers – though this has worked out very well. Here is a plant from one of the world's most remote and least congenial environments that now grows in all corners of the globe – from the deserts of Arabia to the rainforests of the Amazon and Africa, and the coldest fringes of Scandinavia, Asia and the Americas. The potato has come a long way from its origins in the Andes – where, when and how did the process begin?

Defining the origin and evolution of a plant is never a simple matter when the only available evidence is that of its living relatives, and researchers have found the cultivated potato an especially difficult case because it is derived from a group within which species seem to have arisen relatively recently and are still actively evolving, so that the boundaries between varieties and species are often hard to detect.[4] Furthermore, the potato has an exceptionally large number of living wild relatives – far more than any other food crop – and is distinguished by what has been called its 'environmental plasticity'.[5] This means that although potato plants taken from a range of different environments may look like different species, when they are all grown together under identical conditions they can turn out to be the same.

In a classic work, *The Potato. Evolution, Biodiversity and Genetic Resources* (1990), Professor J. G. Hawkes lists 169 species of wild potato, a conspicuous biological feature of which is the contrast (general but not absolute) between the majority which are very variable outbreeders, and the minority which are less variable inbreeders.[6] This distinction accounts for the wide diversity and distribution of wild potatoes, for as their genes were reshuffled with each generation the outbreeders acquired attributes that enabled them to move into new environments, and to thrive under a range of different conditions. Their random mutations also produced the minority that were inbreeders – which then established the plant's permanent presence in a particular environment, where the ability to reproduce clonally, via the tubers, became especially relevant.

This mix of botanical diversity and conservatism established the wild potato over a wide geographical area. According to Hawkes they are found throughout the Americas, from the south-west United States, to nearly every state of Mexico and thence to Guatemala, Honduras, Costa Rica and Panama. In South America they are found in every country except the Guianas, but chiefly in the Andes of Venezuela, Colombia, Ecuador, Peru, Bolivia and Argentina. They also occur on the Peruvian desert coast, in central to southern Chile, on the plains of Argentina, Paraguay and Uruguay, and in south-east Brazil. In recent years the distribution of wild potatoes has been more precisely documented and mapped.[7]

No single wild potato species extends throughout the entire geographical range; some are remarkably widespread, others are restricted to relatively small areas or distinct ecological zones, but, overall, wild potato species seem to have penetrated nearly every natural habitat in the Americas (except for the lowland tropical rain forest) and a number of artificial or man-made habitats too. Adaptability is the key: wild potatoes thrive in a range of altitude, temperature and humidity that few plants can match. Some can withstand extended bouts of sub-zero temperatures; others are adapted to hot, dry, semi-desert conditions; yet others grow in subtropical to temperate mountain rainforest with high humidity. In Mexico and the United States, many species inhabit pine and fir forests. They are also found in the forests of South America, in summer-green woodland and among the cacti of drier habitats. And they thrive in the Andes – on the Altiplano, in the mountains and the valleys.

In botany, as in most things, simplicity generally precedes complexity; which means that if the accumulation of complexity in a living specimen can be unravelled, and sorted into a sequence of stages by which that complexity was acquired, it should be possible to trace the evolutionary history of a plant back to its origins. Such studies draw upon every aspect of botanical science – from the plant's structure and behaviour, to leaf shape and flowers; from the issue of fertility and sterility to the number of chromosomes in each cell and DNA sequencing. The potato's diversity makes it a particularly complicated case. Even after fifty years of dedicated work, Professor Hawkes felt obliged to admit that his investigations into the origin of the potato had been rounded off with a touch of 'inspired guesswork'.[8]

Analysis at the molecular level made possible by advances in technology has gone a long way towards eliminating the guesswork to which Hawkes occasionally resorted. In particular, DNA sequencing has enabled a team led by research botanist David Spooner to trace the origin of all modern potato varieties to a group of about twenty morphologically similar wild species, known as the *Solanum brevicaule* complex, grown by farmers in Peru more than 7,000 years ago.[9]

The simplest and most primitive living relative of the tuber-bearing potato is a small epiphyte – an air-plant – called *Solanum morelliforme* (the name refers to the leaf form, which is similar to that of black nightshade *S. nigrum*, or morel). The plant has simple leaves, small star-like flowers and tiny berries and is found growing in dense shade on moss-covered walls and rocks and the mossy branches of oak trees – never on the ground – in southern Mexico.[10] Hawkes concluded that ancestors resembling these wild species were present in the south-west United States, Mexico or Guatemala some 37–40 million years ago, and migrated into South America when the isthmus of Panama was formed around 3.5

million years ago. Their history thereafter was one of botanical diversification and geographical expansion as the potato advanced and adapted to thrive in the host of ecological niches that South America had to offer. Some lines became stranded in what Hawkes describes as the 'migration race', establishing centres of diversity in Peru and Bolivia, while others went on to colonise parts of Argentina and the surrounding countries.

That's the wild potato – a highly adaptable, diverse, vigorous and widespread group of plants, supremely able to thrive in the natural state. But what about the cultivated form; where did that come from?

It is believed that of the many wild potato species, fewer than ten played any role in the evolution of the cultivated potato, and they were species which had settled, as it were, in the regions of Peru and Bolivia that border Lake Titicaca. It was here, about 8,000 years ago, that people began to manipulate the wild potato's adaptability towards the achievement of a single aim: improving the size and palatability of its tubers. This was not in itself difficult – principally a matter of selecting tubers that seemed promising and nurturing them, season by season.

But if the method is easily explained, the motivation is a complete mystery. The tubers of wild potatoes are generally small, bitter to the taste and contain potentially poisonous levels of glycoalkaloids. Why would people have bothered? But bother they did, and human ingenuity working with the plant's adaptability eventually produced not one but seven cultivated species of potato.[11] The toxic properties remain in the foliage of all species and in the tubers of some; the diversity of the wild potato is retained too, in the huge range of colours and shapes that are found among the numerous varieties that have been raised from the initial seven species. But one cultivated species in particular is of interest here, one in which the tuber's potential for enlargement has been most positively expressed: *Solanum tuberosum*.

S. tuberosum exists in the form of two subspecies. The first, *S. tuberosum andigena*, is a potato that forms tubers only at altitudes of 2,000 metres or more, at latitudes close to the equator, where days are short all year round (they grow so vigorously in the warmth of lower altitudes and where there are more hours of daylight that tuber formation is inhibited). The second subspecies was derived from *andigena* by early cultivators as they migrated south from the potato's cradleland in the vicinity of Lake Titicaca. By planting and selecting for the conditions encountered as they moved along, a potato was gradually created that would produce tubers even at low altitudes in the long days of southern Chile. This is *S. tuberosum tuberosum*.

Today, *andigena* and the other six cultivated species of potato are grown on a large scale only in the Andes (initially because that is where they performed best, but latterly also because export is permitted only for strictly controlled collection and experimental purposes). *S. tuberosum tuberosum* is grown in the Andes too, where it is known as the 'improved' potato and does well at lower altitudes; and this is the potato that is known around the world – grown in the form of many different varieties, but all derived from a single species.

The first tubers of *S. tuberosum tuberosum* to reach Europe were brought in by the Spanish in the 1570s. Those early introductions probably came from both the Andes and the coastal regions of Chile,[12] but were few in number and captured only a fraction of the biodiversity that exists among the wild and cultivated potatoes of South America. It is therefore remarkable that today the potato is grown in 149 countries from latitudes 65 degrees north to 50 degrees south, from sea level to more than 4,000 metres, and has become the world's fourth most important food crop (after wheat, maize and rice). Such achievements reflect adaptations first to the short summer days of the highland tropics and sub-tropics, then to the long summer days of lowland temperate regions, and finally to the short winter days of the lowland sub-tropics and tropics. The distribution also reflects adaptation to a wide range of growing conditions, temperature and the availability of water. But there has been a downside to this profligacy: as a single species, tender and highly bred, *S. tuberosum tuberosum* has become utterly dependent on its cultivators, and highly vulnerable as a result. Hawkes once expressed the opinion that high-yielding cultivated species had 'apparently lost their capacity for survival in a natural environment, possibly because they have been under cultivation for so long'.[13]

Once out of its cradle land, the cultivated potato has advanced only at the hands of the people who grow and eat it, leaving behind a significant portion of genetic diversity and putting it at the mercy of diseases and pests to which it had no inherited resistance. The potato is among the world's most vulnerable crops. Farmers in some regions must spray a dozen times or more in a season to protect their crops from the host of pathogens that could rapidly ruin a field of cultivated potatoes. The annual cost of protecting the world's potato crop is more than $2 billion[14] – and rising, despite the millions more that are spent on research. Without human intervention the *Solanum tuberosum* would almost certainly die out, plagued by disease and unable to sustain viable populations.

TRAVAXOS

PAPAALLAIMITAPA

rha perito haucay ausqui quiella

labrador
pachaca

Junio — yancayausqui   junio

Chapter Three

Domestication

At first glance, the most significant differences between a cultivated potato and its wild relatives are size – it is bigger – and palatability – it tastes better. But, actually, these are merely the consequences of a far more relevant difference, namely that cultivated potatoes (and plants in general) are even more varied in form than their wild relatives. Broccoli and Brussels sprouts, cabbage, cauliflower, kale and kohlrabi may not look very much alike, but they are all cultivated varieties of the same species, *Brassica oleracea*, and can be crossed to produce more variation. It is the same with potatoes, many varieties of which will readily set seed even though their tubers were planted to produce a food crop. The tomato-like fruits contain, on average, about 200 seeds, each one of which, if it germinates and thrives, could be a new variety of its species, *Solanum tuberosum tuberosum*, potentially quite different from either of its parents and possibly possessing new properties which, if deemed valuable, will earn the plant special care and attention.

In the wild, natural selection would promptly eliminate any new forms that were not entirely suited to the prevailing conditions, but in the cultivators' fields these oddities have been cosseted and nurtured to become established varieties. In fact, most modern cultivars are biological 'monsters' that could not survive in the wild. The tubers of cultivated potatoes, for instance, have lost the bitter taste of their wild antecedents and would be at risk of predation – and elimination.

The bitterness derives from the glycoalkaloid compounds that are generally present in wild potatoes.[1] This is the plant's first line of defence, warning potential consumers that what they are about to eat might be poisonous, and potato glycoalkaloids are some of the most poisonous components of the human diet, with a capacity to impair both the digestive and the central nervous systems.[2] They occur in virtually all parts of the plant, and are even present to some degree in the tubers that supermarkets and greengrocers offer for sale today. A study by scientists from the Queen's University of Belfast has shown that even popular and widely produced varieties (Home Guard, Rocket and British Queen) have dangerously high concentrations of glycoalkaloids during the early weeks of tuber growth; in fact, concentrations only fall below the danger line as tubers approach maturity at the end of the growing season and the plant's foliage dies. Thus, even in our times, when farmers, scientists and society are all acutely aware of their responsibilities to the consumer, 'many human poisonings and even deaths have been associated with the consumption of potato tubers with higher than normal glycoalkaloid concentrations', the study reports.[3] So how did the people who domesticated the wild potato and brought it into cultivation 8,000 years ago deal with the problem?

The route from poisonous wild ancestor to tasty domesticated cultivar required a fifteen- to twenty-fold reduction in glycoalkaloid concentrations.[4] Given that glycoalkaloids are the plant's defence against predation, it is improbable that a reduction of this scale could have occurred naturally, as the result of chance mutations. Natural selection (in the form of insightful predators) would have eliminated any such edible plants from the breeding stock. The process must have been gradual, progressive, and must therefore have been driven by initial intent – by people, in other words, who knew what they were doing.

Of course, it is possible that pre-agricultural hunter-gatherers made a practice of searching through stands of wild potatoes for the odd mutants that were non-toxic, but finding them would have involved tasting the majority that were toxic, and the rewards would have been small in terms of quantity. Furthermore, these activities would have served the duty of natural selection, in that every edible tuber they unearthed would have reduced the chance of non-toxic variations becoming more numerous among future generations.

No, potatoes were an unpredictable and dangerous resource until some way of eliminating their potential toxicity was discovered. And here is a paradox: the toxic levels of glycoalkaloids in wild potatoes make it unlikely that pre-agricultural hunter-gatherers exploited them as anything more than a casual resource. But, until people became intensively involved with potatoes, their domestication was even more unlikely. Perhaps it is more a catch-22 than a paradox: people could not make much use of the potato until it was domesticated; but could not domesticate it until they had a lot of experience with its use. Conundrums such as this have puzzled generations of scholars attempting to explain the origins of agriculture and, indeed, culture itself.

Charles Darwin, along with others of his day, was convinced that hunter-gatherers (such as those who first encountered the wild potato) could not have domesticated plants. By definition, he said, their nomadic existence precluded the establishment of settled communities around which the beginnings of cultivation and agriculture might take root:

> Nomadic habits, whether over wide plains, or through the dense forests of the tropics, or along the shores of the sea, have in every case been highly detrimental. Whilst observing the barbarous inhabitants of Tierra del Fuego, it struck me that the possession of some property, a fixed abode, and the union of many families under a chief, were the indispensable requisites for civilisation. Such habits almost necessitate the cultivation of the ground; and the first steps in cultivation would probably result, as I have elsewhere shewn, from some such accident as the seeds of a fruit-tree falling on a heap of refuse and producing an unusually fine variety.[5]

But, while convinced that a settled existence and the beginnings of agriculture were the prerequisites of civilisation, Darwin readily acknowledged that proof of his conviction was beyond the reach of evidence available to him; he concluded that 'The problem . . . of the first advance of savages towards civilisation is at present much too difficult to be solved.'[6]

One might have hoped that the problem would have been solved by now, but although a good deal of research has been aimed at it, a definitive solution is still lacking. If the lives of modern-day hunter-gatherer groups are an acceptable model for those of their prehistoric antecedents, then it was certainly not shortages of food that inspired them to begin growing their own; nor was it the stresses of having to go out and find something to eat – every day. They had plenty of food for everyone; more than enough people to gather it, and all the time in the world. Theirs was, as the anthropologist Marshall Sahlins put it, 'the original affluent society'.[7]

Sahlins's assessment was based on studies of subsistence strategies among Australian Aborigines. One can be affluent, he said, either by having a great deal or by not wanting very much. At the time of European contact in the late eighteenth century, the entire continent of Australia was inhabited by an estimated 300,000 people, with not a single domesticated plant. The Aborigines, in fact, had attained a point of perfect balance between the alternatives of having and wanting: they were well-fed and healthy, and had plenty of time for social, cultural and leisure activities.

The same can be said of the !Kung Bushmen in the Kalahari desert; in the days before foreign influences became overwhelming they too had food and time enough for a lifestyle that was fulfilling without being overly demanding or stressful. And again, not a single domesticated plant. In fact, researchers found that the !Kung Bushmen made use of eighty-four species of edible wild plants, including twenty-nine species of fruits, berries and melons and thirty species of roots and bulbs – not to mention the mongongo nut (*Ricinodendron rautanenii*), a highly nutritious item that because of its abundance and reliability accounted for half of the vegetable diet by weight. Tonnes of these nuts were gathered and eaten each year, and tonnes more left to rot for want of picking. Hardly surprising, therefore, that when asked why his people hadn't taken to agriculture a Bushman replied: 'Why should we plant, when there are so many mongongo nuts in the world?'[8]

And consider the story of wheat. *Triticum monococcum*, the wild ancestor of the grain that today feeds half of humanity, has survived to modern times in parts of the Fertile Crescent (the historic region of the Middle East that sweeps round from ancient Mesopotamia through Anatolia and the Levant to ancient Egypt), where Western civilisation's agriculture began. In 1966 the agronomist Jack Harlan investigated the productivity of natural wild wheat stands in eastern Anatolia. Armed with a crude sickle made of flint blades set in a wooden handle (such as Stone Age gatherers might have used), he found no difficulty in collecting over a kilo of clean grain per hour; furthermore, the grain contained about 23 per cent protein as compared with 12–16 per cent in its modern counterpart.[9]

On Harlan's evidence, a family of four or five could have collected a year's supply of grain with only a few weeks' labour – and a more nutritious grain at that – all of which suggests that the people who lived in the natural habitat of wheat and barley had the least incentive to domesticate and farm the crop.[10] Yet someone did.

Discussions as to who and why generally begin with the idea that population growth and having more mouths to feed must have forced people to find ways of increasing the amount of available food.

Agriculture might have been the answer – but not for people already under stress, with no experience of actually growing food. Further-more, archaeological evidence from the time when agriculture was being adopted in various places around the world shows that pre-agricultural people in general were actually much healthier than the first farmers. They were taller, had better teeth and did not have the diseases that became endemic once people began living permanently in large settle-ments.

So if not population pressure, what about the lucky accident wherein, as Darwin suggested, 'a wild and unusually good variety of a native plant might attract the attention of some wise old savage; and he would transplant it, or sow its seed.[11] Perhaps, but it is hard to imagine that the practice could have been more than a hobby, for to actually advance from occasional domestication to full-scale cultivation requires labour of an order that people probably would be reluctant to provide on a continuing basis while traditional sources of food remained available for the gathering.

Another persuasive idea is that agriculture began as a corollary of the technological developments that enabled people to secure more animal protein. Animals and fish had to be caught – canoes, boats and rafts; nets, spears, bows and arrows would make the job easier and the spin-off would be the invention of tools and techniques that aided the insensible modification of environments towards a cultivated form. Digging sticks churned over the soil. Fires set to trap animals changed vegetation patterns; so did the preference for some plants rather than others. The sago palm of Melanesia, for instance, existed as thorny and non-thorny varieties until people began weeding out the thorny seedlings until eventually only non-thorny palms remained – simply because they were much easier to handle. Similarly, the West African oil palm owes its prominence to the fact that the people who first recognised its usefulness made a practice of ensuring it was not smothered by denser vegetation.[12]

Reviewing the evidence of hunter-gatherer lifestyles in modern times has led the agronomist Jack Harlan to conclude that, in fact, they do everything farmers do except work as hard. They clear or alter vegeta-tion with fire, favour the proliferation of some plants and restrict the spread of others. They are fully aware of the year's seasonal round, they understand the life cycles of plants and know where and when they can be gathered in greatest abundance with the least effort. They harvest grass seeds, then thresh, winnow and grind them into flour. They detoxify poisonous plants for food and extract poisons to stun fish and kill game. They spin fibres, weave cloth, produce string, cord, baskets, canoes, shields, spears, bows and arrows; they make and play musical instruments; they sing, chant, dance and tell stories. They pray for rain, for better yields and for abundant harvests. All this has been amply confirmed among hunter-gatherers in the modern era – and there is no reason to suppose that their pre-agricultural counterparts were any less able to make the most of their environment.

So the development of agriculture would have required very little in the way of additional knowledge or new techniques – just a lot more work. The motivations could have been many and various, but the result was the same everywhere: more people. Farming means more work, but it produces more food; so, whether population pressure actually initiated the process or not, it has certainly driven humanity in a single direction ever since: towards the maximisation of numbers and productivity.

Today, with a global population of over 6 billion, it is sobering to note that most of us would not survive long without a supply of farmed food, even though agriculture has been around for only a small fraction (the last 10,000 years or so) of our 3-million-year existence. We evolved, over thousands of generations, to live as contributing beneficiaries of the environment – a part of the whole; giving and taking. Now we take, but give very little. More than half of us live in cities – beyond even the sight of where our food is grown. Furthermore, the impressive diversity of resources that the pre-agricultural people utilised has been reduced to a handful; where they used dozens of different plants, our huge and complex civilizations are historically based on the cultivation of just six plant families: wheat, barley, millet, rice, maize and potatoes. Other plants have been critical to the survival of some groups, and domesticated animals have also been important sources of protein and power everywhere, but those six plants have been the calorific engines of civilisation.

The advent of agriculture and its consequences are impressive, but the most remarkable thing is that it all happened so quickly, independently, in different parts of the world, in the same relatively brief span of time.

Ten thousand years ago the world was populated entirely by hunter-gatherers. And then, almost simultaneously, people all over the world began growing crops. Within a few hundred years agricultural economies based on rice in China, wheat and barley in south-west Asia, maize in Mexico and potatoes in the Andes had been established. This development is often referred to as the 'agricultural revolution', but in fact it was a human revolution: people changed. And it was a global phenomenon − astonishing for the speed of its development and its independent contemporaneity: the same thing, happening at roughly the same time, at different locations around the world − quite independent of one another. It is as though some global force was responsible, creating circumstances that susceptible groups of hunters and gatherers were obliged to respond to − knowingly or otherwise. How else could it be that people as far apart as China, the Andes and Anatolia should all abandon a way of life that had supported them for millennia, and begin farming?

A global force? Well, how about global climate change? And sure enough, as scientists have fine-tuned their reconstructions of the Earth's climatic history, the detail has revealed cycles of change that could indeed have been severe enough to influence human affairs on a global scale.[13]

The evidence shows that, between about 22,000 and 16,000 years ago, glaciers expanded to cover much of the northern hemisphere, affecting climates around the world. For most of this period, the sea coasts expanded as ocean levels fell. Forests advanced to cover many coastal regions, while grasslands expanded across high inland areas. Then the climate entered a warm phase, and the glaciers began to retreat. As the glaciers melted, the oceans rose − by only about 7–8 millimetres a year, but slowly and inexorably inundating coastlines everywhere. The warming was accompanied by periods of relatively high rainfall between about 14,500 and 11,000 years ago but conditions became increasingly arid for 1,000 years after that.

Looking at the archaeological record against this backdrop of climatic change around 10,000 years ago, researchers have discerned changing patterns of people–plant–animal interactions which could help to explain the advent of agriculture around that time. Drier and more sharply seasonal conditions in the Jordan Valley and adjacent areas of the Middle East, for instance, encouraged the growth and spread of annual cereals and legumes; while dry summers (and a lack of other resources) simultaneously obliged people to harvest and store food for lean seasons ahead. Storage meant establishing secure bases, and thus a more sedentary way of life. And for settled communities, with their extensive knowledge of the plant world and the tools already developed for its exploitation, it was a short step to the development of agricultural practices.

But there are problems with the idea of climate change as the incentive for agriculture around 10,000 years ago. For one thing, the change did not happen overnight, or even over a decade. It was progressive, accumulating year by year, and people probably were already accustomed to a range of extremes that exceeded the annual change – in other words, they were unlikely to have noticed. Furthermore, similar episodes of climate change had occurred many times in the previous hundreds of thousands of years, without prompting the development of agriculture. And when it did occur, the development appeared almost simultaneously in an extremely diverse range of environments: from the humid lowlands of south-east Asia, to the arid plains of the Middle East, and the frosty heights of the Andes. How could climate change alone produce the same result in such a diverse range of environments and conditions?

We do not know. Clearly, there was a significant mix of factors contributing to the beginnings of agriculture – ecological as well as climatic, cultural as well as demographic – in combinations that may never be unravelled. There is a great deal more information available now than in Darwin's day, but his conclusion still pertains: 'the problem . . . is at present much too difficult to be solved'. What we do know, though, is that in every instance where the shift from hunting and gathering to agriculture has been made, a limited number of staple foods have fuelled the subsequent development of civilisations. In the Andes, there was the potato.

But not the potato alone. In fact, the venerable tuber to whose origin and domestication we now return is but one of twenty-five root and tuber crops that were domesticated in the Andean regions, at least ten of which are still grown and marketed today: arracacha, yacón, mauka, achira, ahipa and maca; ulluco, oca, mashua and, of course, the potato. Together, these plants comprise a group of high-altitude species that are ecologically unique – the world's only such numerous and diverse group of domesticated root and tuber crops – and it is worth considering how such a range of choice could have facilitated the domestication of the potato.

The environment is the crucial factor: these plants produce roots and tubers simply because they evolved in regions that regularly experience a long and unbroken dry season. Under such demanding conditions, an underground store of starchy reserves enables them to survive the dry season and regenerate quickly when the rains come. For millions of years they had the place virtually to themselves, exploiting their innate adaptability, proliferating, and colonising the landscape from the forest edge to the Altiplano, with its rocky thin soils where no perennial grasses or herbs could survive.[14]

Although these high bleak landscapes would not have been much of an attraction for gatherers to begin with, the populations of indigenous llama, alpaca and vicuña they supported would certainly have attracted hunters to the scene. And then it was only a matter of time before some hunters discovered the bounty of food that was stored, ripe for the harvesting, in the ground at their feet. The bonus these roots and tubers added to the food budget can be imagined – especially in the dry season, when food of any kind is scarce. At a stroke the mountains acquired a more generous reputation. Hunting forays became gathering expeditions, which in turn doubtless became annual events and the occasions of ceremony, celebration and expressions of gratitude that mark the harvesting of Andean crops even today.

Those early gatherers would have been fully aware that if they wanted to have a harvest worth returning for next year, they must ensure there were enough left in the ground this year. While turning the soil, leaving one tuber or root for every three or four removed became common practice. The wisdom of leaving a harvested area to lie fallow for a few seasons developed then too, and eventually these gatherers became, in effect, farmers – selecting and nurturing the progeny of the tastiest and most productive plants they found in their managed fields of wild stock. In other words, progressively moving the plants from a wild to a domesticated state.

The potato would not have featured much in this process to begin with – but the potato had an advantage which made it more desirable than all the other Andean roots and tubers put together – once a means of dealing with its toxins had been discovered. The advantage was this: while the other Andean roots and tubers shrivel, soften and rot if not eaten within a short time of being harvested, potatoes can be stored and will keep for months – providing sustenance when other foods are in short supply.

It can only have been the selection and nurturing of progressively less bitter progeny, year by year, that brought the wild potato into domestication, but it is interesting to note that those early exploiters of the resource also developed some methods of dealing with its toxic content – methods which persist to this day.

In a study combining ethnobotany and chemical ecology, a team led by the biochemist Timothy Johns found that several of the potato varieties eaten by the Aymará people of the Lake Titicaca region (where the potato was first domesticated) contain dangerously high levels of poisonous glycoalkaloids. They liked the bitter taste, the Aymará said, but were aware that too much of it caused stomach pains and vomiting and could make a person seriously ill. Their solution, the study found, was to eat their bitter potatoes mixed with a quantity of clay that is specifically collected for the purpose. And sure enough, back in the laboratory, Johns' analysis has shown that the clay did indeed contain elements that bind to the glycoalkaloids and so ensured that the potentially lethal elements passed through the system undigested.[15]

Taking a small amount of earth with their food, or geophagy, has been observed among South American monkeys and parrots, so people probably acquired the habit by copying what they had seen as purposeful behaviour in the wild, but while the practice continues in some places (as a matter of taste largely, just as some like their fries with ketchup and others do not), much more efficient methods have been developed by the people who grow bitter potatoes at 4,000 metres and above in the Andes. Taking advantage of the freezing nights and brilliant days that the long dry season brings to these regions, they effectively freeze-dry their potatoes, turning them into hard and chalk-white *chuño* that is free of toxins and stores very well.

The process involves exposing the potatoes to three or four nights of freezing temperatures (while keeping them covered during the day to avoid the darkening caused by direct sunlight), then soaking them in pits or a streambed with cold running water for up to thirty days. After that, they are again put out to freeze at night and the next day walked on to remove the peel and squeeze out most of their water content. When that is finished, the tubers are spread out in direct sunlight for ten to fifteen days, by which time they are almost completely dehydrated. Rubbing them together by hand then removes any remaining peel and gives the *chuño* its characteristic chalky appearance and light firm consistency.

Production is a lengthy and complex procedure, but *chuño* has given the people of the high Andes a food resource that will thicken stews and fill bellies today and for months – even years – ahead. Indeed, archaeologists have found *chuño* in sites at Tiwanaku which dates from about 2,200 years ago. There is no record as to how edible the *chuño* still was, but the discovery certainly testifies to the durability of the product and the antiquity of the process.

Chapter Four

⟨⟩

Whence have they come?

Charles Darwin had found potatoes on the islands of Chile's Chonos Archipelago, where the *Beagle* had anchored early in January 1835, during the five-year round-the-world voyage that prompted so much of his thinking on the origin of species. In his journal he noted that:

> The wild potato grows on these islands in great abundance, on the sandy, shell soil near the sea-beach. The tallest plant was four feet in height. The tubers were generally small, but I found one, of an oval shape, two inches in diameter: they resembled in every respect, and had the same smell as English potatoes; but when boiled they shrunk much, and were watery and insipid, without any bitter taste. They are undoubtedly here indigenous: they grow as far south . . . as latitude 50 degrees, and are called Aquinas by the Indians of that part . . .[1]

Darwin believed he had found wild potatoes, but the absence of bitterness indicates a cultivated origin and, indeed, modern botanical and genetic studies have shown that they were almost certainly the progeny of cultivated potatoes from the mainland, growing from tubers left behind by fishermen who used the otherwise uninhabited islands as a base for their seasonal operations, living on fish and potatoes during their stay.[2] But who were these occasional visitors?

Darwin's first encounter with the inhabitants of Tierra del Fuego, the southernmost point of the Americas, had been a shock:

> It was without exception the most curious and interesting spectacle I ever beheld: I could not have believed how wide was the difference between savage and civilised man: it is greater than between

a wild and a domesticated animal, inasmuch as in man there is a greater power of improvement . . .

These poor wretches were stunted in their growth, their hideous faces bedaubed with white paint, their skins filthy and greasy, their hair entangled, their voices discordant, and their gestures violent. At night, five or six human beings, naked and scarcely protected from the wind and rain of this tempestuous climate, sleep on the wet ground coiled up like animals. Viewing such men, one can hardly make oneself believe that they are fellow creatures, and inhabitants of the same world. . . .

Their country is a broken mass of wild rocks, lofty hills, and useless forests: and these are viewed through mists and endless storms. The habitable land is reduced to the stones on the beach; in search of food they are compelled unceasingly to wander from spot to spot, and so steep is the coast, that they can only move about in their wretched canoes. They cannot know the feeling of having a home, and still less that of domestic affection; for the husband is to the wife a brutal master to a laborious slave. . . . How little can the higher powers of the mind be brought into play: what is there for imagination to picture, for reason to compare, for judgment to decide upon? . . .

Whilst beholding these savages, one asks, whence have they come? What could have tempted, or what change compelled a tribe of men, to leave the fine regions of the north, to travel down the Cordillera or backbone of America, . . . and then to enter on one of the most inhospitable countries within the limits of the globe?

Darwin was appalled by the Fuegians' appearance, way of life and behaviour; they 'resembled the devils which come on the stage in plays', he wrote. They connived, and stole; fought, and were horribly cruel to one another. Even so, the Fuegians did not appear to be decreasing in number and Darwin supposed, therefore, 'that they enjoy a sufficient share of happiness, of whatever kind it may be, to render life worth having' and similarly had enough of whatever was capable of sustaining life in those parts – fish, mussels, limpets, berries, fungi . . . and potatoes. 'Nature by making habit omnipotent, and its effects hereditary, has fitted the Fuegian to the climate and the productions of his miserable country,' Darwin concluded. In other words, the principles of natural selection had ensured that the Fuegians were well-adapted to their environment.[3]

Christopher Columbus and the pioneering adventurers who took Europe's influence across the Caribbean and into the Americas were not surprised to find their landfalls populated by people who clearly had been living there for some time. They had, after all, expected to land in India, or perhaps Japan. But once Europeans realised they were not anywhere near the Orient, but in an entirely New World, confronted by an amazing diversity of hitherto unknown cultures (and strange animals, such as the llama and the three-toed sloth), Europe's intelligentsia wanted to know more about these people and places. The Bible, final authority on all important issues in the Middle Ages, said nothing about even the existence of a 'second-earth' – let alone its inhabitants and whence they had come.

Apparent similarities between Egyptian and American cultures, such as the pyramids of the Nile and Mexico, inspired the idea that one of Noah's sons had somehow found his way to the western shores of the Atlantic as the flood waters subsided. There were also suggestions that Native Americans were the descendants of people who had survived the destruction of Atlantis and other lost worlds; or were Jews derived from the ten lost tribes of Israel. Indeed, by the early 1600s the list of possibilities was long enough for a voluminous compendium of theories to be published, though in conclusion it could only suggest that there must have been many origins, since no single theory could explain all the many customs and languages found among the people of the New World.[4]

Such vagueness was not good enough for José de Acosta, a Jesuit missionary who lived and worked in the Peruvian Andes from 1572 to 1588. He wanted a logical explanation for the existence of living creatures in a hitherto unknown continent – and used the Bible as the means of constructing one. Like most people of his day, Acosta believed the Bible was a chronicle of historical fact – literally true. So, if the book of Genesis said the entire earth had been submerged in the Deluge, eliminating all animal life except that which Noah had taken in the Ark, the inhabitants of the New World could only be the descendants of survivors who stepped ashore when the Ark docked on Mount Ararat. Logical enough; but 'where is the route whereby the beasts and the birds traveled ... How could they have come from one world to another?' Acosta rejected swimming as a possibility and thought it equally unlikely that people, beasts and birds could have reached the New World by boat. Ergo, the migrations could only have been by land:

I conjecture [he wrote in 1590] . . . that the New World . . . is not altogether severed and disjoined from the other world . . . I have long believed that the one and the other are joined and continued one with another in some part, or at least are very near.[5]

Acosta proposed that land bridges into the New World extended either from Europe in the east, or from Asia in the west . . . which solved the question of access, but immediately raised others: why should people and animals have bothered to cross the land bridges, and why were some animals in the New World so different from those existing elsewhere? One might suppose that a man of Acosta's intellectual athleticism could have found answers to these questions in the Bible, but here he used the logic of scientific observation instead, and in so doing put himself two or three centuries ahead of his time.

Having noted that certain regions were more compatible than others with the needs of certain animals, Acosta concluded that if an animal found itself in an unsuitable region it would either move on or die out. So, once off the Ark, the species not suited to life in the environs of Mount Ararat would migrate – driven by the need to find the regions that best suited their specific physiological requirements – and would keep moving until they found a place in which they could live, reproduce and multiply most successfully. That was why the llama and the three-toed sloth were found only in South America, a long way from Mount Ararat, and nowhere in between.

In this analysis Acosta not only gave theologians an acceptable explanation for the existence of people and strange animals in the New World; he also defined the first principles of biogeography.

The term 'biogeography' did not come into use until the late nineteenth century, but the principles Acosta had deployed to explain the puzzles of animal life in South America were nonetheless a starting point for scientific investigations into the origins and diversity of plants and animals around the world. They were fundamental to the idea that while God might have created life, environmental circumstance had been a powerful influence on its subsequent development. Biogeographical principles guided the observations of Charles Darwin on the Beagle's circumnavigation of the world, during which he gathered so much of the evidence upon which his theory of evolution would be founded.

Meanwhile, José de Acosta's conjecture regarding the existence of a land bridge between Asia and North America was confirmed, and by

1781 Thomas Jefferson could describe the peopling of the New World in terms that remain valid to this day:

> . . . late discoveries of Captain Cook, coasting from Kamschatka to California, have proved that, if the two continents of Asia and America be separated at all, it is only by a narrow strait. So that from [Asia] . . . inhabitants may have passed into America: and the resemblance between the Indians of America and the Eastern inhabitants of Asia, would induce us to conjecture, that the former are the descendants of the latter, . . .[6]

For Jefferson and everyone else it was obvious that once people had entered the New World across what was later to be called the Bering land bridge, they must have gradually trickled down and spread out to populate the entire region, from Alaska to Tierra del Fuego, as though the force of gravity had drawn them southward, down the familiar face of Mercator's map of the world. They had crossed the land bridge during one or more of the warmer and ice-free episodes that occurred between 60,000 and 10,000 years ago; once across, a limitless prospect lay before them – such as none had confronted before: 40 million square kilometres of virgin territory, one-third of the total inhabitable area of the earth's surface. Not that the pioneers would have been aware of this; they were nomadic hunters, simply doing what they had always done, moving on and doubtless hoping that conditions ahead would be as good or better than those they were leaving behind. Their advance proceeded erratically, as groups 'budded-off' from the 'growing edge' of the clans, dividing, redividing, dispersing and colonising new territories.

In the 1930s, archaeologists discovered stone projectile points and blades lying among the bones of extinct animals at a site near the town of Clovis in New Mexico. These tools matched discoveries at other sites scattered across North America, the oldest of which dated back to about 11,200 years ago. This date fitted in nicely with what was known of conditions on the land bridge around that time and so persuaded many that the first immigrants must have arrived in the New World not long before then. And the Clovis culture became firmly established as the earliest evidence of a human presence in the New World.

Meanwhile, though, Clovis-style artefacts were being found at sites in South America too, which effectively extended the range of the technology from the Arctic to Tierra del Fuego. And raised a problem. All dates for Clovis sites in North America clustered tightly between 11,200 and 10,800 years ago, while sites at the southern tip of South America were dated at 11,000 years ago. Could people have populated an entire hemisphere in such a short span of time – 300 to 500 years – from the initial crossing of the land bridge to the appearance of artefacts in Tierra del Fuego?[7]

It seemed improbable, but so long as there was no contradictory evidence to hand, the all-embracing concept of a Clovis culture throughout the Americas held. Indeed, it became an article of faith, generating not a little rancour during the late twentieth century as archaeologists sought and disputed evidence of a human presence in the Americas that predated the Clovis culture. Literally scores of pre-Clovis contenders came forward, 'only to wither under critical scrutiny', as an authority close to the issue reported.[8] So many failed that the archaeological community grew highly sceptical of any and all pre-Clovis claims. Few went so far as to absolutely exclude the possibility that earlier evidence might be found, but most were unwilling to take such claims at face value. The evidence was always flawed in some way: the dating was not secure enough; the geology was confused, or the artefacts were open to doubt. Clearly, if a site was going to break through the Clovis barrier it must be unimpeachable, with unambiguous artefacts or human skeletal remains in an unquestionable geological and stratigraphic context, chronologically anchored by absolutely secure radiocarbon dates.

As a graduate student, Thomas Dillehay had been trained to believe (and never seriously question) the veracity of Clovis as the first culture of the New World, so he was 'startled', to say the least, when radiocarbon tests on archaeological material from a site at Monte Verde in southern Chile yielded dates of more than 12,000 years ago. If the Clovis culture was the first in the New World and the people responsible for it had come to North America no earlier than 11,200 years ago and reached South America perhaps 800 years later, how could there have been people living at Monte Verde more than 1,000 years earlier? Dillehay was sceptical. The chronology must be wrong, or the site must have been disturbed by erosion or flooding that left artefacts of different ages mixed together. And besides, there were none of the spearpoints that distinguished the Clovis culture.[9]

The puzzle of Monte Verde began in 1976, while Dillehay was doing a spell of teaching and archaeological research at the Southern

University of Chile. A student brought in a large mastodon tooth and other bones which had been exposed where some local men had been clearing a path for their ox carts. Since the bones bore marks which could have been made by people cutting meat from them, Dillehay decided that an exploratory excavation was merited. The following year, he and his team found more bones with unmistakable cut-marks, clay-lined hearths with charcoal and burned food plants, and stone tools – all buried in the same thin geological layer. Because the material included mastodon remains, Dillehay believed the site probably dated from the late Ice Age, between 11,000 and 10,000 years ago, when the animals were known to have inhabited the region.

With the site appearing to be so old, Dillehay proceeded cautiously – as well he might, given the scathing scepticism with which pre-Clovis claims were customarily greeted. Over the next ten years he directed a programme of excavation and research with a team of more than eighty professionals at Monte Verde. They found a wide variety of wooden, bone and stone tools, as well as scraps of animal hide and chunks of meat, human footprints, hearths, and fragments of edible and medicinal plants, all scattered in and around the remains of wooden hut foundations. Additional excavations and radiocarbon dates 'proved conclusively that the site was a valid human locality, at least 12,500 years old'.

Dillehay and his colleagues were convinced, but another ten years of painstaking analysis was undertaken before the findings were published – in two volumes, totalling over 1,400 pages. 'Analytical overkill,' said a reviewer, but necessary given the volume (in both quantity and intensity) of doubt expressed about Monte Verde's antiquity since the site was first reported. In 1997 a party of experts and specialists – staunch sceptics among them – was invited to examine the site and its collections. They could not find fault with any aspect of the work and conclusions: the Monte Verde site was unimpeachable and 12,500 years old.

As Dillehay reports in his popular book on the settlement of the Americas,[10] Monte Verde was an open-air settlement on the banks of a small freshwater creek, surrounded by sandy knolls, and backed by a cool damp forest. A bog developed in the creek basin some time after the settlement had been abandoned, steadily burying everything under a layer of peat. Because the lack of oxygen in the bog inhibited bacterial decay, and because constant saturation stopped anything drying out, all kinds of perishable materials that normally disappear from the archaeological record were preserved, giving an unprecedented glimpse of life on the banks of that creek. And there – in the cracks of wooden mortars and in food storage pits set in the corners of shelters – were the preserved remains of potatoes.[11] The Monte Verdeans had gathered, processed and eaten potatoes, 12,500 years ago.

The settlement had been occupied throughout the year by perhaps twenty to thirty people, who had built a 20-metre-long tent-like structure – its frame made of logs and planks and its walls of poles covered with animal hides. The tent's dirt floor was imbedded with hundreds of microscopic flecks of hide tissue, suggesting that it was probably covered with skins. Inside, planks and poles divided the floor space into individual living areas, each with a clay-lined firepit surrounded by the remains of vegetable foods, and stone tools. Outside the tent there were two large communal hearths, a store of firewood, wooden mortars with their grinding stones, and even three human footprints near a large hearth, where someone had walked on clay brought in to reline some firepits.

The remains of a wide variety of edible and medicinal plants were recovered from the hearths, living floors and small pits, along with the remnants of mastodon, paleo-llama, small animals and freshwater molluscs. Aquatic plants provided the greatest variety and, along with meat, the bulk of the Monte Verdeans' diet. Most of their food came from ecological zones on the Pacific shore, about 70 kilometres to the west, or from the Andes. More than half of the purely medicinal plants found at the site came from distant parts too – one from arid regions about 700 kilometres to the north. All of which indicated that the Monte Verdeans either travelled regularly to distant environments or were part of a complex social and exchange network.

Monte Verde broke the Clovis barrier; the paradigm shifted and the old school was now obliged to confront the profound implications of a site so old, so far south. The fact that Monte Verde dated from 12,500 years ago meant that the initial crossing from Asia into the Americas must have occurred much earlier. How much earlier depended largely on obstacles encountered along the way: routes south from Alaska were blocked by glaciers from about 20,000 to 13,000 years ago, for instance, and remained an ecological barrier for several millennia. The timing also depended on how well the migrants maintained their reproductive viability while living in relatively small numbers spread thinly over vast and unpopulated continents.[12]

Current knowledge suggests that people first crossed the Bering land bridge into the New World at least 20,000 years ago. But even this has awkward implications. If people entered the New World that long ago, why is no site in North America older than 11,200 years? What were people doing for those several thousand years? Or could the New World have filled up from the bottom, as any container would when a flowing mass pours in from the top? This idea is not as fanciful as it might seem, and finds support in the contention that a Pacific coastal route would have been the best way for people to enter the Americas.

In this scenario,[13] hunting groups with relatively simple watercraft could have successfully migrated along the coastal zone from Asia to the Americas even at the height of the last glaciations. Compelling geological and biogeographical evidence shows that well-spaced breaks in the chain of coastal glaciers retained ample terrestrial and marine life to support migrants as they advanced. And once past the glaciers, people could have followed the coast down to the southernmost tip of South America. It all sounds plausible, but will remain no more than hypothesis until hard confirmatory evidence is found. The best would be a string of occupation sites along the coast. Unfortunately, though, any that might exist in the appropriate locations are invisible, deep underwater, drowned by rising sea levels as the glaciers melted.

Invisibility is a major problem in archaeology. The 'out of sight, out of mind' principle creates a danger that if something cannot be seen its absence generates a belief that it did not exist − as the discoveries at Monte Verde demonstrated. Of course, the collapse of the Clovis barrier did not mean that previous arguments against it suddenly became valid − sites that were not genuinely old before Monte Verde were no older afterwards − but it did open the field to more discussion and hypothesis. And this, along with the new avenues of enquiry that were developed in the interim − genetics and linguistics, for example − reinvigorated investigations into the number, timing and antiquity of migrations into the Americas.[14]

Another issue that Monte Verde brings to light is more general, concerning some very deeply rooted beliefs about the nature and lives of people before the advent of agriculture: the concept of Man the Hunter.

'Man the Hunter' was the title of a symposium held in Chicago in 1966 that brought together seventy-five scholars from around the world for 'the first intensive survey of . . . man's once universal hunting way of life'. The undisputed tenet here was that hunting defined humanity; participants declared that 'hunting is the master behavior pattern of the human species'; 'our intellect, interests, emotions, and basic social life are all evolutionary products of the success of the hunting adaptation'.[15]

War and cowboy films were two aspects of life in the second half of the twentieth century which helped to ensure that boys grew up believing males were born to fight and prevail, while females bore children and kept the home fires burning. Hunting was the respectable adult expression of this; red meat its reward. Not surprising, then, that the prevalence of spearpoints, arrowheads and animal bones that archaeologists unearthed at prehistoric sites around the world was seen as proof that hunting had been the primeval driving force of human evolution: 'for those who would understand the origin and nature of human behavior there is no choice but to try to understand "Man the Hunter",' the Chicago symposium was told.[16]

And once a belief like that is established, research on the subject tends to become self-fulfilling, with evidence assessed by the extent to which it conforms with the paradigm. Here, too, Monte Verde broke through the barrier. The site had been preserved in a bog, which inhibited the decay of organic matter and left indisputable evidence of a far more diverse and bountiful economy than hunting. The occupants had occupied the site throughout the year; they were not exclusively nomadic; nor were they principally big-game hunters – they ate meat, certainly, but the acquisition and preparation of vegetable foods and medicines had clearly occupied a good deal of their time and energies too. Yet if the Monte Verde site had been in a more typical location, none of the organic matter would have been preserved. Only the hundreds of stone artefacts and bones would have been found. And then it would have been another classic 'Man the Hunter' site – important for its antiquity, but adding little or nothing to the understanding of the origin and nature of human behaviour.

Monte Verde is a rare – if not unique – case. Most archaeological evidence of early human activity in the Americas has been recovered either from sites in open locations, as at Clovis, where the preservation of organic material is poor to non-existent, or in caves, where it is not much better. How many sites that have been so readily attributed to Man the Hunter would have been classified in more general terms if the preservation had been as complete as at Monte Verde?

In the Peruvian Andes, for instance, numerous cave sites are listed under 'The Central Andean Hunting Tradition' by virtue of the bones and stone points, blades and scrapers they contained.[17] Dating from up to about 10,800 years ago,[18] the caves are located at elevations of between

2,500 and 4,500 metres. Since protein and fats are essential elements of the human diet (and skins, bone and sinews have practical uses), we can be sure that the cave-dwellers used some of the points and blades for hunting. Even so, they would have needed a dependable source of vegetable foods for even a relatively brief stay in the region. So perhaps it was not merely fortuitous that their caves usually overlooked valleys or lakes, where the local vegetation, with its host of edible seeds, roots and tubers, could have been as much of an attraction as its animal population. Indeed, these are exactly the locations where the domestication of the potato (and other Andean crops) probably began.

Scraps of organic material do occur in some of the high Andean cave sites, and even the remains of edible plants have been found, but archaeological investigations still draw more attention to the hunter than to the gatherer – unsurprisingly, given that the evidence of hunting activities is more readily preserved, but frustrating to those wishing to trace the use and domestication of the potato through the millennia. All we have is the evidence of potatoes being consumed at Monte Verde around 12,500 years ago, and then a gap of several thousand years before any sign at all of the potato appears in the archeological record.

In 1970, shrivelled tubers found during the excavation of a cave site on the high western slopes of the Andes, 65 kilometres south-east of Lima, were identified as domesticated potatoes,[19] and said to be 10,000 years old. But this claim is treated with extreme caution,[20] since it is based on the plants' position in the deposit, not on radiocarbon dating of the specimens themselves (the danger here is that such items can easily slip down through cracks in the deposit, thus encouraging a belief that they are older than they are). In fact, after Monte Verde, the first reliable evidence of potatoes as part of the human diet comes more than 8,000 years later and 4,000 kilometres to the north.

Archaeologists have found tubers to which secure radiocarbon dating gives an age of around 4,000 years near Casma, in the coastal desert of central Peru. But this was not a bog site – nor even a cave site; it was an agglomeration of domestic and civic ruins spread over more than two square kilometres of dry desert sands – larger than London's Hyde Park. Extreme aridity (the present rainfall average of less than 5 millimetres per year has prevailed for millennia) preserved organic matter as effectively as the bog at Monte Verde, and it is equally clear that people at the Casma locations also enjoyed a varied diet and participated in extensive trade networks. Their potatoes, for instance, were most definitely domesticated (comparative analysis of starch cells proved that), but could not have been grown in the coastal desert conditions at Casma[21] without extensive irrigation (of which there is no evidence). They must have come from the highlands – probably exchanged for fish – and could even have been brought down as *chuño*, the dried form that both preserves potatoes and detoxifies them. All of which indicates that by 4,000 years ago at the latest, the potato was domesticated and grown extensively enough in the Andes for it to serve both as a food crop and an item of trade.

In South America, as in all centres where civilisation first took root, the transition from hunting and gathering to agriculture and a settled way of life was accompanied by profound cultural and social change. Within a few generations of abandoning the nomadic way of life that had sustained their ancestors for untold thousands of years, the settlers' villages grew to the size of cities and their egalitarian communities were subsumed into states under the control of a ruling elite. In South America the process began along the Andean coastline, where numerous settled communities were established by 4,000 years ago. And no sooner had some developed successful economies than they began 'spending' their surplus wealth on the construction of temples, tombs, grand plazas and massive pyramids – just like their counterparts in Egypt, Mesopotamia and China. Dozens of such places were built along the coast, each with its monumental architecture demonstrating the conspicious extravagance that has characterised the early formative stages of civilisation around the world.

There was art too – paintings, sculpture, carvings, tapestries and wonderful ceramics. A diverse series of ceramic styles evolved, each with a wide range of examples, but the most interesting from the point of view of this narrative is the pottery of the Moche, who ruled the coastal and immediate inland regions of northern Peru from the beginning of the Christian era until about AD 600. The Moche took the potter's art to an exceptionally high standard, producing vessels whose purpose must have been more decorative, or ceremonial, than utilitarian. Every aspect of Moche life is depicted in the finely worked clay: men in the fields, people chasing deer with spears and clubs, hunters aiming blowguns at brilliantly feathered birds, fishermen putting to sea in small canoes, craftsmen at work, soldiers in battle, and scenes of human sacrifice – all beautifully painted and burnished. There are also scenes of people being carried in sedan chairs, seated on thrones, receiving tribute and engaging in sexual activities both commonplace and remarkable – all shown in exquisite detail.

Potatoes feature prominently among the Moche ceramics. Of course, the tuber's globular form is easily reproduced, and there are plenty of what might be called conventional potato pots, in that they are shaped like a potato, but there are also some oddities that combine the potato and the human form in a disturbing manner. The simplest just make a head or a face of the potato, or use naturally occurring shapes to represent the human form – like the tubers that occasionally turn up with knobbly heads or limbs attached – but others are more sinister. On one, several heads erupt through the skin; on another, a man carrying · a corpse emerges from the deeply incised eyes; a 'potato' head has its nose and lips cut off; potato eyes are depicted as mutilations . . .

We can never know whether any particular significance should be attached to the combination of human and potato forms in Moche pottery, but surely must agree with an authority on most things relating to the potato, the Cambridge scientist Redcliffe N. Salaman, who concluded that the pots illustrate 'the overwhelming importance to certain sections of the population of the potato as a food, . . . to the people both of the coast and the sierra' – especially in times of famine or war.[22] For, as we know, the potato could not be cultivated on the hot and arid coastal desert. Imports from the highlands were the only source, and for coastal people who had become dependent on the potato a disrupted supply could spell disaster.

The Moche civilisation disintegrated around AD 600, and if the collapse was precipitated by a failure in potato supplies, it was probably caused deliberately – especially if the Moche had been getting their potatoes from around the shores of Lake Titicaca; for it was here that a number of groups coalesced into what became the Tiwanaku state. And the rise of Tiwanaku precisely coincided with the fall of Moche. They were all states for whom warfare and bloodshed were the principal means of gaining and governing territory, but depriving an opponent of an essential food would have been a no less effective strategy.

Tiwanaku was the first state to be based largely on the cultivation of potatoes. It was also the first state in the Americas to build its numerous huge monuments in stone (Moche and others had used clay and mudbricks) and it was the exceptional productivity of their farming practices that enabled them to afford such extravagances – a first instance of the economic, social and political influence the potato would have throughout the world.

Today, Tiwanaku is a UNESCO world heritage site administered by the Bolivian government. It stands at an altitude of 3,845 metres above sea level, close to the southern end of Lake Titicaca. The site is a popular venue for tourists visiting the region, though much of its architecture is in a poor state of preservation after centuries of looting and amateur excavations. During the nineteenth and early twentieth centuries substantial amounts of its stonework were taken for building and railway construction, and the remainder was used for military target practice. Nonetheless, some impressive monuments and statues remain.

At the height of its powers between AD 800 and 1200, Tiwanaku was a huge and powerful state, controlling an empire of some 600,000 square kilometres from its capital of state buildings, palaces, pyramids, temples, plazas and streets, apparently all built to an integrated design by legions of stonemasons and master craftsmen. In its heyday, 100,000 people are said to have lived at Tiwanaku. This is impressive by any standard, but at 3,845 metres above sea level – where the air is thin, the sun is fierce and temperatures regularly fall below freezing – the achievement merits even greater admiration and further examination. The key to Tiwanakuan success was the judicious husbanding and manipulation of the region's natural resources. They domesticated and herded vast numbers of llamas, for example, which not only provided transportation for their voluminous trade with the lowland regions, but also converted the Altiplano's widely dispersed grasses into a compact and easily gathered source of energy. Dried llama dung has a high calorific value; it has fuelled the cooking fires and heated the dwellings of Altiplano farmers for hundreds of years.[23]

The llama herds would also have supplied the Tiwanaku communities with meat – but the entrenched view of Man the Hunter as the formative imperative of human development should not be allowed to exaggerate the significance of this. The Titicaca region was also endowed with native plants of exceptional nutritional value, and while it might have been hunting that first attracted people to the area, it was the food plant resources that enabled them to establish permanent settlements there. There were several tasty options to be dug from the soils of the Altiplano, as we have seen, including the potato, but also above-ground food plants such as quinoa and kañihua – two pseudo-cereals which, although not of the grass family, yield prodigious quantities of cereal-like seeds. Both quinoa and kañihua typically have a protein content of 14–18 per cent (enough to temper the hunting imperative), and a most useful capacity to thrive under the extreme conditions of the Altiplano. Indeed, kañihua will germinate and start to grow at minus

3 degrees Celsius, and some varieties of quinoa are similarly able to begin growth at or near freezing point.[24]

The practice of allowing livestock to feed on the stubble of newly harvested fields and thus manure the fields and improve productivity was adopted by Tiwanaku farmers at an early stage. They also developed the practice of planting their crops on ridges one metre or more high, and 3–5 metres wide, with ditches in between. The ridges were set typically in a pattern of ten or more; the ditches were open-ended, neither closed off such as might serve to keep water in or out nor forming a network typical of drainage or irrigation systems.

When Tiwanaku first came under scientific scrutiny in the 1960s, investigators were puzzled as to what the function of the ridged fields could have been – especially as surveys revealed that they had once covered a total area of more than 500 square kilometres. Neither irrigation, drainage nor land reclamation made sense in that region on that scale, but in the 1980s a series of studies showed the raised fields functioned extremely well as a means of keeping the land frost-free. It was found that when the ditches contained a reasonable depth of water (as they usually did), its temperature, and that of adjacent soils, could be as much as 6–9 degrees Celsius higher than the surrounding air temperature on cold nights.

Differentials on this scale can raise productivity significantly. In trials, quinoa and kañihua yields were four to eight times larger on the ridges than on flat fields, and potato yields were equally impressive: 10.6 tonnes per hectare compared with regional averages of between 1.6 and 6 tonnes.[25]

Thus, although they had settled in one of the most demanding inhabitable environments on earth, the Tiwanaku were blessed with a bounty of food. Even without the innovation of heat-conserving ridges, their domesticated animals and cultivated food plants could have sustained sizeable populations. But with potatoes growing in temperature-controlled soils, the potential soared. Even if only three-quarters of the ridged fields was in use at one time (which would allow for a four-year rotation), potatoes alone would have produced enough calories to support a population of at least 570,000 people,[26] while quinoa, kañihua and llamas provided the protein they required.

In fact, the Tiwanaku population was never so large, which invites the conclusion that, at the peak of operations, there was a sizeable surplus of potatoes to dispose of. And here the freezing nights and dry sunny days of the Altiplano worked to the advantage of the Tiwanaku, facilitating the conversion of their surplus potatoes into *chuño* – a durable, valuable and highly marketable commodity. With herds of domesticated llamas to provide the transport, Tiwanaku potatoes must have been distributed far and wide. There are the remnants of several large ancient causeways in and around Tiwanaku that were probably built to facilitate the export traffic, and it is significant that some of Peru's major roadways appear to have been constructed as Tiwanaku rose to supremacy, for they would have been essential for the efficient movement of goods to distant markets – such as Moche.

Potatoes thus not only filled Tiwanakuan bellies, but also fuelled long-distance trade and the emergence of the bureaucracy needed to run the operation – which in turn called upon the state's communal organisations for the massive labour forces required to produce, process, store and transport the goods.

The demise of Tiwanaku appears to have been a relatively slow process, and certainly not due to sudden capitulation. The ridged fields fell into disuse; the power of Tiwanaku dwindled. It seems that no single cause was responsible, though factional differences between leaders on what are now the Bolivian and Peruvian sides of Lake Titicaca cannot have helped, and climatic changes could have made the matter worse. Ice cores taken from glaciers on mountains to the north-west show that the Titicaca basin was already in the grip of a serious drought from 1245 to 1310, and limnological studies at the lake itself confirm that lake levels were at their lowest for over 500 years by that time. Researchers conclude from these findings that from about AD 1100 or a little earlier, the entire southern Altiplano was affected by a major long-term drought, which steadily eliminated the elaborate farming system and, with it, the power of the Tiwanaku state.[27] And left the stage clear for the appearance of the mighty Inca.

The Inca went beyond mere statehood to found an empire that was the largest and most highly integrated political system ever to appear in the Americas before the arrival of Europeans. Their origins are not definitively known. Oral histories recorded by the Spanish tell of Quechua groups uniting on the fertile lands of the Cuzco valley sometime around AD 1200 under the leadership of Manco Capac, to whom legend attributes the founding of the Inca dynasty. Subsequently they captured the town, formed an alliance with neighbouring groups and progressively added new provinces to the empire by conquest, treaty or simple annexation.

Perhaps inspired by the construction work they saw at Tiwanaku,[28] the Inca transformed their capital city, Cuzco, into an orderly arrangement of streets, houses and monumental buildings, complete with a municipal water supply and drainage system. From here, they ruled an empire they called the Tahuantinsuyu – 'the parts that in their fourness make up the whole' – which embraced over a million square kilometres of South America. The empire stretched from the Pacific coastline eastward across the Andes into the Amazonian lowlands and from Columbia southward to central Chile and Argentina, and brought many diverse regional economic and political systems under the administration of a single royal lineage. At its height, 10 million people were living under Inca rule in one of the most intricately ordered societies of all time.[29]

The strength of the Inca system was their determination to establish a permanent presence in the territories they took over. Instead of the invasion, plunder and withdrawal that had characterised expansion tactics until that time, the Incas installed local administrators and located military garrisons throughout the empire. To facilitate communications, pre-existing land routes (such as had carried the Tiwanaku export trade) were linked and upgraded to create a network of paved roads that gave all corners of the empire direct access to Cuzco. This involved cutting tunnels through mountains; laying causeways across swamps; building embankments along the flanks of precipitous ravines, and spanning rivers with suspension bridges made of fibre ropes hung from stone towers. In all, about 40,000 kilometres of roads were built – enough to encircle the globe – with food stores and administrative outposts placed along them at strategic points and runners stationed about a kilometre apart so that a message passed from one to another could travel as much as 2,400 kilometres in just five days, it is said.[30]

The economic basis of the Inca empire was an integrated system of farming, herding, fishing, mining, craft manufacture, state service and so forth. Starvation was not a threat under the Incas, but people lived at the order of the state and, in one way or another, food was the *sine qua non* of Inca administrative policies. Flights of terraces were built to bring hitherto unusable steep mountainsides into cultivation; canals and aqueducts brought water from distant sources to irrigate dry land; existing irrigation systems were extended to increase productivity (though the Tiwanaku raised fields were not reinstated, perhaps because appreciation of the technology had been lost, or climate still militated against it); guano and fish remains were brought from the coast to fertilise the soil. Throughout the empire, the agricultural land accessible to each community was divided into three parts: one for the Gods, one for the State, and one for the community. Farmers were obliged to cultivate all three, but lived off the produce of their community's land. The harvests they reaped from the other two categories were consigned to the stores of the Gods and the State, to be used in ceremonies, to feed soldiers and the armies of masons, miners and craftsmen working for the greater glory of the Inca, and also for distribution to those whom local crop failures might have left in need.

But the masterstroke of the Inca was the spread and intensification of maize production. Maize was not a native Andean crop, having been introduced from its Mexican homeland even before the Inca rose to power. In their hands, however, it achieved new heights of utility. Highly productive and easily transported, maize flowed continuously through the Inca's arterial network, nourishing their physical, economic and strategic systems. But the greatest benefit was that while it fuelled the expansion of the empire, maize production did not completely replace the traditional agricultural system.

By Inca times, potatoes were well and truly established as the staple food of the high Andes, grown in rotation with the indigenous quinoa and kañihua, on land lengthily fallowed and fertilised by herds of domesticated llama and alpaca. Maize displaced potato production at lower altitudes, but this intensified its continuation higher up, at 2,500 metres and above, where maize would not grow. Under the Incas, people were obliged to build terraces and irrigation systems for maize, and tend the crop, but organised labour also increased all-round efficiency. The traditional systems persisted, and people lived off the produce of traditional agropastoralism even while they worked on state and religious lands or on civic projects for the benefit of the Inca empire. Thus, although the Inca used maize to extend and maintain their power, the grain supplemented rather than supplanted the most valuable subsistence crop of the Andes – the potato.

Maize was important to the Inca not only as an easily transported food commodity, but also as a grain from which a beer they called *chicha* could be brewed. *Chicha* is nutritious as well as alcoholic – a welcome and altogether palatable brew that became a prestige item, associated with the imperial power and theology of the Inca state. Throughout the empire people were regularly brought together for communal feasts at which large quantities of *chicha* were consumed; in this way, the elite reinforced their status and reminded the peasantry of how much they owed to the state and its religion.

The Inca worshipped the gods of sun and thunder, of the Earth, the sea, the moon and the stars. They recognised that the sun was the giver of life in the cold highlands and so, lacking a distinguished past or any inherited property, the founder of the Inca dynasty, Manco Capac, had declared that his father was the sun, his mother the moon, and his brother the day-star, Venus.[31] Manco Capac ordered the building of the Coricancha, the Sun Temple, in Cuzco, a massive building demonstrating the finest skills of Inca stonemasonry, with exterior walls measuring 68 metres by 59 metres and interior structures more than 30 metres high. A gold frieze about a metre wide ran around the exterior wall and the entrance was similarly sheathed in solid gold. It is said that 4,000 attendants watched over the various shrines and treasures of the Coricancha, the most precious of which symbolised the Inca belief in their divine descent from the sun – a massive disc of solid gold, with sunbeams radiating from a human face at its centre.

There was also a garden dedicated to the sun at the Coricancha, where golden cobs of maize stood life-size on stalks of silver and the ground was scattered with lumps of gold resembling potatoes.

The Inca empire had existed at its fullest extent for less than 100 years when its rule was brought to an end by Spanish conquistadors in 1532. Given the size and power of the empire, it seems odd that it should have fallen so readily to Francisco Pizarro and his force of less than 200 men, but the seeds of downfall had been sown some years before. The death of the Inca Huanya Capac in 1527 had been followed by eruptions of opposition to Inca rule in several parts of the empire (so much so that some factions actually welcomed the Spanish when they arrived). Huanya Capac had died suddenly in the Inca's Ecuadorian capital, Quito, in an epidemic of smallpox that spread from Spanish exploratory landings on the coast that year. He had died without declaring which of his three sons, Ninan, Huascar or Atahuallpa, should succeed him as absolute ruler and further confusion ensued when the first-born, Ninan, died of smallpox shortly after his father, leaving Huascar and Atahuallpa each claiming the right of succession. Their political intrigues culminated in civil war, from which Atahuallpa had only just emerged victorious, in 1532, when Francisco Pizarro and his men reached Cajamarca – an Andean town in what is now Peru, on the Inca road from Quito to Cuzco.

By then, Huascar was in captivity, the systematic slaughter of his family and followers had been completed and Atahuallpa was journeying to Cuzco for his installation as ruling Inca. He stopped to meet the Spaniards, who were virtually imprisoned in Cajamarca by encircling Inca armies. A formal meeting was arranged, and an eyewitness, Francisco de Jerez, recorded how Atahuallpa entered the town at twilight with a party of his senior generals, all splendidly dressed and bedecked with gold and silver regalia. Retainers swept the road before them, dancers and singers accompanied them, and Atahuallpa was carried on a litter lined with red, yellow and blue parrot feathers. In the town square, an ambush awaited them. Atahuallpa was captured and his companions killed before the armies outside the town could be alerted.

With their divine ruler captive and leading generals dead, the Inca armies fell into disarray. Pizarro played one disaffected faction against another and eventually gained control of them all. Atahuallpa was held hostage while a huge ransom of gold and silver treasure was collected to secure his release; then he was tried on charges of offending the laws of Spain, found guilty and executed.

'The earth refused to devour the Inca's body – rocks trembled, tears made torrents, the Sun was obscured, the Moon ill,' a sixteenth-century account laments, and with the death of Atahuallpa, the last divine image of the Sun on Earth, the New World's most imposing indigenous civilisation fell to the power of Europe.

Atahuallpa's ransom was melted down to 11 tons of pure gold and silver ingots. This was only the beginning of the fabulous wealth that flowed from the Andes into Spanish coffers – and it was to have a profound effect on the economies and history of Europe. So too would another Andean treasure which the Spaniards almost entirely overlooked: the potato.

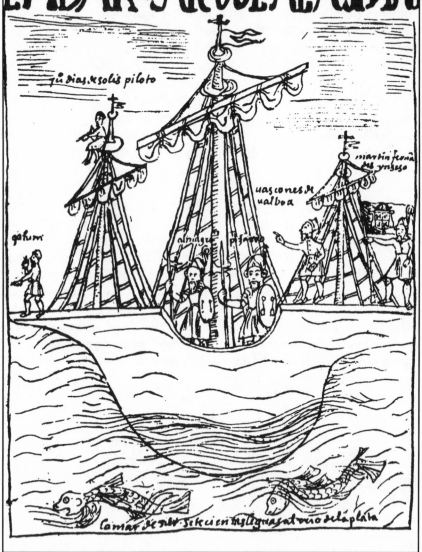

CONQVISTA
ENBARCAROSEALASINDIAS

juan dias. de solis piloto

martin feona
des ynsuso

uascones de
ualboa

alniigro pisarro

gahun

la mar de nor se ken leguas al rio dela plata

Chapter Five

⌒⌒⌒

A dainty dish

Huge amounts of gold and silver were shipped to Spain in the decades following the discovery of the Americas, but, even so, it was not the prospect of treasure that attracted most of the 13,000 men and 700 women known to have left Spain for the New World between 1520 and 1539.[1]

They were not all soldiers or romantic adventurers by any means, more an advance guard of European economic expansion, with a realistic outlook and the uncompromising demeanour of entrepreneurs who would acquire land, engage in trade, and change the ecological and human landscape to suit their needs. In research that looked beyond the facts of conquest into the nature of Spain's colonisation of South America, the historian James Lockhart investigated the life stories of Pizarro and his men: who were they, where did they come from, what were their occupations, their ambitions, and what became of them?

Lockhart was able to do this because when the Inca treasure was melted down and distributed among Pizarro and his men after the ransom and execution of Atahuallpa at Cajamarca in 1532, records were made of exactly who received how much. Over a period of nearly four months, 11 tons of treasure were melted down, producing 13,420 pounds of 22.5-carat gold; silver objects yielded 26,000 pounds of silver. The ingots emerging from the furnaces were officially stamped with the royal mark, to show that each had been legally melted and the obligatory one-fifth of its value paid to the royal treasury. Francisco Pizarro received the largest share – roughly 600 pounds of gold and over 1,200 pounds of silver – and every one of the other 167 men received a precise fraction of the total according to his status and role on the expedition.[2]

Each allocation of gold and silver was recorded and notarised, and if this attention to detail seems surprising in a newly discovered land where even the paper it was recorded on had travelled thousands of miles and a pen would need to be cut from an eagle's quill, then consider the occupational qualifications of the men that Pizarro selected for his expedition. The men of Cajamarca were a diverse lot, coming from every region of Spain, representing every social position from the son of a slave to the relative of a courtier, and between them practising all the major callings and crafts. The maintenance of the expedition and the bureaucratic needs of a new colony were as well provided for as the demands of conquest.[3]

Every man accompanying Pizarro was obliged to take arms when called upon to do so, but there were only four professional soldiers among the men whom Lockhart identified by occupation. The expedition's largest contingent consisted of artisans: six tailors, two blacksmiths, two carpenters, one cooper, one swordsmith, one stonemason, one crier and one barber. Next came the professionals: notaries, secretaries and accountants – twelve in all, who were required to make records of all transactions, double-check the arithmetic, certify the legality of agreements and generally ensure that the bureaucratic foundations of the new colony were soundly laid (as well as compensate for the fact that Francisco Pizarro himself could neither read nor write).

As Lockhart points out, it is because there were notaries and secretaries on Pizarro's expeditionary force that so much is known about the men of Cajamarca. And it is overwhelmingly evident that, among them, as with most Spaniards who left their homeland for new horizons during the sixteenth century, the driving ambition was to amount to something. First as an individual, but most importantly as the means of raising the position and prestige of one's family and lineage. Once they had wealth, the men of Cajamarca longed to get back to Spain – to buy property, to acquire a position at court or in regional administration, to marry well, have children and ensure the continuity of a wealthy and respected family line.

If they had been free to go, the majority of Pizarro's men probably would have taken their treasure and returned to Spain forthwith. Why else did Pizarro order that most should stay and assist in the task of consolidating the Spanish presence in Peru? A general exodus would have dangerously weakened the Spanish position, so only a few were permitted to leave in the immediate aftermath of the conquest: among them officials accompanying the treasure due to the Spanish crown, and the married men who had been away longest. The yearnings of those obliged to remain, their thoughts of the homeland and dreams of how they might use their new wealth to further themselves and their families, are poignantly illustrated in a letter Gaspar de Marquina wrote home to his father from Cajamarca in July 1533.

Gaspar was from the Basque country, an illegitimate son whose father had recognized him, brought him up, and given him an education that could have qualified him to become a merchant or a notary. But instead of settling down in Spain, Gaspar set off for the New World at an early age, where he adopted the name Marquina. He was still in his early twenties when he became a footman to Francisco Pizarro on the expedition to Peru. His letter is the only one to survive of the many personal letters the men of Cajamarca must have sent back to Spain with the first returnees. James Lockhart gives a translation:

A mi muy deseado señor padre Martín de Gárate
Muy deseado señor padre,
To my longed-for father, Martin de Gárate
Dear Sir,

It must be about three years ago that I got a letter from you, in which you asked me to send some money. God knows how sorry I was not to have anything to send you then, because if I had anything then there wouldn't have been any need for you to write; I've always tried to do the right thing, but there wasn't any possibility till now . . . God knows . . . I give you my word that I never had a penny the whole time since I came to these parts until six months ago, when God was pleased to give me more than I deserved, and now I have over 3,000 ducats; please God that it will be for his holy service.

Sir, I'm sending you 213 pesos of good gold in a bar with an honorable man from San Sebastián; in Seville he'll have it turned into coin and then bring it to you. I'd send you more except he's taking money for other people too and couldn't take more. His name is Pedro de Anadel . . .

Sir, I would like to be the messenger myself, but it couldn't be, because we're in a new country and haven't been here long, and they aren't giving license to leave except to married men who have been in these parts for a long time. I expect to be there with you in two years with the aid of our Lord; I swear to God that I have a greater desire to be there than you have to see me, so that I can give you a good old age.

Sir, I'll tell you something of my life since I came to these parts [Gaspar then writes of how he came to join Pizarro's expedition, the capture of Atahuallpa and the riches of Peru: 'where there's more gold and silver than iron in Biscay'] ... it would be too long to tell if all were told; the bearer of the present letter can inform you, and I won't say more because as I say, it would be too long to tell.

Give my greetings to Catalina and my brothers and sisters and my uncle Martín de Altamira and his daughters, especially the older one, because I am much in her debt, and also to my uncle San Juan de Gárate and my uncle Pedro Sánchez de Arizmendi and all the rest of my relatives ... I really want you to greet them all from me and tell them that I greatly desire to see them, and pleasing God I'll be there soon. Sir, the only thing I want to ask you is to do good for the souls of my mother and all my relatives, and if God lets me get there, I'll do it very thoroughly myself. There is nothing more to write at present except that I'm praying to our Lord Jesus Christ to let me see you before I die. From Cajamarca, in the kingdom of New Castile, July 20 1533.

Vuestro hijo que más ver que escribir os desea,
Your son who would rather see you than write to you,
Gaspar de Gárate[4]

But sadly, Gaspar's prayers were not answered. He bought a horse after Cajamarca and was riding with the vanguard of Spanish forces advancing on Cuzco in November 1533, when he and four others were killed in a battle with an Inca contingent on the steep slopes of Vilcaconga.[5] Dragged from his horse, his head split open in the hand-to-hand fighting at which the Inca excelled, Gaspar's life, dreams and ambitions were extinguished before his father even received the letter his son had written, or saw the gold he had sent.

Of the men who each received a share of the Inca treasure at Cajamarca, sixty-six are known to have returned to Spain within a few years of the conquest. Among them, Juan Ruiz, like Gaspar de Gárate and many others, was from a family of commoners – but schooled more in the training of horses than in the education required of a merchant or a notary (Ruiz could sign his name, but his ability to read and write did not extend much beyond that). He sailed to the New World around 1525 at the age of eighteen, shortly after the death of his father. Having tried his luck – without success – in Jamaica, Honduras and Nicaragua, he caught word of operations in Peru and signed up as a horseman with Pizarro's expedition.

With a share of treasure amounting to more than double that which Gaspar de Gárate had received, Juan Ruiz was among the first to return to Spain after restrictions were relaxed in 1534. By September 1535, he was at the royal court in Madrid, negotiating substantial annuities in return for gold and silver he had brought back. He was granted a coat of arms too, and with that retired to his home town of Alburquerque in western Extremadura. He was not yet thirty years old, but lost no time in outfitting himself and his family line for the seigneurial life that every Spaniard dreamt of, but very few ever achieved.

Having made a will and testament ensuring that his descendants would be citizens of substantial means for generations to come, Juan Ruiz revelled in a life of extravagant magnificence. A palace in the town, a noble wife, and ostentatious display:

'He had twelve squires who served him at table, and many more servants, pages, lackeys, Negroes and horses, armour, and much table ware, silver and gold, and many mules at his service; the pitchers he sent to the fountain were all of silver of much value. When he went out to hunt or other places he took along many horsemen, the cream of the town, and his squires as servants. He kept hunting dogs, falcons and hawks, horses, parrots and other animals. At his death [around 1560] they gave mourning clothes to twenty-four people besides all his servants and squires.'[6]

The trickle-down effect of the wealth that Juan Ruiz and others brought back to Spain doubtless gave local economies a boost – bene-fiting trade and providing employment for many who might otherwise have struggled to support themselves and their families. But the effects were patchy, more urban than rural, and hardly touched the 80 per cent of the population that was dependent on subsistence agriculture – there were simply not enough wealthy men to improve living stan-dards for more than a small fraction of the population as a whole. Indeed, ironically – and tragically – the influx of so much gold and silver from the new world actually made the already deteriorating prospects of most Spaniards even worse.

Like all of Europe, Spain in the sixteenth century was suffering the pains of transition from an agricultural subsistence economy to one based increasingly on money and the market forces of supply and demand: the beginnings of capitalism. Crucially, the profits to be made from wool and textile manufacturing encouraged landowners to convert tillage to pasture, thereby reducing the amount of land devoted to grain production and exacerbating the problems of an agricultural economy that had to contend with poor soils and a testing climate at the best of times.

Most of Europe's sixteenth-century farmers could expect to harvest about six times the amount sown in an average year; but in Spain 'A year which yielded four times the amount sown was considered to be abundant; very good if it gave five times; extraordinary if six or seven times were harvested.[7] For Spain, then, even more than for the rest of Europe, 'Grain was a preoccupation simply because it was always scarce, a matter of life and death.[8] The country was already struggling with the effects of repeated and prolonged grain shortages as the sixteenth century dawned, and prospects for the future were not improved when more and more sheep were put out to graze where wheat had previously grown.

As wool production soared and Spain began to dominate the international markets, the country became increasingly dependent on grain imports from the Middle East and the Baltic to make up for the deficiencies in home production – a precarious state of affairs which the influx of so much wealth from the New World might have been expected to alleviate. But, in fact, the sheer volume of gold and silver flowing into Spain had the effect of devaluing the currency, precipitating a price revolution that saw the cost of staple goods and foodstuffs rise threefold in the course of the century.

This ominous trend had begun even before the New World was discovered, as silver production in Europe rose to meet the demand for money in the growing market economies. The trend accelerated with Spain's acquisition of so much treasure in so short a period, and the discovery of silver at Potosí in the 1540s[9] intensified its effects. The amounts of treasure then at the disposal of the crown (with the confident expectation of plenty more to come) fuelled Spain's imperialist ambitions, invigorated the country's determination to defend the Catholic faith against Protestantism and Islam, financed wars and, in short, became the bedrock upon which Spain's aggressive foreign policy was founded. In those days of relatively undeveloped international finance, gold and silver were highly prized means of supporting military operations in distant lands.[10]

Thus, by way of its military and economic activities, Spain flooded the markets with more wealth than could be absorbed and the consequences were felt wherever nations and merchants engaged in trade. There was simply too much money around for the amount of available goods and services. Prices rose as the value of silver fell. The economist Adam Smith wrote of this in *The Wealth of Nations* (1776):

'By the abundance of the American mines, those metals have become cheaper. A service of plate can now be purchased for about a third part of the corn, or a third part of the labour, which it would have cost in the fifteenth century.'[11]

So, although hopes of finding (or making) a fortune will have sharpened the enthusiasm of many who left Spain for the New World in the early sixteenth century, most were looking for a chance to satisfy needs and ambitions they believed could not be fulfilled at home, where the price revolution was making life difficult for all but the very wealthy. The emigrants wanted a livelihood of some sort, and prospects of advancement. But whatever had forced them to leave, they took their homeland's social and cultural standards with them. A new world yes, but one moulded to resemble the old. Religion, law, society and culture must replicate the forms they had known in Spain. They strove to live like Spaniards – and especially to eat like Spaniards.

After weeks of hardtack and salt meat on the crossing, new arrivals welcomed the abundance of fresh fruit and green vegetables that was available, but were far less enthusiastic about the indigenous staple foods of the Caribbean, central America and the Andes. Few deigned to touch the edible rodents that ran through the fields and forests; nor did they fancy the iguana lizards which local people ate with such relish. In central Mexico only the most desperate Spaniards would eat any of the many wild animals found in and around the lakes. In the Andes, the llama, vicuña and the alpaca were similarly regarded as useful sources of protein in an emergency, but no substitute for beef and mutton as part of a day-to-day diet. Likewise, Andean hares and guinea pigs were little more than novelty local foods to the Spanish. Nor did breads made from maize and cassava meet with much approval; nor native grains such as amaranth and quinoa. All in all, the emigrants generally regarded the native foodstuffs that sustained central and south America as fit for livestock, poultry and the indigenous population, but not for Spaniards – except in an emergency.[12]

And the potato? We read of Pizarro and his party subsisting on guinea pig, llama meat, maize, potatoes and chicha (a fermented maize drink tasting 'like stale cider') while at Cajamarca,[13] and there is some suggestion that they may have resorted to eating potatoes in the absence of anything else at Túmbez on the northern coast, but first-hand accounts of sightings (and tastings) of the potato are few and far between. The earliest known have been uncovered by scholars delving through contemporary manuscripts in the archives and libraries of Madrid and Bogotá, Lima and Seville, Quito and Paris.

Credit for the first description of potatoes being seen by Europeans goes to Juan de Castellanos, whose *Élegías* of 1601 record the exploits of an expedition which set out in 1536 from Santa Marta on the Caribbean shore of what is now Columbia. The expedition was led by Jiménez de Quesada, and on entering the high valleys of the northern Andes in 1537, they found the local people cultivating a crop which they likened to the European truffle. It was not identified by name, but can only have been the potato:

> The houses were all stocked with maize, beans and truffles, spherical roots which are sown and produce a stem with its branches and leaves, and some flowers, although few, of a soft purple colour; and to the root of this same plant, which is about three palms high [24 inches, 61 centimetres], they are attached under the earth, and are the size of an egg more or less, some round and some elongated; they are white and purple and yellow, floury roots of good flavour, a delicacy to the Indians and a dainty dish even for the Spaniards.[14]

The first writer to identify the potato by its name was Pedro Cieza de León, who travelled extensively through the Andes in the late 1530s and '40s and left voluminous accounts of the region's history, the places he visited and the people he saw. Cieza de León's writings extend to around 8,000 pages. He writes of the Inca, and their history before the arrival of the Spanish; he gives the details of Pizarro's expedition, the events at Cajamarca, and the battles that established Spanish dominion over Peru; he describes mountains, rivers and valleys where there were 'large palm groves, and palm hearts were taken from some varieties, and they bore coconuts that were used for milk, and they even make a cream and lard from them that can be used in lamps, for they burn as oil'. He writes of land so fertile that one hundred bushels of maize are harvested for every bushel sown; of farmers who put two sardine heads with the maize in the same hole that is made for the seed, 'and in this manner the grain grows and yields abundantly . . .'[15]

But amidst such copious detail, Cieza de León makes scant mention of the potato – surprisingly scant, given what is now known of the potato's importance as a staple food of Andean peoples at the time, and the benefits it has subsequently brought to the wider world:

> Of provisions, besides maize, there are two other products which form the principal food of these Indians. One is called potato, and is a kind of earth nut, which, after it has been boiled, is as tender as a cooked chestnut, but has no more skin than a truffle, and it grows under the earth in the same way. This root produces a plant exactly like a poppy. The other food is very good and is called *quinoa*.

Elsewhere he notes that 'many Spaniards have enriched themselves and returned prosperous to Spain by merely taking . . . *chuñus* to sell at the mines of Potosí', where food for the thousands of workers was always in demand.[16] And that's it. A few sentences that could be easily overlooked on a crop that would ultimately be of more value to Europe and the world than all the gold and silver of the Spanish Main.

A clue to the explanation for this apparent neglect is to be found in Cieza de León's repeated reference to the fertility of the lands he saw, the extensive pastures, the plentiful supplies of water – in short, how well the lands were suited to the requirements of Spanish crops and livestock. Like the majority of his countrymen, Cieza de León was not interested in the indigenous agriculture of the Andes as a food production system the Spanish might adopt. His purpose was to illustrate the early achievements and future potential of Spanish settlement; the creation of New Spain – or rather, the re-creation of old Spain in the New World.

It is worth remembering that by the time Cieza de León was recording his observations on South America, fifty years had passed since Columbus made his first landing in the New World and throughout that time settlers had been pursuing Spain's determination to establish a permanent presence in the colonies. Columbus had written of:

> many harbours on the coast of the seas, and many rivers, good and large. Its islands are high and there are very lofty mountains. All are

most beautiful, of a thousand shapes, and all are accessible and filled
with trees of a thousand kinds and tall, and they seem to touch the
sky. And some were flowering and some bearing fruit. And the
nightingale was singing, and other birds of a thousand kinds. . . . The
people go all naked, men and women . . . They are so guileless and
generous with all they possess that no one would believe it who has
not seen it.[17]

Columbus's reports had persuaded the Spanish crown and administrators that self-sufficient colonies could be established in the New
World – not least as a means of relieving land-use and food supply
difficulties in the old. But it was not intended that the colonies should
achieve self-sufficiency by making use of resources available in the
colonies themselves. No, an entirely new agricultural system would be
introduced, one that would supply the settlers with the staple foods of
a traditional Spanish diet. As the historian John Super writes in an illuminating review of the issues involved, 'the scope of the vision was
staggering . . . nothing short of recreating the alimentary life of Spain
on a still-unknown island'.[18]

Blithely unaware of the numerous obstacles the settlers would
confront, administrators drew up plans for the establishment of the
colonies. At first thousands of sacks of wheat flour, barrels of hardtack,
and jars of wine, vinegar and olive oil were shipped out. Then wheat
and barley seed, grape and olive cuttings, dozens of common vegetables and fruits. Along with the plants went cattle, oxen, sheep and goats,
pigs, horses and farming equipment such as ploughs, spades, hoes and
rakes. Thus a policy of official support for settlement was established
at the very beginning of Spain's colonisation of the new world; one
that encouraged subsequent adventurers to call for the same degree of
attention to the needs of their newly taken lands. Hernán Cortés, for
example, urged Charles V to ensure that no ship left Spain without
bringing plants for farming. Taking the policy a stage further, in 1531,
the crown promised immigrant farmers free passage, food, land, stock,
Indian labour, exemption from tithes and yet more lands for their
descendants.

The result was a steady flow of immigrants and the remarkably rapid
establishment of Spanish farming practices and crops in the new world.
For instance, although it was only in November 1519 that Cortés and
his party had first set foot in Tenochtitlan – soon to be renamed Mexico
City – by 1526 even the introduction of European kitchen vegetables

was advanced enough for commentators to remark that carrots, cauliflowers, beans, turnips, horseradish and lettuce were cheaper in the city markets that year.[19] Bananas and plantains also spread rapidly. First planted on the Caribbean islands in 1516, then on the mainland in the 1520s, they supplied abundant carbohydrates, vitamins and minerals in return for much less labour than was required for traditional crops and this – along with greater productivity and a capacity to fruit all year round – made them especially attractive as subsistence crops. Within a generation bananas and plantains had spread through much of tropical America and become staple items in the diets of indigenous communities wherever conditions favoured their cultivation.

But wheat and meat were the out-and-out successes of Spanish agricultural introductions in terms of a capacity to 'recreate the alimentary life of Spain' in a foreign land. As John Super writes, 'wheat was a cultural imperative for the Spanish, a driving force that shaped the social and physical landscape.' Despite many obstacles, the settlers worked with unremitting determination to establish wheat production and livestock husbandry. Where they succeeded, Spanish society took root and grew. The advance was swift.

From the first tentative steps in the Caribbean, numerous towns and rural communities were established and major cities founded: Vera Cruz (1519), Mexico City (1521) and Guatemala City (1524). Meanwhile, other adventurers had crossed the neck of land dividing the Caribbean from the Pacific Ocean and founded the city of Panama (1519). Here the ships were built (using native forest timber) which would transport and service Spain's advance into South America. Following Pizarro's crushing defeat of the Inca in 1532, Spanish rule was exercised from Cuzco (1534), Lima (1535), Bogotá (1538) and Santiago (1541). In little more than fifty years the Spaniards had achieved as much if not more than they could have wished for.

By the end of the sixteenth century the Spanish had established a presence from the desolate northern rim of Mexico to the bleak subarctic regions of southern Chile and Argentina. But they could not have achieved so much without the certainty of reliable food production systems to the rear. Pizarro and his men doubtless felt some trepidation as they climbed the Andes towards Cajamarca, but, as the vanguard of forty years of Spanish expansion, they knew that conquered lands and thousands of settlers lay behind them, with ships, reinforcements and supplies. They were well-prepared, and not only with notaries and writing paper: Pizarro even had in his baggage two goblets of

Venetian glass that were to be sent ahead as an introductory gift to Atahuallpa.[20]

But re-creating the alimentary life of Spain in foreign lands proved especially difficult at the start. No amount of determination could persuade wheat to grow productively in the climatic regime of the sub-tropical Caribbean islands; they were dependent on imported flour until wheat from the mainland became available, where it was introduced with more than enough success to compensate for the failures in the Caribbean. The crop was first planted in the Valley of Mexico soon after the fall of Tenochtitlán in 1519 and within a decade was yielding abundant harvests throughout the region. Contemporary observers were impressed by the productivity of the wheat fields, citing harvests of twenty, forty, sixty and up to 400 bags for every bag of seed sown. Not all of these reports can be true but it is certain that yields were at least two or three times greater than in Spain. Furthermore, fertile soils, adequate water and an especially amenable climate enabled some farmers to harvest not just one but two or even three crops a year. All in all, grain rapidly became plentiful in the New World and – in stark contrast to conditions in Spain – dependable. Harvests seldom failed; one poor harvest rarely followed another. And here contemporary reports are confirmed by long-term statistics showing that only once every thirty to fifty years were there two bad harvests in succession.

From Mexico, wheat farming followed the Spanish advance into South America. Virtually everywhere it could be said that '[w]hile many of the sights and smells of the New World bewildered visitors, they could usually count on fresh-baked bread in the Iberian tradition to remind them of home.'[21] And as with bread, so with meat.

Wherever the Spanish went, they took livestock with them. 'Pigs, sheep, and cattle were as much a part of the conquest as Toledo steel and fighting mastiffs.' From the Caribbean to the central regions of Mexico and the highlands of Peru, European livestock found excellent pasture and an amenable climate. Without predators or serious competition from indigenous grazing animals, livestock of all kinds quickly multiplied and spread. Even before 1500 there were huge numbers of livestock and poultry on the first Caribbean islands that had been settled, and livestock threatened to overrun some islands; by the 1520s, officials were calling for a livestock guild to control the herds. In the 1560s wild dogs were reportedly killing 60,000 head a year, without seriously affecting the size of the herds. Of course, with meat so plentiful, not only the settlers but also the ships returning to Spain were assured of a good supply. This was important. Live pigs were especially valued. Fed with maize stored on board they provided a very welcome feast of fresh meat during the long voyage.

Central Mexico soon surpassed the Caribbean as a producer of protein and by 1526 – barely seven years after the fall of Tenochtitlán – production was rising so fast that the price of pork in Mexico City, for example, had fallen to a quarter of the price in 1524. In fact, pigs were so numerous that the city council had to devise ways of keeping them off the streets. Vast tracts of land were awarded to livestock owners and soon herds and flocks of 20,000 and even 40,000 animals were grazing on the plains to the north of the central valley.

The valleys of the Andes also supported large populations of cattle and sheep, and even though altitude and competition with Andean cameloids restrained their proliferation in the highlands, they were an important factor in the introduction of Spain's alimentary life. By the middle of the sixteenth century, almost everyone – from wealthy Spanish settler to poor indigenous farmer – ate meat, and plenty of it. In places where cattle were exceptionally plentiful, their hides were worth more than their meat. Laws were passed ordering that labourers should be given a pound of meat a day; soldiers serving in Mexico received two pounds a day – twice the amount those in Spain could hope to get. A Peruvian resident summed up the situation: 'Meat is dirt cheap in this country.'

Plenty of meat, plenty of bread, cheese, fruits and vegetables – with plenty of home-produced olive oil and wine becoming available as the vineyards and olive groves matured . . . much of Spanish America achieved self-sufficiency in food supply within a generation of colonisation. While sixteenth-century Europe suffered repeated shortage and famine compounded by remorselessly rising prices, Spanish America regularly produced surpluses.[22] The tragedy was that declining numbers of native Americans were alive to enjoy them.

The population collapse that followed the Spanish conquest was both swift and devastating. The Spaniards brought diseases to which the indigenes had no resistance. From the Caribbean islands to the far reaches of Mexico and Peru, smallpox, measles, typhus, influenza and plague all took their toll, precipitating a demographic catastrophe of unequalled proportions. The extent of the collapse is impossible to assess accurately, because no one knows precisely how many people lived in the region before the arrival of the Spanish in 1492. Even so, the work of historical demographers strongly suggests that the total population probably fell by over 90 per cent in little more than a century. An authoritative estimate of the decline in the Andes, for example, concludes that where some 9 million people had populated the region in 1520, there were just 600,000 in 1620.[23]

Like secret allies, European diseases effectively cleared the way for the Spanish colonisation of South America. There was little contest for the best arable lands when traditional owners were succumbing to smallpox, and little conflict between tillage and pasture when such vast tracts of both were being vacated and left untended. While European Spain was struggling to produce enough, Spanish America was consistently producing the surpluses that hastened conquest and enabled Spaniards to establish viable communities and build new cities. It is both sad and ironic that one of the greatest population losses in history occurred during a period when food surpluses were regularly available,[24] and a terrible indictment of Europe's expansionist ambitions.

The simultaneous collapse of the indigenous population and successful establishment of European-style agriculture in South America also explains why the Spanish did not make more use of the potato. At first it seems strange that seed tubers were not shipped back to be grown as a food crop capable of alleviating Spain's chronic food shortages. But then, why should anyone have bothered? After all, the potato was peasant food, grown and consumed by people who were dying in their thousands.

Part Two
Europe

Chapter Six

The lonely impulse of delight

> I have fine potatoes,
> Ripe potatoes!
> Will your Lordship please to taste a fine potato?
> 'Twill advance your wither'd state.
> Fill your Honour full of noble itches.[1]

John Fletcher, who wrote these lines for his play *The Loyal Servant*, was one of a band of dramatists who, in the early 1600s, made London the world's first centre of the entertainment business. The theatre was a popular novelty and better value – at the basic admission price of one penny – than even a beer or a meal. Thirteen per cent of Londoners went to see a play every week in 1605; which works out at some 3,500 a day or 21,000 theatregoers a week for London's then population of 160,000.[2]

The demand for new works was insatiable. In the fifty-two years between 1590 and 1642 (when the civil war started, and Parliament declared that 'publicke Stage-playes shall cease and be forborne') a total of over 2,500 plays are known to have been written by named authors. Shakespeare contributed thirty-eight, but for every one of his at least another twenty were written by other dramatists. Many have been lost, but 900 are known, of which no fewer than 850 were the work of just forty-four dramatists. Among these, Thomas Heywood claimed he had written or 'had a maine finger in' 220 plays. Thomas Dekker wrote at least sixty-four, forty-four of them in the five years from 1598 to 1602. And John Fletcher wrote or collaborated in a total of sixty-nine plays.[3]

The dramatists knew their market, and even Shakespeare was not above including the salacious exchanges that would provoke a laugh

77

and might encourage the audience to return next week, keen for more. Thus in *The Merry Wives of Windsor* he has Falstaff in Windsor Park, dressed as a stag, awaiting 'a cool rut-time' and greeting Mistress Ford as: 'my doe with the black scut! Let the sky rain potatoes; let it thunder to the tune of "Green Sleeves", hail kissing-comfits and snow eringoes; let there come a tempest of provocation, I will shelter me here.'[4] And in *Troilus and Cressida* Thersites declares: 'How the devil luxury, with his fat rump and potato-finger, tickles these together! Fry, lechery, fry!'[5]

The potato was believed to be an aphrodisiac in Shakespeare's day and it is in this context – rather than as food – that Falstaff and Thersites are speaking of it. But Shakespeare was an innocent when compared with his contemporaries, and it is among their writings that more frequent and direct references to the sexually arousing properties of the potato appear.[6]

John Fletcher again:

> A Banquet! – Well! Potatoes and eringoes
> And, I take it, cantharides! Excellent!
> A priapism follows; and as I'll handle it
> It shall, old lecherous goat in authority.[7]

But belief in the potato as an aphrodisiac arose before Shakespeare started writing and continued long after he had died. The historian William Harrison wrote (in 1577) of 'the potato and such venerous roots as are brought out of Spaine, Portingale and the Indies to furnish up our bankets'.[8] In 1622 Dr Tobias Venner, a physician noted for his advocacy of healthy living, recommended potatoes because 'they . . . doe wonderfully comfort, nourish and strengthen the bodie, and [are a food that] incites to Venus'. And a century later, as though to perpetuate a myth that has no basis whatsoever in fact, the herbalist William Salmon declared that potatoes 'are moderately Diuretick, Stomatick, Chylisick, Analeptick, and Spermatogenetick. They nourish the whole Body, restore in Consumptions, and provoke Lust.'[9]

One might imagine that with so many references to the potato, over an extended period, the year and location of the tuber's first appearance in Europe and England would be well known by now. After all, here was an item renowned for characteristics that were likely to attract interest even where serious discussion was unlikely, and expensive enough to be known of even by those who could never afford it (Sir

Joseph Banks, director of the Royal Botanical Gardens at Kew, wrote that potatoes were 'purchased when scarce at no inconsiderable cost, by those who had faith in their alleged properties'[10]).

Surely, someone must have claimed credit for its introduction? Or at the very least, first knowledge of its properties and availability must have been recorded? But scour the literature and primary sources, and far from discovering a precise name and date, the pursuit is soon overtaken by confusion. Not least in respect of which potato the writers were referring to; for there were two candidates: the common potato *Solanum tuberosum tuberosum*; and the sweet potato *Ipomoea batatas*. The two are in no way related, as we have seen.

Columbus had encountered sweet potatoes on his first voyage, in 1492, and reported that they looked like yams and tasted like chestnuts. They were included among the curiosities he exhibited to the Spanish court on his return, and stocks of both roots and planting material were shipped back to Spain on subsequent voyages. By the second or third decade of the sixteenth century the sweet potato was already widely cultivated in southern Europe wherever conditions were suitable. Northern Europe was too cold, so for London it was an imported delicacy – and costly, but presumably worth the expense to those in need of its alleged properties. Though a tasty fare whether boiled, baked or fried, it was as a sliced and candied 'sucket', or sweetmeat, that the sweet potato is most often mentioned. It is said that Henry VIII was especially partial to its delights.

Sixteenth-century writers were undoubtedly referring to the sweet potato, since the common potato was unknown in Europe during their time, but when writers during the seventeenth century attributed aphrodisiacal properties to the potato they could be referring to either, since both were available by then and neither was cheap.

But the difficulty in discovering who brought the common potato to Europe and when is more than a confusion over names; it is also a reflection of what was known in the fifteenth and early sixteenth centuries. The investigative study of botany and natural science had yet to begin. The description of plants still followed the classical tradition established by Pliny the Elder's *Natural History* and the work of Dioscorides (both compiled in the first century AD). Though their work was thorough (Dioscorides described about 500 species of plants), they and their successors were motivated principally by a desire to produce a catalogue of useful (or dangerous) plants and to describe how they should be used (or avoided). It was plants with medicinal properties that excited the most interest, and they were described in works (first manuscripts then printed books) that went under the general title of Herbals.

The Herbal was essentially a medical reference book which identified the 'vertues, vices and values' of particular plants and listed the illnesses and conditions to which they might be applied.[11] Avowedly practical, with an index directing readers to the cure for each malady, the Herbals were something every household should have, and understandably popular (one author claimed to have sold 30,000 copies)[12] – and for centuries their authors were content to reiterate and often plagiarise the works of their predecessors. In the early sixteenth century, however, a new perspective was introduced by authors who attempted to advance knowledge with an explanation of the relationship between condition and cure that they called the Doctrine of Signatures. This could be seen as an early step in the direction of investigative science, but serious respect was forever disqualified by the lengths to which it was taken, and by the boastful arrogance of its most famous proponent, Theophrastus Bombast von Hohenheim. In the fashion of the day, von Hohenheim took the latin name Paracelsus, but his second name, Bombast, is the clue to his character.

The Doctrine of Signatures held that the most effective medicinal plants were those which in some way mirrored the condition to be treated. It recommended red beetroot juice for anaemic women, for instance, and prescribed the yellow celandine as a cure for jaundice. 'The flowers of St John's wort, when they are putrified, they are like blood,' Paracelsus noted, 'which teacheth us, that this herb is good for wounds, to close them and fill them up.' Similarly, the Doctrine proposed that long-lived plants would lengthen life (while short-lived ones shortened it); herbs with a rough skin would heal diseases that destroyed the natural smoothness of the skin. Plants with flowers like butterflies would cure insect bites. The maidenhair fern, with bare stalks and flowing greenery above, was recommended where baldness threatened[13] . . . and so on, to the English herbalist William Cole, who in 1657 gives a supreme example of the Doctrine of Signatures in both its principle and its fatuity:

Wall-nuts have the perfect Signature of the head. The outer husk or green Covering, represent the *Pericranium*, or outward skin of the skull, whereon the hair groweth, and therefore salt made of those husks or barks, are exceedingly good for wounds in the head. The inner wooddy shell hath the Signature of the Skull, and the little yellow skin, or Peel, that covereth the Kernell of the hard *Meninga* and *Pia-mater*, which are the thin scarfes that envelope the brain. The *Kernel* hath the very figure of the Brain, and therefore it is very profitable for the Brain, and resists poysons; For if the Kernel be bruised, and moystned with the quintessence of Wine, and laid upon the Crown of the Head, it comforts the brain and head mightily.

The belief that walnuts are good for the brain and the idea that potatoes will incite Venus are equally fanciful, but while the Herbals and the Doctrine of Signatures provided one sort of botanical information, another approach was gaining strength – an approach that would ultimately throw light on the question: who brought the potato to Europe, and when?

It has been said that the scientific study of 'natural history was invented in the Renaissance';[14] the first botanists were a diverse community of men from the Low Countries, France, Germany, Switzerland, Italy and England; some of independent means, others from humble homes, who were united by a passionate interest in the diversity and beauty of the living plants – not simply their medicinal value. They were driven by an aesthetic imperative, 'the lonely impulse of delight'. They wanted to see, discover and describe, but soon found that the classical tradition did not have the last word on plants and their distribution. At first, loyally, they tried to squeeze their discoveries into the traditional format. But there was too much that simply did not fit; too much that either contradicted the received wisdom or was indisputably new.[15]

Among the pioneers, Leonhardt Fuchs and Mathieu L'Obel are for ever memorialised in the popular flowering plants that bear their name, fuchsia and lobelia, and it is a pity that others are not similarly remembered: Pietro Mattioli, Conrad Gessner, Valerius Cordus, Rembert Dodoens and – most especially – Carolus Clusius, which was the latinised name of Jules Charles de l'Écluse. As a scholar and investigator Clusius was in a class apart, applying a degree of industry and rigour to the study of plants that raised him above all his contemporaries. His work was central to the expansion of floristic knowledge by which the Herbal was transformed into, and finally replaced by, the Flora.[16]

When Clusius was born in 1526 it was still possible for one man to know every plant that had ever been described. By the time he died in 1609, thousands had been added to the catalogue – from Europe and around the world. More than any one man could know. As Adriaan van de Spiegel wrote in 1606:

> No human mind, however hard-working, will ever come to a wholly perfect knowledge of plants, for their variety is infinite in form, use, and other accidents. We see that rivers, swamps, the sea, mountains, fields, valleys, sand, walls, stones, meadows, vineyards, woods, and uncultivated places – to sum up, Europe, Asia, Africa, and the Indies – always produce something new.[17]

Botany had become a collective endeavour and it is clear from books published towards the end of the sixteenth century that the potato had become a plant of interest in several parts of Europe by then. The first written, but unillustrated, mention of it occurs in Gaspard Bauhin's *Phytopinax*, where it was given the Latin name *Solanum tuberosum esculentum*, a name Linnaeus retained as the binomial *Solanum tuberosum* in his *Species Plantarum* of 1753. Bauhin's *Phytopinax* was published in Basle in 1596, and a year later the English botanist John Gerard published his *Herball or Generall Historie of Plantes*, which has as its frontispiece an engraved portrait of the author holding a spray of potato flowers, to which he draws attention in the text:

> ... whereon do grow very faire and pleasant flowers, made of one entire whole leaf, which is folded or plaited in such a strange sort, ... The colour whereof it is hard to expresse. The whole flower is of a light purple colour, stripped down the middle of every folde or welt, with a light shew of yellowness, as though purple and yellow were mixed togither ... the roots [of the plant] are ... some of them round as a ball, some ovall or egge fashion, some longer, and others shorter: which knobbie rootes are fastened unto the stalks with an infinite number of threddie strings ...

John Gerard had trained as a physician, but his energies were chiefly devoted to gardening and botany. For twenty years he maintained a much-visited garden in London and supervised two others. In 1596 he, like Bauhin, had published an unillustrated catalogue of his garden plants, but his reputation as a botanist was founded on the much larger and illustrated *Herball* mentioned above. Unhappily, however, that reputation founders on the revelation that not much of the book's content was Gerard's own work. In an otherwise measured and temperate account of English naturalists published in 1947, the Cambridge scholar Charles Raven makes no bones about it, describing Gerard as 'a rogue. Moreover, botanically speaking, he was a comparatively ignorant rogue.'[18]

The original proposal for *The Herball or Generall Historie of Plantes* had been that of a London printer, John Norton, who had commissioned a scholar, Dr Priest, to translate from Latin into English a botanical work that one of the fathers of botany, Rembert Dodoens, had published in 1583. Norton purchased 1,800 woodcuts from another source to illustrate the translation but unfortunately Dr Priest died before his text and the illustrations could be faithfully united. The material passed to Gerard for completion and he, noting that Priest had closely followed the original Dodoens, set about rearranging the material so that it should be recognised as his (Gerard's) work, rather than a mere translation. But his knowledge of botany was not advanced enough for the task of accurately matching text and illustrations. Many were misplaced, and once this had been pointed out by a third party, John Norton brought in another famed botanist, Mathieu L'Obel, to sort out the muddle. L'Obel made numerous corrections, but not as many as he would have wished, for Gerard became impatient and stopped the process – angrily claiming that L'Obel didn't know enough English to do the job properly. Thus about two-thirds of *The Herball or Generall Historie of Plantes* published in 1597 is reasonably accurate, but the other third is less reliable.

John Gerard died in 1612. His *Herball* was redeemed by an amended edition published in 1633, but his name was forever blighted by the editor's introductory comment:

> For the author Mr John Gerard I can say little . . . His chiefe commendation is that he out of a propense goodwill to the publique advancement of this knowledge, endeavoured to performe therein more than he could well accomplish; which was partly through want of sufficient learning.[19]

The accounts of Gerard's plagiarism and inaccuracy are well-founded. Even so, his descriptions and illustration of the potato must have been original. There was no source from which he could have copied them. It is true that Gaspard Bauhin had described the potato in his *Phytopinax*, published in 1596, but Bauhin's account was not illustrated. Furthermore, Gerard's original garden catalogue (published before Bauhin's work was available) also included the potato and here he described the growing plant in enough detail for modern experts to make authoritative comment on the species and variety.[20] For all the doubt that Gerard's reputation engenders, one must conclude that the potatoes he illustrated and described with such feeling in *The Herball or Generall Historie of Plantes* had come from his own garden, and it seems likely that he had been growing them for at least two seasons. The question is: where did he get them from? In *The Herball* Gerard writes:

> It groweth naturally in America, where it was first discovered, as reporteth *C. Clusius*, since when I have received rootes hereof from Virginia which growe and prosper in my garden, as in their own natiue country. The Indians call this plant *Papus*, meaning the roots.[21]

It is confusing that Gerard should claim his tubers came from Virginia, for the potato was unknown there until introduced by settlers after his time. But it is possible the potatoes arrived on ships that had sailed from South America *via* Virginia, and not impossible that Gerard set the facts aside in an attempt to ingratiate himself with Queen Elizabeth I by claiming that this new food plant was the first fruit of a colony which Sir Walter Raleigh had named after the Virgin Queen herself.[22] It is interesting, also, that whereas Gerard frequently omitted any reference to help received from other botanists, in this case he quotes Clusius. But how did he know of Clusius's report when, as we shall see below, it was not published until 1601, four years later?

Clusius visited England several times in the late 1570s, but there is no evidence that he ever met Gerard (who would surely have made something of the fact if they had), nor did they exchange correspondence. But they did have a friend in common: a London apothecary, James Garret. Assuming that information on the potato passed among the three, it seems that Gerard in London, and Clusius in Vienna must have received their potatoes from different sources between 1588 and 1593.[23] We will probably never know exactly where Gerard's came from; is the source of Clusius's any clearer?

Clusius was in no doubt that the potatoes he described at length in his 1601 publication were the same as those from the Andes that Pedro Cieza de León had seen in 1538. They had been growing in his garden for several seasons, but he could not explain how they had become so widely distributed in Europe (he says potatoes by then were common – even fecund – in Germany and Italy). Clearly, the original stock must have come from either South America, or Spain, but Clusius could only say that his first knowledge of the plant had come from Belgium, at the beginning of 1588, when Philippe de Sivry, Prefect of the city of Mons, had sent two potato tubers to him in Vienna. De Sivry apparently had been given the tubers by a friend of the Papal Legate in Belgium, who had brought them from Italy. The Italians had no idea where their stock had originally come from, and Clusius could only wonder that knowledge of the plant had not reached him earlier, since by then it was so common in Italy that, apart from eating potatoes themselves, people were also using them as fodder for pigs.[24]

Clusius had good reason to wonder. Apart from being Europe's foremost botanist, with a right to expect that his generous sharing of knowledge and material would be reciprocated, he had also spent several months travelling around Spain in 1564, specifically looking for rare and interesting plants. The meticulous account of his discoveries was published in 1576 – with no mention of the potato. Meanwhile, he had also been making condensed and annotated translations of Spanish reports on New World plants[25] – again, with no mention of the potato. And Pedro Cieza de León's published account of the potato in Peru had not come to Clusius's attention either. For most commentators, this absence of the potato from Clusius's work in Spain means that the potato was not there. But it could also mean that the Spanish did not want foreigners to know of it. There is evidence that some reports on what the Spanish had found in America were not published, but 'remained in manuscript in Seville, locked away by cautious Castilian bureaucrats worried about divulging commercial secrets'.[26]

One should always be wary of conspiracy theories – especially those relating to events 400 years ago. But then one should be suspicious of negative evidence too – especially when it is all that is on offer. And the fact that Clusius did not see or hear of the potato while he was in Spain is a long way from proof of its absence. And so the suspicion mounts: there is something distinctly odd about the Spanish and the potato's relatively sudden appearance in various parts of northern Europe in the late sixteenth century without any previous mention of it in Spain. After all, it is not as though the Spanish were not keen on bringing things back from the New World. As one commentator put it, 'the Spanish, always diligent imitators of all things foreign, who know so well how to exploit other people's inventions'.[27]

Maize, for instance, had been discovered for Europe by Columbus and was so commonly grown in Spain and beyond by the 1530s that its New World origin had been forgotten. Leonhardt Fuchs believed it had come from Turkey. He included a splendid woodcut of the plant in his flora published in 1542, naming it *Turcicum Frumentum* or 'Türckisch Korn' and went on to remark that the Turkish grain 'is now growing in all gardens'. It was not until 1570 that its New World origins were reconfirmed, when the Italian botanist Pietro Mattioli declared that 'it ought to be called *Indicum*, not *Turcicum*, for it was brought from the West Indies, not out of Turkey or Asia, as Fuchs believed.'[28] Then there were tomatoes, cocoa, chilli, squash, tobacco – all from the New World. And the sunflower, now known to have been domesticated in North America but long believed to have come from the land of the potato itself, John Gerard having described it in his *Herball* as the marigold of Peru. The sunflower had become so popular in Europe by the 1590s that it was grown 'everywhere', a contemporary source reports.[29]

We should not forget, of course, that relations between Spain and much of Europe were not always cordial during the sixteenth century. Envy of the wealth that discovery of the New World had brought Spain, plus religious animosity engendered by the Reformation, setting Protestant against Catholic, had caused friction. Wars between the factions erupted. Francis Drake famously 'singed the King of Spain's beard' in 1587, when he sailed a fleet into Cadiz, one of Spain's main ports, occupied the town for three days and destroyed twenty-six enemy ships as well as a large quantity of stores. This attack delayed Spain's attempt to invade England, but Drake again routed the Spanish Armada when it sailed into the English Channel a year later. In these circumstances, one can imagine that the English were unlikely to grant the Spanish credit for anything commendable, while Sir Francis Drake could do no wrong. He was even credited with introducing the potato to Europe.

A statue of Drake holding a flowering potato plant, complete with tubers and haulm, once stood in Offenburg in southern Germany, commending the circumnavigator for bringing the potato to Europe in 1580. The plinth was decorated with a frieze of potato tubers and bore an inscription that offered (in paraphrased translation): 'his immortal memory the blessings of millions who cultivated the precious gift of God as the help of the poor against need and bitter want'. The statue was destroyed during the Second World War, presumably because it memorialised an Englishman, but the legend lives on: having brought some potatoes back from his trip around the world, Drake gave them to a friend, so the story goes, who grew them successfully enough but cooked the berries instead of the tubers. They tasted terrible, so the gardener was ordered to root up the remaining plants and burn them. The gardener did so, but happened to break open a potato that rolled from the fire, nicely baked. He sniffed it, then tasted it. Delicious – and the potato was saved.

The story is invalidated, however, by the facts. Drake certainly knew about potatoes, having encountered them on an island off the coast of Chile in November 1578, as his journal reports (but it was not published until 1628): 'We being on land, the people came down to us to the water side with shew of great curtesie, bringing us potatoes, rootes and two very fat sheepe . . .'[30] But his voyage home was via the Pacific and the Cape of Good Hope, and Drake arrived in Plymouth a full two years later, by which time any remaining potatoes would have been incapable of regeneration. It is also significant (though negative evidence, admittedly) that Clusius, who knew Drake and had actually stayed with him on a visit to England in 1581, makes no mention of the potato among his description of items Drake had brought back from his voyage around the world (Clusius even named a plant after Drake).[31]

Sir Walter Raleigh, another hero of English adventures in the Americas and against the Spanish, is also said to have brought the potato to Europe. Indeed, the precise date of the discovery was set at 27 July 1586 by Sir Joseph Banks, whose credentials include not only the directorship of Kew Gardens but also his work as botanist on Captain Cook's voyage to the Pacific. Rather less precision can be attached to the story that Raleigh actually served a plate of boiled potatoes to Queen Elizabeth I on his return to England, and all versions of the story crediting Raleigh with the introduction of the potato founder on what can only be called a case of mistaken identity.

Raleigh never actually went to the stretch of North American coast that he named Virginia (now North Carolina), and even the settlers he had sent there could not have found the potato, for the simple reason that it was not native to North America. That they found and sent back to Raleigh *something* resembling a potato seems certain, but it is most likely to have been the roots of a native tuber-bearing climber called 'openawk' (which is confused with the potato in some accounts), or even sweet potatoes; there is no evidence to connect Raleigh with the introduction of the true potato to England and Europe.

By the early 1600s the potato was regularly illustrated and described in botanical treatises, but no author could cite an irrefutable source for the route and date of its introduction – or even give an instance of its cultivation prior to 1588. There was nothing conclusive, only a haze of confusion. And that remained the case for more than 300 years, until it came under the scrutiny of the Cambridge scientist and potato expert, Redcliffe N. Salaman.

A feature of Salaman's research technique was the stream of enquiries he addressed to any authority and every institution that he thought might offer a glimmer of information on aspects regarding the potato that were currently engaging his attention. Always courteous (and thrifty: some of the carbon copies archived at the University of Birmingham are on the reverse side of letters from his stockbrokers), these letters winkled out the many unexpected insights and odd gems that make his book *The History and Social Influence of the Potato*, published in 1949, entertaining as well as a monument of scholarly endeavour. Among his correspondents was a Harvard Professor of Economics, Earl J. Hamilton, whose research matched Salaman's own in its depth and diligence.

Hamilton was studying the effect that the influx of so much gold and silver from the New World had had on the economies of Spain and Europe during the sixteenth century. In search of figures that would reveal changes in the cost of living over the decades, he scoured city archives – and those of any other establishments where the price of commodities and essential items were consistently recorded. He spent months in Seville, hunting down relevant sixteenth-century documents; unravelling their often obscure manner of compilation; deciphering the handwriting, translating the archaic Spanish and finally transcribing any useful information that he had found. The search took him to the Hospital de la Sangre, one of several hospitals for the poor and infirm that were established in Seville and other Spanish cities during the fourteenth to sixteenth centuries. The Hospital de la Sangre, however, was distinguished by the detailed and almost unbroken records of its accounts, both receipts and purchases, from 1546 on. Here, page after page gave Hamilton details of what the hospital had paid for its supplies of bread, honey, chickens, fish, meat and lard, vegetables, wine and vinegar, soap, linen, wool and sheets, firewood and kindling, medicines – and so on. The list was exhaustive, showing how prices had changed year by year, and showing also that on 27 December 1573 the Hospital's purchasers bought something they had never bought before: 19 pounds of potatoes.[32]

Potatoes become a regular feature of the Hospital accounts in subsequent years, first bought by the pound and later by the 'arroba' (a unit of 25 pounds) – so they must have been a rarity or luxury to begin with, but gradually became more commonly available (and cheaper).

Furthermore, all the purchases Hamilton had noted took place in December and January, indicating that the potatoes had been grown and harvested in Spain rather than imported, since South American potatoes were harvested in March and April and would have reached Spanish markets by June, or August at the latest. And if potatoes were available in Seville during those months, the Hospital surely would have bought them then too.

Salaman concluded that this new evidence permitted him to put the date of introduction of the potato into Spain at least as early as 1570, which allowed three years for the seed tubers to grow on and multiply into a crop that was large enough for producers to market profitably. This in turn meant that the original tubers could not have been gathered in South America later than in the previous year, 1569.[33] On the strength of these conclusions Salaman was generally credited with having given us the earliest-yet known evidence of the potato in Europe. But a doubt remained, one which bothered Birmingham's former Professor of Botany, J. G. Hawkes, for many years: Hamilton was an economist, not a botanist; what if the purchases he had found in the Hospital de la Sangre accounts were in respect of sweet potatoes, not true potatoes – would he have known the difference?[34]

Professor Hawkes had worked on the taxonomy and cytogenetics of South American potatoes for his Ph.D. thesis at Cambridge University. He had known and worked with Redcliffe Salaman, and had published papers with him, but it was not until 1991, at the age of seventy-six (and nine years after he officially retired), that he was able to put that nagging doubt to rest. In that year Hawkes travelled to Seville with J. Francisco-Ortega, a visiting scholar from the Canary Islands, and together they re-examined the account books of the Hospital de la Sangre.[35] They found that although the records were reasonably legible and in many instances very clear, several books were in a very bad state indeed, owing sometimes to damp or decay, and sometimes to the nature of the ink used, which had destroyed the paper almost entirely, leaving the writing as a kind of stencil. Moreover, both sides of the paper were used, adding further confusion. First impressions were of admiration for the dedication which Earl Hamilton had applied to his research, then delight as 'Domingo xxvii [de Diciembre] de deiz y nueve libras de patatas' stood out from the page: 'Sunday 27th [of December]. Of nineteen pounds of potatoes', the word 'patatas' instantly recognisable to these botanists who on occasion needed local experts to help them decipher the handwriting.

So, like the economist sixty years before, the botanists were rewarded for 'the lonely impulse of delight' which had taken them to Seville, to the archives, and to the florid script in which the accounts of the Hospital de la Sangre were recorded. All the records of potatoes (and there were many) in the account books used the Spanish word 'patata' and never the South American term 'papa'. Furthermore, they did not mention the sweet potato, for which the Spanish words 'batata' or 'camote' (another New World term) would have been used. This was enough to convince Hawkes and his colleague that Hamilton and Salaman had been correct in assuming that the records referred to the true potato, *Solanum tuberosum*, and not the sweet potato, *Ipomoea batatas*. The nagging doubt was eliminated, potatoes were being grown in Spain from 1570 – but the investigators were not finished yet. What about the Canary Isles, Francisco-Ortega's home – could they not hold clues to the arrival of the potato in Europe?

Descriptions of these Atlantic islands by several authors – both historical and modern – had already invited the conclusion that many New World plants were brought to the Canaries before they reached Spain. And sure enough, on closer inspection Hawkes and Francisco-Ortega found references to both potatoes and sweet potatoes in the literature.[36] An account published in 1583 by the English adventurer Thomas Nichols mentions the sweet potato ('batatas') only: 'This iland hath singular good wine, especially in the towns of Telde, and sundrie sortes of good frutes, as batata, melons, peares, apples, oranges, lemons, pomegranads, figs, peaches of diverse sortes . . .', but authors writing in Spanish refer to the presence of 'patatas' *and* 'batatas' on the islands. Sometimes they write 'papas' or 'patatas', showing that both names were used for the true potato, as well as 'batatas' for the sweet potato. Thus the South American word 'papa' was used as well as the Spanish word 'patata' in the Canary Isles, while in Spain only 'patata' was used. This in turn suggested that the islands might have an older and more entrenched connection with the potato and its South American origins than was the case in Spain.

The investigators enquired further, and finally came to 'the most interesting records from the Canary Islands so far discovered':[37] a document from the archives of the public notary in Las Palmas de Gran Canaria dated 28 November 1567 which read (in translation) '. . . and also three medium-sized barrels [which] you state contain potatoes and oranges and green lemons'. This nugget of information was found in a document – probably a bill of lading – listing the goods which Juan de Molina had shipped to his brother, Luis de Quesada, in Antwerp, Belgium. Another entry by the public notary, written on 24 April 1574, states: 'Also came from Tenerife two barrels of potatoes and eight . . . of aguardiente [a fiery brandy]'. This consignment was shipped with other items to Hernando Qunitana in Rouen (France), also by Juan de Molina.

For Hawkes and Francisco-Ortega these intriguing records were a clear indication that potatoes were being grown on the Canary Islands in commercial quantities by 1567, and were exported from there to ports in continental Europe. The tubers could not have come directly from South America, they say, for after such a long journey they would have been far too shrivelled and sprouted to be sent on as articles of commerce to Antwerp and Rouen. 'They must undoubtedly have been grown and harvested in the Canary Isles.'[38] To allow five years for the bulking up of stock to commercial levels, potatoes would have to have been introduced directly from South America to the Canary Isles no later than in 1562. Which puts the date of the potato's arrival in the Old World back to only thirty years after the presumed first sighting of them by Pizarro in 1532, and not even ten years after they were mentioned by Pedro Cieza de León in 1553.

It follows that the most likely explanation for the absence of the potato from Clusius's 1564 account of Spanish plants is that it had not yet been transferred to continental Spain from the Canaries. He did not see the potato in Spain because it was not there. But what about Antwerp, where Clusius also had lived for a time during the 1560s? Did he know about the potatoes that Juan de Molina was then shipping from the Canaries to his brother in the city? He does not mention them; nor do potatoes crop up where the relevant years are covered in the standard biography. Negative evidence again, but allowing us to conclude – as Hawkes and Francisco-Ortega have done – that Luis de Quesada and his family probably just cooked and ate their potatoes, blithely unaware that in the same city lived Clusius, the man who could have made them famous for introducing the potato to Europe – had they invited him to share a meal.

NE POUR LA PEINE

Reueille matin de Campagne

But
des gens
de Campagne
Taille payée

L'ABEILLE
mouche à miel
Chacun a part à
ses trauaux

LA
VACHE

par mon moien tone boit et mange

LE COCHON
Il est meprisé et necessaire

LA POULE
sa journée est d'un petit pris

qui ne nourrit rien na rien

attribue

N. Guerard inu. et fecit

Chapter Seven

⌒

The way it was

Four hundred years after Luis de Quesada and his family had been eating their potatoes in Antwerp the tuber had become such a familiar item in kitchens around the world that few who ate Kartoffel klösse, pomme frite, french fries, rösti, mashed, boiled, fried, roasted or baked potatoes were even aware of the tuber's origin in the South American Andes. The potato was now a dietary institution, a primary source of energy for most of Europe and North America, plus a rapidly expanding number of other nations.

Oswald Seematter, for instance, had been growing potatoes on the family lands at Törbel, a village high in the Swiss Alps, all his life when I met him in the 1980s – just like his father and grandfather before him. The Seematters had been making cheese for generations too. These two products – potatoes and cheese – were key elements in the staple diet of farming families in the alps. Together, they made an easy meal that was eaten daily by past generations, but these days was more often served on occasions when there were visitors to be entertained – raclette.

There has been a village at Törbel for over 1,000 years, and the same families have been tending its lands and raising children for most of that time. In 1340, Seematter was one of fourteen family names among the signatories to a document drawn up to regulate use of the community's commonage. Today, thirteen of those family names are still to be found among the villagers – and no others. One family line has died out in the past 650 years; none has come in. The same families, on the same land, century after century. Such remarkable continuity speaks of judicious social management and land use practices that take care to nurture the land as well as feed the landowners.

Out on the patio, Oswald set a half-round of cheese edge-on to the coals in his custom-made fireplace; the cheese melted, bubbled, scorched and formed an appetisingly crisp crust. Deftly, he scraped a portion onto each warmed plate; Mary added boiled potatoes, steaming and floury on the outside, waxy inside – just as they preferred them. A sprinkling of chopped parsley, salt if you insisted, and there was a meal that filled and satisfied.

'How long have we been growing potatoes in Törbel?' Oswald paused only briefly. 'We've always grown potatoes; the village couldn't have existed without them,' he said.

In fact, the potato was unknown in Törbel until the 1750s, and its arrival heralded what has been described as 'a genuine, perhaps even revolutionary, change in the local environment that in turn directly affected the peasant standard of living'.[1] The nutritional status of the villagers improved with the increased food supply that the potato brought to Törbel. Better fed, the villagers became more resistant to disease, especially the respiratory illnesses to which the malnourished are particularly susceptible. The death rate declined as a consequence, while at the same time birth intervals shortened – primarily because well-nourished women generally resumed ovulation sooner after child-birth than their poorly nourished antecedents had done. Similarly, boiled potato mashed up with milk or butter, or cooked into a thick soup, provided an easily prepared and digestible supplement for infant feeding, thereby reducing the duration and intensity of breast feeding.

Fewer deaths and more births brought an overall increase in popu-lation, but this did not strain resources as might be expected, simply because the potato was adopted in Törbel as a supplement to the village's established staple crops, not a substitute for them.

Before the arrival of the potato, the year-to-year survival and well-being of Törbel was utterly dependent upon the size of its grain harvests. An ascending sequence of fields enabled villagers to plant according to which cereals grew best at particular altitudes – wheat and oats at lower elevations, barley and rye higher up – but not even rye would ripen above 1,100 metres. Potatoes, on the other hand, could be depended upon to produce a useful harvest at 1,500 metres or more; and even in years that saw grain crops parched by drought or flattened by storms there were always some potatoes to be harvested.

Thus the potato slotted neatly into the ecological niches of the Törbel landscape which previously had been unproductive, and brought a greater degree of food security than ever before to the village, as well as an improved diet. Hardly surprising, then, that a distinct upturn in Törbel's fortune is detectable from that point on. As indeed can be said of communities everywhere which successfully added the potato to their suite of staple crops. And on an expanding scale, it can be seen that the fortunes of entire regions, nations and continents were hugely influenced by the arrival of the potato.

The historian William H. McNeill has said that the availability of the potato as a food source in northern Europe during the eighteenth and nineteenth centuries:

> changed the world's history . . . without potatoes Germany could not have become the leading industrial and military power of Europe after 1848, and no less certain that Russia could not have loomed so threateningly on Germany's eastern border after 1891. In short, the European scramble for empire overseas, immigration to the United States and elsewhere, and all the other leading characteristics of the two centuries between 1750 and 1950 were fundamentally affected by the way potatoes expanded northern Europe's food supply.[2]

These are bold words, the truth of which is perversely obscured by the commonplace image of the potato in everyday life today. We take it so much for granted that even William McNeill feels obliged to begin his discussion of the subject with a disclaimer: 'My [claim] is not as absurd as it sounds . . .'

Why should it be absurd to suggest that the potato changed world history? Perhaps because it is so difficult to imagine life without it. Like Oswald Seematter, people who regularly eat potatoes tend to believe they have always been available. What else goes so well with raclette? What would have been roasting alongside the beef of old England if not potatoes? What else could have filled the bellies of van Gogh's potato-eaters? There are plenty of other options today, of course, as well as whole nations for whom rice, maize, cassava, millet, sorghum, pasta and so forth are the staple foods. But not in sixteenth-century northern Europe. So what kept the wheels of human endeavour turning before the potato arrived? And if northern Europe derived such impetus from the arrival of the potato, what were the limitations from which it freed the continent, empowered its talents and fuelled an industrial revolution? Doubtless people complained about conditions and called for improvement but − as hardly needs saying − they did not live with any sense of lacking the conveniences we enjoy today. Whatever they had, and whatever life encumbered them with, was nothing more or less than to be expected: normal.

Some aspects of sixteenth-century normality seem very familiar. Then, as now, curmudgeonly commentators deplored the falling standards of the times, convinced the country was going to the dogs: '. . . when our houses were builded of willow then we had oaken men,' William Harrison wrote in the *Description of England* he published in 1587, 'but now that our houses are come to be made of oak, our men are not only become willow but a great many . . . altogether of straw.'³ Other aspects of sixteenth-century normality are starkly, frighteningly different. Consider this: a man found guilty of killing his wife in sixteenth-century England would be hanged for murder, whereas a woman who killed her husband would be burned at the stake for treason. Treason? Yes, because the law regarded a husband as the king of his household (and, moreover, granted him the right to dispose of his wife's money and property without her consent – or even her knowledge).⁴ That was normal in the sixteenth century. So too was the fact that childbirth was a foremost cause of death among women – and birth was no guarantee of a long life for the child either. Infant and child mortality was appalling. For instance, of every 100 babies born in St Botolph's parish during the years that Shakespeare and his fellow dramatists were drawing the crowds to London's theatres, fewer than seventy lived to see their first birthday. Only forty-eight saw their fifth, and at the age of fifteen only twenty-seven or thirty of the original cohort were still alive.⁵

These figures relate to an urban community. One might expect to find better survival rates away from the sinks and slums of the towns, but such similarly detailed records of births and deaths as are available for rural communities show that an infant's chances of becoming an adult were not much better in the countryside than in the towns. Overall, across the length and breadth of Europe, six of every ten children born during the sixteenth century did not live to the age of five. And it was not only disease, deprivation or accident that threatened their chances of survival. Some destitute parents, struggling to house and feed the children they already had, resorted to desperate measures when the arrival of another threatened their already precarious existence. When abortion had failed, infanticide was the remaining option – particularly if the infant was a girl.

Wherever baptismal records or tax censuses show a disproportionately small numbers of girls compared with boys in a community, female infanticide is probably the explanation, and the motivation is not hard to deduce: poverty. A study of population control in rural France in the early Middle Ages, for example, cites instances of a direct correlation between economic circumstance and a skewed sex ratio. The larger the family, the more males there were in proportion to females and thus the more likely it is that female infanticide was practised, 'of necessity, to rid families of potentially unproductive and economically unsupportable mouths,' the author concludes.[6]

Necessity has always been a hard taskmaster, but normality can provide an ameliorating context. In early medieval England at least, anyone desperate enough to contemplate infanticide would have been aware that the authorities of the day – while disapproving – did not regard the crime as especially heinous. After all, the edicts on leading a good and godly life issued by Bartholomew of Exeter in the twelfth century had amended the sixth commandment to read: 'Thou shalt not kill but needst not strive officiously to keep alive',[7] and in England those found guilty of not keeping their newborn infant alive were not executed, physically punished, imprisoned or even fined – they were sentenced to a penance of two or three years on a diet of bread and water[8] (which may have been all an impoverished penitent could afford to eat anyway). But those found guilty of infanticide in continental Europe were not so fortunate.

Medieval European sources tell of convicted women being tied in sacks, along with a dog, a cock or some other uncongenial companion and thrown in the river to die. Such reports are anecdotal and open to question but there can be no doubting the documentary evidence of court and prison records from Nuremberg, for instance, which list by name the eighty-seven women who were executed for infanticide between 1513 and 1777. Most were drowned, though prior to 1500 the customary penalty in Nuremberg as in most of Germany had been live burial, often with gruesome refinements.[9]

In France, church and state raged against infanticide, typically claiming that a woman who killed her own child was devoid of 'all natural and human affection and piety' and could only commit the crime if she had made a pact with the devil. Laws making infanticide a capital offence were enacted in 1556, and rigorously enforced. In the 120 years from 1560 to 1680 alone, a total of more than 5,000 women were executed for infanticide in Paris and other jurisdictions of France.[10]

Yet the rivers and latrines of medieval Europe continued to 'resound with the cries of children who have been plunged into them', literary sources declare.[11] Clearly, the threat of execution was no deterrent.

The state of mind that induces a mother, or a father, to wilfully kill their own newborn child is beyond comprehension, and utterly inexcusable in any civilised context of normality. But even uncivilised behaviour deserves an explanation, and here is a clue: between the tenth and eighteenth centuries France endured eighty-nine famines that the historian Fernard Braudel regarded as widespread and severe enough to have been national disasters.[12] There were also hundreds of local and short-lived calamities and while Braudel refers specifically to France, all the countries of Europe were similarly afflicted at one time or another. As is demonstrated by England's 'constant local famines of the sixteenth and seventeenth centuries . . .'[13] The deadly threat of famine was a fact of life in the context of Europe's sixteenth-century normality.

So the fortunate four out of ten children that reached their fifteenth birthday would have seen famine among the afflictions that carried off the other six. They had another twenty-five years ahead of them on average, and could expect to suffer more famines before they died. The most unwelcome and perhaps the hardest to bear came with the marauding armies that were fighting over Europe throughout the Middle Ages. Those glorified landmarks of history − 1066, Agincourt, Magdeburg − doubtless were pivotal events, but at what cost?

This poor country is a horrible sight; it is stripped bare of everything. The soldiers take possession of the farms and have the corn threshed, but will not give a single grain to the owners who beg it as an alms. It is impossible to plough. There are no more horses; all have been carried off. The peasants are reduced to sleeping in the woods and are thankful to have them as a refuge from murderers. And if only they had enough bread to half satisfy their hunger, they would indeed count themselves happy . . . Of the 450 sick persons whom the inhabitants [of Saint-Quentin] were unable to relieve, 200 were turned out, and these we saw die one by one as they lay on the roadside . . .

We certify to having ourselves seen herds, not of cattle, but of men and women wandering about the fields between Rheims and Rhétel, turning up the earth like pigs to find a few roots; and as they can only find rotten ones, and not half enough of them, they become so weak that they have not strength left to seek food. The parish priest at Boult, whose letter we enclose, tells us he has buried three of his parishioners who died of hunger. The rest subsisted on chopped straw mixed with earth, of which they composed a food which cannot be called bread . . .[14]

And then there were the famines brought about by Europe's fickle climate: drought and a scorching sun that withered the sprouting seed and left a mocking stand of tough useless weeds. Or too little sun and torrential rains that left the crop flattened, soddened and rotten. Even in good years, the threat of famine – or just the fear of not being able to feed the household – was never far away. Let illness, misfortune or improvidence get a foot in the door and the unwanted guest would swiftly force an entry. Nagging fear was then transformed into an uncompromising reality of want and hunger which, paradoxically, was greatest when the season was fairest: in midsummer.

July was the cruellest month, when the grass stood high in the meadows, demanding to be cut and dried and stacked before a turn in the weather spoiled it. Haymaking was the first great harvest of the year – but to feed livestock during the winter, not haymakers at midsummer. People toiling in the hayfields were hungry, burning up at least 3,000 calories a day at the time of year when their available supplies of energy-packed carbohydrates were lowest. The store of last year's harvest was nearly finished – if there was any left at all – and crops planted in the spring would not be ready to reap for weeks yet. Thus, summer was not a sunblest romp for the rural majority in sixteenth-century Europe – it was 'the hungry gap',[15] when people worked hardest and ate least, and many were starving if last year's harvest had been poor. Brueghel painted hayfield scenes of bucolic fun. Midsummer madness? Perhaps, though as likely induced by the lightheadedness of starvation as by the excesses of consumption.

But despite the setbacks of famine, warfare and high infant mortality, the population of Europe was rising steadily throughout the sixteenth century. The continent had been home to around 80 million before the Black Death struck in the 1340s; by 1400 the number had sunk by up to one-third and then began to climb again – to about 60 million in 1550, 72 million in 1680[16] and then past its pre-Black Death levels on a rising curve to the total of modern times (about 340 million for a comparable area). The distribution was uneven, with about half of Europe's sixteenth-century population living in just three countries – France, Germany and England[17] – and wherever people had settled the landscape was heavily used.

Surrounded by conveniences, we forget that prior to the development of manufacturing economies, humanity's dependence upon the landscape and its resources was absolute, and stark – there was nothing else. Those fields and pasture, mountains, woods, valleys, rivers and forests – plus the animals and birds they sustained – were the totality of what was available to keep people alive. And livelihoods had to be wrested from the landscape. That was the normality of sixteenth-century life, and never forgotten. A lad hearing the corncrake call would not pause to wonder – he heard a clue as to where some fresh-laid eggs might be available. People did not stumble over fallen branches in the wood – they carried them home for the fire. Families did not gather on the brows of hills in golden summer evenings to sigh over the beauty of the view laid out before them – the fields of waving corn, the hay securely stacked, the cattle contentedly grazing, the sheep gathered in for shearing – at least, I do not believe they did.

I believe that when people scanned the landscape from the brow of a hill in the Middle Ages, their purpose was primarily to assess how much they could get out of it that year, and what a lot of hard work it would be. The beauty of nature had nothing to do with their appreciation of the view. In fact, the modern capacity to see beauty in a landscape is probably a deep-seated sigh of relief. We do not have to cut down and saw up that oak to make a new barn, nor milk the cows, shear the sheep, or reap the corn.

How much would those people on the hill have known of the world beyond their immediate horizon in the sixteenth century? Quite a lot is the conclusion to be drawn from parish and community records of the period. Although significant numbers were born, lived and died without ever venturing beyond the bounds of their community, by 1600 (and probably earlier) two-thirds of England's rural population changed their village of residence at least once in the course of their lives[18] – and this was a trend that accelerated in succeeding centuries. Many went into service on the great estates (visitors from the continent remarked that the English gentry would rather have servants than children), but cities and the attractions of urban life were the foremost incentive for leaving the village. Indeed, no city in those days could have existed – let alone grow – without a continuous influx of migrants from the rural areas (urban death rates in Europe persistently exceeded birth rates until the sanitary and healthcare measures of modern times were introduced).[19]

Apprenticeship records from some of London's professional companies show that before 1640 (and the crisis of England's civil war), as many as 30–40 per cent of their apprentices had come from places 300 or 400 kilometres away. So how did they get there? It was not as difficult as might be imagined. In his history of the English countryside, Oliver Rackham says that '[i]n the Middle Ages the road system of England was rather denser than it is now . . . Every wood, meadow, house, and barn and most fields and furlongs had vehicle access, and there were also footpath rights-of-way across fields. Moors and heaths were criss-crossed with tracks linking hamlets and farms.'[20] Even in September 1066 communications were good enough for King Harold to travel 200 miles from London to York in four days, defeat Danish invaders at Stamford Bridge then, on hearing three days later that William of Normandy had landed at Pevensey, march his army 250 miles south to confront William at the Battle of Hastings on 13 October. As Rackham points out, few campaigns before the age of helicopters can have packed more action into three weeks; a tribute to organisation and endurance, but also to the country's road system.[21]

It was the arterial network of Roman roads, strategically routed and magnificently engineered, that enabled Harold to move armies up and down the length of England so expeditiously, but the hinterland of rural communities played an important role too. Simply by being there, viable and economically active, they kept the network functioning and serviceable. Overlay a map of Roman Britain with the location of villages and towns that existed in medieval times, and the regions the roads traverse are splattered with dots representing rural settlements of everything from just a few to several dozen houses – hamlets, villages and towns.

The Romans are remembered as conquerors, but far from supressing an indigenous rural economy, their network of roads actually facilitated its development. The immediate hinterland of the roads was especially well-populated: in medieval times, for instance, there were over 100 villages and towns within an hour or so's walk of the Fosse Way, a 220-mile Roman road running diagonally across southern England from Exeter to Lincoln, via Ilchester, Bath, Cirencester and Leicester.[22] Other major routes were similarly endowed. No one in Britain (or wherever else in Europe the Romans had laid roads, for that matter) was more than a day or two from one of these major highways.

Though news could travel no faster than a man on a horse in medieval times, and goods at the speed of an ox-wagon or packhorse, information was widely shared – simply because its relatively slow passage through any region gave ample time for it to be picked up and passed on by interested parties. And for an indication of the volume of traffic passing ponderously through the landscape, Exeter, at the southern end of the Fosse Way, is a good example. The port had been handling a wide range and volume of merchandise since Roman times, local and from overseas. Such as foodstuffs: hundreds of fishing boats supplied Exeter markets with fish, for instance, which was then distributed throughout the south-west and beyond – pilchards, herring, cod and salmon; lamprey, eels, mackerel and sprats; fresh, salted, smoked or dried.[23] And wine: even in the aftermath of the Black Death, while times were still hard, Exeter was importing a yearly average of more than 500 tuns of French wine[24] for its customers – enough to fill over half a million bottles.

By the sixteenth century, Exeter was exporting a greater value of wool than anything else, part of a development that would see increasing numbers of English (and European) farmers moving away from food production as their primary activity, and committing themselves more and more to the business of producing the raw materials that manufacturing industry would pay good money for. Exeter was one of numerous provincial centres that found themselves ideally placed to serve this aspect of Europe's nascent market economy. But no other town in England grew so fast. The census of 1520 reveals a booming mercantile centre, with widespread connections, handling an impressive volume and variety of trade: there were hundreds of importers, wool merchants, wholesalers, fish dealers, brewers, butchers, bakers and candlestick makers . . . And how many people lived in the city at that time? Seven thousand[25] – in present times, not even enough to fill the city's new £15 million football stadium at Sandy Park (capacity 8,200), and little more than 5 per cent of its 2006 population (113,073), but in the sixteenth century enough to sustain a thriving centre of commercial activity and the social interactions required to service it.

The volume of activity generated by relatively small populations in the sixteenth century is one of the more striking features of life in medieval times, though it was always constrained by the rights and obligations of a strict social hierarchy in which everyone knew their place – and that of anyone else they may encounter in the daily round. Inevitably, wealth tended to concentrate in the hands of those at the top of the hierarchy. In fifteenth-century England, for instance, the upper echelons of society – who totalled about 50,000 and comprised no more than 2 per cent of the population – shared an annual income of close to half a million pounds; more than ten times the peace-time state budget of the country.[26] And this disparity contributed to the friction which a century later provoked a fundamental change in the hierarchical arrangement of English society.

In the early 1530s the church in England was earning about £400,000 per year from its properties and landholdings, while the crown estates were providing Henry VIII with an income of only about £40,000. What followed is generally known as 'the dissolution of the monasteries', though some historians prefer to speak of 'the plunder of the church'. In 1536 the lands and incomes of 374 lesser monasteries were confiscated by the crown, followed in 1539 by the confiscation of over 180 greater monasteries and in 1545 by the property of various colleges, chapels and hospitals, and 700 Irish monasteries. In this way more than 60 per cent of the church's wealth passed to the crown; and of course the crown gained not just income, but also the capital value of church lands, properties and treasures. The lands appear to have passed through the crown's hands quickly, however, and into the possession of many smaller landowners – royal courtiers and favourites of the crown prominent among them.[27]

The poor are always with us and deserving of attention, the Bible says.[28] The church had been a source of relief, but not all its charitable obligations were taken over by the new owners of its properties. In fact, legislation enacted during the late sixteenth century explicitly required local authorities to provide care for the poor in their communities. The need was considerable, widespread and persistent throughout the Middle Ages, with between half and one-third of Europe's population reduced to abject poverty at some time in the course of their lives. Rural poverty was scattered, out of sight and not widely reported, but reports of urban poverty abound. 'You cannot walk down the street or stop in a square or church without multitudes surrounding you to beg for charity; you see hunger written on their faces, their eyes like gemless rings, the wretchedness of their bodies, with skins shaped only by bones', a visitor to Vicenza near Venice wrote in 1528. Nearly 40 per cent of Bergamo's population were registered as paupers in 1575. In 1630, Madrid too found that 40 per cent of its population were paupers.[29]

Urban poverty was of course directly linked to rural poverty. When harvests failed or warring armies rampaged across the landscape, starving country people crowded into the towns. They had no other option. Some had the money to buy food (though prices may have risen three- or fourfold); others looked for work – offering their labour in exchange for bread and gruel alone if necessary. Riots ensued when and wherever the point of total desperation was passed. Fernand Braudel writes of Europe experiencing 'thousands of bread riots' (one of which culminated in the French Revolution).[30] In England alone, the most acute of several hundred grain shortages sparked off sixty serious riots during the century after 1550, spurring the authorities to a more meticulous application of the poor laws (even when it meant price controls and ensuring that available grain supplies went to bakeries rather than breweries). In France, where grain riots became virtually endemic during the sixteenth century, the authorities were less sympathetic. Their response, a commentator reports, was almost always the same: 'an invasion of troops, summary trials and gibbets groaning under the weight of corpses'.[31]

Clearly, Europe's food supply was often strained to the limit, but the underlying cause was not a rapidly expanding population (prior to the Black Death, Europe had supported more people than in the sixteenth century), nor the growth of urban centres (the ratio of urban to rural populations remained roughly the same). The principal factor was the change in farming practices that saw farmers turning away from food production as their primary activity and concentrating instead on the production of raw materials for manufacturing industries at home and abroad. Especially wool. Increasingly, cornfields were transformed into sheep pastures. Add to this the fact that agricultural productivity was inherently low and you have what is politely called 'the agrarian problem of the sixteenth century'.[32]

It is astonishing that at least three-quarters of the land being farmed in England today was also under cultivation in the sixteenth century. The difference is that today's cornfields produce twelve times more than their counterparts 500 years ago. Furthermore, while we can acquire the necessities of life from any number of places, in the sixteenth century everything – not just foodstuffs – came directly from the land, and probably from not very far away. Clothes were made from wool, linen and leather; sheep and cattle fat (tallow) was used for lighting; people wrote with a goose quill pen on vellum (calf skins) or parchment (sheep skins). All forms of transport – from sledges to ships – were made of wood, and land transport was powered by animals fuelled with hay and oats. Hemp was grown to make rope; flax for linen; hops for beer; woad, weld, madder and saffron for dyes; teasels to prepare wool for spinning.[33]

The labour requirement was immense, with only wind- and water-mills to ease the burden of men and beasts. It took five or six experienced sickle-wielding reapers a day to harvest a hectare of wheat[34]

– which yielded on average less than a tonne of grain (one-third of which must be kept as seed for the next year), and in bad years might not be enough to cover the food requirement of the harvesters. There was livestock to be provided for too – and haymaking called for equally large inputs of labour over a short period of time. And throughout the year there was ploughing, harrowing, sowing and weeding to be done; ditches and drains to be dug out, hedges to be cut back, fuelwood to be gathered, buildings to be repaired, and always the goading demand of land to be cleared. Shortfalls in production always provoked calls for more land to be brought into cultivation. Even three centuries on, administrators were urging: 'Let us not be satisfied with the liberation of Egypt, or the subjugation of Malta, but let us subdue Finchley Common; let us conquer Hounslow Heath, let us compel Epping Forest to submit to the yoke of improvement.'[35]

With agriculture and related occupations so labour-intensive, up to 90 per cent of Europe's population were tied to the land in the sixteenth century. In effect, nine out of ten people were supplying the needs of themselves and one other individual not similarly engaged. Which would have been fine if every farmer consistently produced a surplus of 11 per cent or more. But medieval agriculture rarely achieved such efficient productivity. In England, for example, four out of five farmers grew just enough food for the needs of the family household.[36] Any surplus they reaped and sold in good years would pay for essentials such as salt and iron goods, and could provide some insurance against bad years, but the wholesale production of grain for sale was beyond contemplation: they simply did not have enough labour – or land. Farms were too small, and yields too low. Meanwhile, however, wool was in high demand, and the price rising.

Ever since biblical times – and probably before then – the conflicting needs of cultivators and herders have caused trouble. One wants a field to plough, the other needs pasture for grazing. It is possible for them to work together. After all, people need both protein and carbohydrate and while livestock are grazing a fallow meadow they fertilise next season's plantings. Likewise, stubble on a harvested field is good supplementary feed. But if either seeks to maximise production and sell the surplus beyond the local community, difficulties arise. The wholesale transition from cereal-growing to sheep-grazing, inspired by the high price of wool, characterises 'the agrarian problem of the sixteenth century'. It changed the face of England and – even more critically – set the economies of Europe on a course which moved society from the world of the seasons, the village, and a sense of community and natural justice, into the world of the marketplace and its remorseless sense of competitive individualism.

'Enclosure' is the catch-all word that describes the process by which ploughland was converted to pasture, but it involved much more than the erection of fences to enclose flocks of sheep. The scattering of small fields which previously had served to feed a number of households were combined in single united areas; big landowners consolidated their properties by combining the farms they leased out, evicting tenants and destroying buildings; commonage was seized, with the simultaneous decrease or even complete abolition of the rights of commoners. There were advantages: consolidation rationalised production, saving both on the cost of labour and haulage costs of horses or oxen; land which had formerly kept scores of men busy could now be worked by a few shepherds; wool production was less susceptible to the vagaries of climate than wheat, and fetched a good price; the value of land went up. From a production and economic point of view there can be no doubt that enclosure was sensible. But it caused much anguish and suffering. 'The gentle sheep was more voracious than the wild beasts of Africa; it ate men, ploughland, houses and whole villages.' Tenant farmers complained that the large landowners: 'leave no grounde for tillage, thei enclose al into pastures, thei throw doune houses, thei plucke down townes, and leave nothing standynge, but only the churche to be made a shepe-howse.'[37]

The result was a breakdown in land-based self-sufficiency. Where families previously maintained at least the means of producing food for themselves – to which every relation felt entitled to claim a share in difficult times – increasing numbers were cast off their land and became dependent on paid employment for survival. By the first half of the sixteenth century this disengagement from self-sufficiency had already reached the point at which 60 per cent of people in England aged between fifteen and twenty-four were servants and labourers working on large farms. In southern England a quarter of all adult men were landless and dependent on working for others as the sole means of supporting themselves and their families.[38]

Meanwhile, the conversion of arable land to pasture, and the economics of the marketplace, was pushing up the price of foodstuffs – especially wheat and bread, which were the measures against which people judged their standards of living. Wages did not rise to match; indeed, in terms of the quantities of wheat a working man could afford to buy, wages fell steadily throughout the sixteenth century.[39] Seventeenth-century records show no improvement: if the harvest was 10 per cent below expectations, the price of wheat rose 30 per cent; if the yield was only half, a working man had to pay four times the usual price for a loaf of bread.[40] And if these demand-driven fluctuations of a market economy were making life hard for the wage-earner, self-sufficient small farmers who had managed to hold on to their land were having a no less difficult time. Indeed, they had the worst of all worlds; caught in the marketing trap that forced them to sell cheap and buy dear: whenever harvests were good and they produced a surplus, the market was flooded and prices low; conversely, when harvests did not cover their subsistence needs, supplies were scarce and the cost of making up their shortages correspondingly high.

Food was the principal concern of most households 500 years ago. Every other aspect of their lives was subservient to the challenges of putting sufficient food on the table, and the surrounding landscape – urban as well as rural – was simply the place where they hoped to acquire it.

So how well did people eat? We read of London cookshops offering three roast thrushes for twopence.[41] Since a skilled medieval craftsman earned only around eightpence a day this was a fast-food snack that cost the equivalent of about £20 in today's money; hardly something that any but the very well-off could afford. Only the nobility sat down regularly to meals the sixteenth-century chronicler William Harrison describes, consuming 'beef, mutton, veal, lamb, kid, pork, cony, capon, pig, or so many of these as the season yieldeth';[42] nor can many ever have shared a meal such as the Duke of Buckingham hosted on the feast of Epiphany in 1508, when a total of 459 people consumed 36 rounds of beef, 12 sheep, 2 calves, 4 pigs, 6 suckling pigs, numerous chickens and rabbits, geese, swans, capons, peacocks, herons, mallard, woodcock, snipe, other unspecified birds great and small, as well as oysters, salmon, sturgeon, cod, ling, flounder . . . and precisely 678 loaves of bread. All washed down with French wine and 259 flagons of ale.[43] In fact, while attention focuses on extravagance at one extreme, and on the peasants' monotonous potage and bread at the other, a wider view reveals simply that food was the largest single item in everyone's budget – from aristocrat to labourer – with the proportion of expenditure devoted to food increasing with each step down the social ladder:[44] the rich spent most, but the poor spent the greatest proportion of whatever they had on food.

Clearly, those who could afford to ate well. But among those who spent the greatest proportion of their available income on food – the small farmers, artisans, labourers and the very poor – rising prices eroded their diets, in terms of both quality and quantity. While the food of the rich became increasingly varied and their tables groaned with meat and luxuries, the changing economic climate forced many to eat less meat than formerly and to depend more heavily on cheap bread grains.[45] Malnourishment ensued. Then, towards the end of the century a succession of harvest failures brought starvation. A contemporary observer reported:

> [They] die, some in ditches, some in holes, some in caves and dens, some in fields . . . rather like dogs than christian people . . . yet they are forced to walke the countries from place to place to seeke their releefe at every mans doore, excepte they wil sterve or famish at home . . . Yea, in such troups doe they flocke, and in such swarmes doe they flowe, that you can lightlie go any way, and you shall see numbers of them at everie door, in everie lane, and in everie poor cave.[46]

Nothing short of the agricultural revolution which the landholding and land-use revisions of the enclosures had set in motion could effect lasting improvement. As scattered landholdings were reduced to fewer, larger units, there was more incentive to intensify production by making better use of available resources. Ploughing one large field was obviously more efficient than ploughing several smaller ones. Crop rotations and the benefits of manuring became more widely appreciated. Clover was planted as a fallow and forage crop. The full benefits of these early developments would become evident towards the end of the eighteenth century, as machinery began to supplement muscle as the powering force of agriculture. The light two-horse plough, the horse-drawn seed drill, reaper and binder, the threshing machine, the winnower – even the move from sickle to scythe boosted productivity. There were new crops too. And here we find one of those remarkable synergies which come along from time to time: the potato arrived in Europe and established itself as a staple food just as economic developments were pushing the price of wheat beyond the means of many households, just as fewer people were needed to work on the land, and precisely when Europe's burgeoning industries were beginning to cry out for workers.

It would be stretching the point to say that the potato actually fuelled the industrial revolution. Many factors were involved. Even so, the potato's contribution was huge and incontestable. Indeed, it is hard to imagine where Europe would have been without the potato.

ENGLANDS
Happineſs Increaſed,

OR

A Sure and Eaſie Remedy againſt all ſucceeding Dear Years;

BY

A Plantation of the Roots called *POTATOES*, whereof (with the Addition of Wheat Flower) ex-cellent, good and wholeſome Bread may be made, every Year, eight or nine Months together, for half the Charge as formerly.

ALSO

By the Planting of theſe Roots, Ten Thouſand Men in *ENGLAND* and *WALES*, who know not how to Live, or what to do to get a Maintenance for their Families, may of One Acre of Ground, make Thirty Pounds *per Annum*.

Invented and Publiſhed for the Good of the Poorer Sort,
By JOHN FORSTER *Gent.*.

LONDON, Printed for *A. Seile*, over againſt St. *Dunſtans*-Church in *Fleetſtreet*; 1664.

Chapter Eight

The demoralising esculent

People eat and prefer the foods they have grown up with. And for centuries wheat, barley rye and oats – the cereal grains – had been 'the staffs of life' in Europe. It was a matter of belief as much as anything else. Whether they ate bread at the high table or could afford only barley to thicken a soup, the sentiment was the same; there was no issue of taste or fashion, just an unquestioning, deep-rooted and universal conviction that grain was essential.

In 1716 – more than a century after John Gerard had first grown potatoes in his London gardens – market gardeners in southern England still regarded radishes as a more worthwhile crop than potatoes.[1] Clergymen and priests banned their parishioners from planting the potato, saying it was unworthy of human consumption because it was not mentioned in the Bible, and an early edition of the *Encyclopædia Britannica* lent its weight to such contentions by describing the potato as a 'demoralising esculent'. Not until the nineteenth century did the potato achieve anything like the status it has today: Europe's most widely consumed, cheap and nourishing food – 250 years after its first arrival on the scene.

The early botanists and herbalists of northern Europe must bear some responsibility for the potato's slow progress. Driven by that 'lonely impulse of delight', they were more interested in describing the botanical features of a plant than in considering the usefulness of the parts that lurked underground. After all, it was the visible portion of a plant – the stem, leaves and flowers – that most readily distinguished one plant from another. And the potato plants that botanists were describing in the first flush of investigation seem to have been especially interesting above ground, with flowers so attractive and abundant that the Finnish botanist Olaus Rudbeck (memorialised in the popular garden plant *Rudbeckia*) even recommended potatoes more for garden borders than for the dining table.[2]

In mitigation, the botanists' discounting of the potato's culinary potential had a lot to do with the fact that the original stock had come only recently from the equatorial Andes, and so was adapted to complete its cycle of growth, flowering and tuber production in an environment where the days were about twelve hours long all year round. When they were planted in northern Europe, where summer days lasted up to eighteen hours, the cycle was distorted. With so much warmth and light the plants grew prodigiously, producing tier upon tier of leaves and flowers but no tubers until late September, when twelve-hour days at last brought the conditions under which they were adapted to tuberise. By then, though, temperatures were falling, and the days getting shorter. To stay alive at all, the plants then had to allocate a large proportion of available nutrients to the maintenance of their stem and leaves. There was little left over for making tubers and those that were produced before the growing season ended were not very large. Numerous yes, but mostly the size of marbles or smaller, and few even as big as a chicken's egg.

To select and breed a line of potatoes that would produce acceptably large tubers at high latitudes was beyond the early botanists' interest, so it was fortuitous that the Spanish had begun growing them in the Canary Isles – a halfway house, as it were, between conditions in the potato's Andean cradle land and those in northern Europe, where the plants' potential was to be most thoroughly exploited. The Canary Island farmers succeeded in breeding varieties adapted to their variable day length very soon after its discovery in Peru, so must have been persuaded that the potato merited serious attention. In northern Europe its virtues were not so rapidly appreciated.

Above all, there was the influence of the herbalists' 'Doctrine of Signatures' to be overcome. Though mistaken in prescribing the walnut as a cure for troubles of the brain simply because the one resembled the other, the doctrine's principle of similarity – that both the cause and cure of an affliction could be found in plants which resembled the condition or the part of the body affected – was a deeply entrenched piece of folklore. Old wives' tales, most of it, but offering explanations and treatment when nothing else could. And sometimes the signatures were right. For instance, the willow thrives in marshy ground, and we now know that salicylic acid (aspirin) extracted from its bark will indeed ease the rheumatic pains of those who live in such places, just as the doctrine advised.

So what did the doctrine's advocates make of the potato? They found its signature in the tubers – those weird and unfamiliar products of dirt and darkness. And the first potatoes to arrive in Europe were not uniformly shaped, like those we know today; nor were they all the same colour, but could be red, black or purple – or deathly white, all of which emphasised the sinister connotation of the nodules and the bulbous finger-like protuberances that many of them bore. In the eyes of the doctrine's followers, potatoes resembled the deformed hands and feet of the leper – the shunned outcast of the Middle Ages. Ergo, their signature was leprosy, that most loathsome disease.

This diagnosis should have meant that the doctrine would prescribe potatoes as a treatment for leprosy. But there is no sign of that, probably because leprosy was less prevalent in the early seventeenth century – rarely seen but widely known and feared. And since little need of a cure was evident, the principles of the doctrine of signatures were inverted. Instead of being regarded as a treatment of leprosy, the potato was deemed to be its cause – and proscribed.

This was more than enough to deter potential consumers from eating potatoes – especially as it related to a vegetable that was entirely new to Europe, that grew underground, and without which people had been getting along well enough. Certainly the belief that potatoes caused leprosy became widespread, and was taken seriously enough to evoke instances of official condemnation: 'I am told that the Burgundians are forbidden to make use of these tubers, because they are assured that the eating of them causes leprosy,' says the second edition of John Gerard's *Herball* (1633).

Not everything that Gerard wrote was beyond dispute, but in this case the *Herball* was repeating – almost word for word – what a more reputable botanist, Gaspard Bauhin, had written a few years before. And there were other objections, among them complaints that potatoes were difficult to prepare (all those knobs and deep-set eyes); they could not easily be made into bread; they were 'windy' and caused indigestion. All in all, even those undeterred by the threat of leprosy tended to regard potatoes as food fit only for animals and indigents. But it was not just potential consumers that found the potato an unattractive proposition. Potential producers – the farmers and market gardeners – had their objections too.

At a time when meat and wheat (or other cereals) were considered to be the diet that all should aspire too, and agricultural productivity was low, there was little time, labour, land or enthusiasm to spare for anything new. And the novelty of the potato was more than just that it grew underground, in a variety of shapes and colours. The potato was also the first crop Europeans had seen that grew from tubers, not seed. This was completely different from customary practice, and imposed heavy burdens on a farmer and his resources: whereas a field of wheat could be sown by a single man walking back and forth, casting handfuls of seed to left and right, each tuber in a potato field had to be planted individually. And as with planting, so with harvesting: cereal crops could be reaped more quickly and cheaply than a field of potatoes could be dug.

Furthermore, growing potatoes conflicted with traditional patterns of land use. Cereals rotated with fallow and stock grazing in the old scheme of things, and while we think of fallowing as a means of resting the land, early farmers did it to control weeds. By ploughing the fallow fields in summer, before weeds had set seed, the presence of invading plants was much reduced and farmers could expect (or least hope for) a relatively weed-free harvest when the field was sown again the following year.[3] There was no space (temporal or territorial) for the potato in this pattern of rotation. In order to grow potatoes, farmers would either have to give up a portion of their cereal production, or bring some new land into cultivation for the crop. Both options would demand a major investment – of conviction as well as resources.

This is not to say that root crops were unknown in Europe. Carrots, turnips and parsnips were a familiar feature in the gardens of monasteries and houses great and small, as were leaf vegetables, leeks, onions and garlic, herbs and such profusion of ingredients as would go into the everyday potage and stew. But gardens and the taste for vegetables were not universally popular – even among kings. When Henry VIII's first wife, Katharine, wanted to eat vegetables such as she had enjoyed at the table of her father, Ferdinand II of Aragon, for instance, she had to hire a gardener from Flanders to grow them. And whatever that gentleman introduced seems to have been lost among the succession of wives that followed Katharine, for Henry's last wife, Catherine Parr, reportedly sent agents to Holland whenever she needed so much as a salad.[4]

The botanists grew potatoes in their gardens in early seventeenth-century Europe, and doubtless a few adventurous yeoman householders did too, but only in the course of the eighteenth century would the potato finally break through the garden fence and become a field crop, capable of supplementing and eventually competing with grain. By thus enlarging the food supply, potatoes were then destined to fulfil their potential as an influential factor in the economic and demographic development of Europe. The process had already begun in Ireland, where potato-growing was widespread and arousing comment in the first half of the seventeenth century. The crop was quite well-known in England and Scotland then too, and English immigrants could have played an important role in the spread of the potato to Europe. Prime candidate for this is a community of English Carthusian monks who settled in Nieuwpoort, close to the Channel coast of Belgium in 1626.

Another clue to the potato's escape from garden to field has been found at Tielt, a small town 20 miles inland from Nieuwpoort, where an official writing in 1678 notes that 'for better than thirty-six years potatoes have been planted outside the gardens [and] almost all the inhabitants of the parish [are growing them], each for his [own] consumption and convenience'. This would put the beginnings of the potato's influence as a field crop in that region at around 1642 – and Tielt is close enough to Nieuwpoort for the development to have come from England, courtesy of the Carthusians. It is also not far from Antwerp, which brings to mind the barrels of potatoes that were shipped from the Canary Islands to a resident of that city, Luis de Quesada, in 1567. They too could have been a factor.

Anxious to take investigations from speculation into the realm of verifiable fact, the Dutch historian Chris Vandenbroeke opened up an illuminating line of enquiry in the 1960s, when he began looking at the lawsuits between tenant-farmers and tithe holders which had been brought to court during the period in question. This was a master-stroke of research.[5] In the Middle Ages landowners throughout Europe were entitled to levy as tax, or rent, one-tenth (a tithe) of their tenants' agricultural produce. But on 1 October 1520 Charles V, ruler of the Holy Roman Empire, had declared that new crops should be exempt from tithes for forty years after their introduction. Tithe holders tended to ignore the royal edict, however, and continued to tithe any crop that was grown in open fields – new or otherwise. Numerous lawsuits ensued as farmers protested that the crops being tithed were new introductions. The cultivation of tobacco, clover, buckwheat and carrots all featured as subjects of litigation. And, finally, potatoes too.

It follows that the number of lawsuits increased as the crops in question began to be more extensively cultivated. Thus they could show that at the time of litigation the crops were being grown in open fields, on a scale that justified the effort of appealing to the courts for collection (or cancellation) of the tithe. Furthermore, since litigants had to convince the courts that the crops in dispute had (or had not) been under cultivation for more than forty years, the lawsuits were also a good indication of when the crop had first been grown in open fields. There were problems of biased testimony, as Vandenbroeke readily admits, since all parties would be inclined to exaggerate the evidence that supported their case. Nonetheless, the numerous lawsuits he examined in dozens of towns collectively show 'a definite evolution in the diffusion of potato-growing' from north-west to south-east Belgium.

Tielt is among the first towns in which the potato-tithe lawsuits were noted (in 1723). Thirty-three years later they appeared for the first time in the Brussels area, and a couple of years after that in Antwerp and Limburg. Thus the evidence reveals that potato-growing started in central Belgium around 1710–20 and that potatoes were a firmly established field crop from 1740 on – so much so that the bakers and millers of Schaarbeek (now a suburb of Brussels) were 'complaining about the reduction in the grinding of grain and sale of bread, since potatoes have been planted in such great quantity'.

The trail of lawsuits continued south and east, to Namur (where a document from 1762 noted that potatoes were being harvested everywhere in the country), and on to Limburg and Luxemburg. But here some of the dates overlapped, indicating that the potato had been advancing from the south, as well as from the north. Vandenbroeke concluded that Luxemburg's potatoes had come from Alsace. And Alsace, the evidence reveals, was where the potato first broke through the garden fence to become established as an open field crop that could save people from starvation. A document quoted by Vandenbroeke explains what it was that had persuaded people to set aside their prejudices and begin growing potatoes as their staple food – war:

> . . . this vegetable spread and gradually multiplied in the Vosges because of the proximity of Alsace. Since this province was nearly always the first arena of war in Europe the peasants valued a ground-crop that could feed the people, their cows and pigs, and give a good yield. It was never exposed to damage by . . . the ravages of war, for when an army camped for a month on a field of potatoes, the farmer could still harvest them . . . when the army had left . . .[6]

Warfare was frequent and widespread in Europe during the seventeenth and eighteenth centuries, and it coincided with the beginnings of large-scale potato cultivation often enough to persuade scholars that the disruptions and upheavals inflicted by marauding armies were indeed the factors that changed the diet and tastes of the continent. This was a huge and relatively rapid change – on the scale of a seismic shift – with massive demographic and economic consequences.

So it was not choice, but a lack of options that put potatoes in the bowl. People would never have taken to the cultivation and consumption of potatoes as a staple food if circumstances had not forced them to, but once they began eating potatoes regularly they came to appreciate the beneficial qualities of the crop. In fact, since potatoes would yield up to four times more calories than grain from the same piece of land, half a hectare of potatoes and the milk of just one cow was enough to feed a whole family for a year. Monotonous, but nutritious, and more than enough to keep even the poorest rural communities in vigorous good health. Grow another quarter hectare of potatoes and they could raise a pig too, whose sale would supplement wages and help to pay for rent, clothes and other essentials. War may have forced the rural populations of Europe to grow and eat potatoes, but potatoes in turn opened up new horizons of opportunity.[7]

Above all, though, and from the individual farmer's point of view, the spread of the potato from gardens to the open fields of Europe radically reduced the destructive consequences of war. Because armies lacked the resources and transport facilities that would have enabled them to maintain adequate supply lines, they had long since been accustomed to getting most of the food they needed from the lands they were fighting over. Foraging parties took all they could carry – and resorted to violence if necessary. Some armies added a gloss of legality to their requisitioning by handing out promissory notes which offered payment at a later date for the supplies taken. Such procedures may have lessened the destructive effects of the seizures (and sometimes even paid up what had been promised), but any delay or unhelpful turn of events (the issuing army's defeat, for instance) would make the chits as good as a death warrant to families whose entire stocks of food had been carried off.

So, wherever local communities depended on a store of grain for their survival, outright starvation was the usual and anticipated result of an extended military campaign. And as the size of armies and the frequency of war increased through the seventeenth and eighteenth centuries, the demographic and monetary costs mounted rapidly. At the point of desperation, villagers turned to the potato. Their prejudices and reluctance to accept an unfamiliar food crop were set aside – outweighed by the simple fact that potatoes could keep a family alive even when foraging troops had emptied the barns, leaving only a piece of paper that may or may not be worth something. At first the villagers ate potatoes because there was nothing else. But soon they realised that the potato offered more than just nutritional benefits. By planting them extensively and leaving tubers in the ground until they were needed for eating, people could survive even the most ruthless military requisitioning. Foraging parties would always prefer to take grain if there was any in the neighbourhood. And if the barns were empty because everyone was growing potatoes, even then the foragers were unlikely to linger and dig long enough to take every last tuber.

As the historian William H. McNeill points out,[8] the Thirty Years War (1618–48) marks a climax in the all-too frequent eruptions of destruction and privation that warfare had been inflicting upon the civilian populations of Europe for centuries. Its devastations were especially terrible in Germany, and remembered with shuddering horror. Many died – but the survivors could be thankful for small mercies: the Thirty Years War was the last to be fought in Europe before potatoes became widespread enough to forestall rural starvation and thus cushion the human cost of military requisitioning.

Thereafter, the coincidence of war and adoption of the potato is well documented.[9] Alsace in the second half of the seventeenth century; Flanders during the War of the League of Augsburg (1688–97); the War of the Spanish Succession (1701–14); the War of the Austrian Succession (1740–48 – when harvest failures exacerbated grain shortages); and in Germany. Here, the first major advance occurred during the Seven Years War (1756–63), giving the potato a foothold that the failing grain harvests of succeeding years served to consolidate and extend. By the late 1770s the potato was firmly established as the staple crop of rural communities throughout Germany and central Europe, just in time for the War of Bavarian Succession (1778–9) – which must count among the least enlightened episodes of Frederick the Great's luminous career.

Anxious to ensure that Bavaria should become part of Prussia following the death of its ruler, Frederick declared war on the other claimant – Austria. The Prussian forces invaded by way of Bohemia and eventually confronted the Austrians across the breadth of the Elbe river, at Königgratz. These were positions from which neither army could achieve victory. The opposing forces could do no more than threaten each other, while steadily munching their way through the region's bountiful potato crop. At the onset of winter both armies terminated the inglorious campaign and retreated – not victorious, but undefeated and well-fed. The episode is commonly known as the *Kartoffelkrieg*, the Potato War.

The value of potatoes as a means of keeping peasants (and soldiers) alive during military campaigns was a useful lesson that Frederick the Great had picked up during the early battles of the War of the Austrian Succession (1740–48), an escapade which extended Prussian territories and ultimately involved all the major powers of Europe. In 1744 he ordered his government to distribute free seed potatoes and instructions on growing them throughout Prussia. Consequently, when French, Austrian and Russian armies invaded Prussia during the Seven Years War, potatoes kept Frederick's subjects alive. Indeed, the precarious survival of the Prussian state itself owed much to potatoes. Not surprisingly, the invading armies took note of the reason for Prussia's remarkable resilience and the governments of Austria, Russia and France all subsequently began encouraging their farmers to grow potatoes.

It was not always easy. The belief that eating potatoes was likely to cause leprosy and sundry other afflictions lingered on. Pockets of resistance to the new crop existed even in Prussia, so that when a cart-load of Frederick's free potatoes arrived in Kolberg, a small town on the Baltic coast, the farmers refused to have anything to do with them. Officers responsible for the delivery reported that peasants believed that potatoes gave rise to scrofula, rickets, consumption and gout. Furthermore, they complained that 'the things have no taste; not even dogs will eat them. What is the use of them to us?'[10] Frederick is alleged to have responded to such ungrateful behaviour with a threat to have the ears and nose cut off any Prussians who persistently refused to do as they were told. There is no evidence that the threat was ever carried out, but the cart-load of potatoes sent to Kolberg the following year (1745) was accompanied by a soldier from southern Germany, where the potato was already well-established, who was charged with the task of demonstrating how the tubers should be cultivated and cooked.

The overall result of the Prussian Wars and Frederick's initiatives was that whereas the potato was either unknown or despised through much of central and eastern Europe in 1700, by 1800 it had become an indispensable part of the diet from the Alps to the steppes of Russia. Its adoption in France was sluggish – though there, too, it was a war that eventually propelled its introduction: not so much in the direct effects of warfare on French communities as in the fact that a young pharmacist, Antoine-Augustin Parmentier, was taken prisoner by the Prussians while serving with the French army during the Seven Years War. While in captivity he was fed almost exclusively on potatoes. On his release in 1763, delighted to find that he had not only survived for three years on a diet of potatoes, but was also in remarkably good health, Parmentier returned to Paris determined that all of France should enjoy the benefits of this hitherto despised crop. Thereafter he devoted much of his energies to gathering and disseminating information on potatoes.

To begin with, Parmentier initiated a series of pioneering studies in nutritional chemistry – inquiring into the essence of food and the means by which it promoted growth and maintained good health. 'A thing which will always appear astonishing . . .' he wrote, 'is that we have lived centuries without having the curiosity to seek to know the nature of the substance that nourishes us.' How ironic and sad, he noted, that savants have devoted volumes to exotics, while the simplest and most familiar things remained a mystery.[11] Parmentier was actually referring to wheat in that instance, but when harvests failed yet again in 1770 and the Academy of Besançon offered a prize for the best 'study of food substances capable of reducing the calamities of famine', he was uniquely poised to enter a pro-potato 'Inquiry into Nourishing Vegetables That in Times of Necessity Could Be Substituted for Ordinary Food'. Parmentier's potato proposal won the Besançon prize and was subsequently expanded into his *Examen chimique des pommes de terre* (Paris 1773), which gave a thorough and convincing demonstration of the potato's nutritional attributes and advantages.

Paris was home to more than half a million people in the 1770s, and putting a loaf of bread on the table was a major concern for many of them. The government was under constant pressure to ensure the city was adequately provisioned, and its failings contributed in no small measure to the events of 1792 – the French Revolution. The rumblings of Louis's downfall were already evident on the eve of his coronation in 1775, when hordes of ill-nourished subjects looted the bakeries of Paris in what became known as the Flour War. Rioting went on for several weeks, threatening postponement of the coronation. It went ahead on 11 June as planned, with troops deployed to quell the riots; hundreds of people were arrested and two publicly executed before the government regained control.

Parmentier was closely involved with government efforts to secure and guarantee adequate food supplies for Paris throughout these troubled times, but it was not until 1785 – a decade after the Flour War – that he was able to get a royal seal of approval for the potato.

It was 23 August, the king's birthday. Accounts differ as to exactly what happened, but an engaging summary[12] declares that Louis and his wife Marie Antoinette were so enchanted when Parmentier presented them with a bouquet of potato flowers that the king pinned a spray of the blooms to his lapel and his consort put a garland in her hair. Potatoes were on the menu too, and all this was enough to inspire a degree of emulatory haste among the king's guests. Lords and ladies of the court began serving potatoes – some even had potato flowers painted on their best china and society florists were able to charge outrageous prices for potato flowers.

Now that the potato was served at court, and had achieved respectability among the aristocracy, Parmentier began promoting its virtues with the panache of a modern-day public relations consultant. He hosted dinners at which his guests ate nothing but potatoes – from soup to liqueur. Benjamin Franklin, then America's Commissioner in France, is said to have attended one of these and perhaps Thomas Jefferson did too, after taking over the Paris post from Franklin. Jefferson certainly seems to have been interested in potatoes and Parmentier. A copy of Parmentier's prize-winning essay ended up in the Jefferson library and a White House dinner which included a dish Jefferson had particularly enjoyed in Paris is said to have been the occasion at which America was introduced to french fries.

High society was one thing, but persuading impoverished Parisians that the potato could save them from starvation quite another. Indeed, the fact that aristocrats were making such a fuss about potatoes condemned them by association. By far the greatest benefit to accrue from royal approval was the King's permission for Parmentier to plant 40 acres of potatoes at Les Sablons, near Neuilly, on the western edge of Paris. This was a lot of potatoes, many tonnes – more than enough to feed the proverbial 5,000. But there was lingering prejudice to overcome; potential consumers would have to be convinced that the crop was worth having. So Parmentier arranged for soldiers to patrol the field as harvest-time approached, and chase away the curious. Predictably, people in the neighbourhood assumed that whatever merited that sort of protection had to be immensely valuable. The soldiers were instructed to withdraw at dusk and sure enough, the locals sneaked in to steal the forbidden fruit during the night.

Eating potatoes became routine. They could be bought on the streets of Paris, either raw or roasted like chestnuts,[13] and soup kitchens supplied the needy with bowls of potato soup. The King told Parmentier that 'France will thank you some day for having found bread for the poor.'[14] France did. Louis was destined to meet his country's judgement at the guillotine, but Parmentier became a hero. His potatoes, fortuitously available in quantity when everything else was in very short supply, were declared to be the food of the revolution. In an apt conjunction of the symbolic and the practical, the extensive ornamental gardens of the Tuileries Palace were dug up and planted with potatoes.

Antoine-Augustin Parmentier was among the first members of the *Légion d'Honneur* that Napoleon created in 1802 – an emperor's accolade for the man who had consorted with kings and survived a revolution. He died in 1813 at the age of seventy-six. It was once customary for potatoes to be planted each year at his grave in the Père Lachaise ceme-tery. Nowadays, though, he is remembered as a station on the Paris Métro, and by restaurateurs who feel that 'Potato Soup' looks vulgar on the menu and so call it 'Potage Parmentier' instead.

On the damp north-western fringes of Europe, where wheat grew poorly, the potato was accepted with far greater alacrity than in France, or Germany. In Ireland especially, climate and social conditions favoured potato cultivation and the crop was already popular with subsistence farmers by the late 1600s, when it crossed the Irish Sea to England. With deep soils and a moist mild climate, north Wales and north-west England were also well suited for potatoes. Lancashire in particular became a centre of production, to the extent that in 1686 a rector successfully sued thirteen of his parishioners for a tithe on the pota-toes they had grown in the previous three years – which implies that the potato had become a field crop of marketable proportions by then. In other words, a commerical crop – grown to produce an income, not simply as a subsistence food for its producers. And, indeed, by the middle of the eighteenth century potato production in north-west England was such that considerable quantities were being exported from Liverpool to Gibraltar and other ports (there are even records of twenty shiploads being dispatched each year to Dublin).[15]

This move into the sphere of commerce is significant, for it marks the stage at which people were prepared to buy potatoes and thus signals a beginning of the economic and social influence that the potato was destined to exercise in the modern history of Europe. Increasingly, people were growing or buying potatoes because they appreciated their merits and could afford them, not because they were driven to it by famine and the lack of anything else. Salaman cites an instance of this development from the Rochdale district of Lancashire. In 1773 exceptionally heavy crops had made potatoes so abundant that the price of wheat fell to levels that gave 'the poor an opportunity of buying bread'.[16] A solitary instance of the economic influence that potatoes could exercise – and a hint of far-reaching implications.

For centuries, over 90 per cent of all human activity was devoted to the production and distribution of food. Grain was the staple food that sustained those activities, and thus an indispensable factor in the maintenance of national stability. But grain supply was a highly unstable foundation. The size and quality of harvests were no more predictable than the weather. No one could be certain that grain supplies would be adequate – yet all were aware of the consequences that would ensue if there was not enough: people rioted and threatened to overthrow governments. Tiberius had warned that failure to maintain the grain supply of Rome would result in the utter ruin of the state,[17] and no governments since could disregard the warning in respect of their own domains.

But grain supply was entangled with government policy by more than issues of national stability. Grain was also a commodity – and therefore a powerful agent of economic activity. While governments struggled to ensure availability and keep prices under control, fortunes were being made (and lost) by speculators gambling on the fluctuations of supply. The markets were driven more by the profit motive than by any pious concern to get food from producer to consumer; in fact, the nation's principal food might have been intended to do more for the pockets of rich men than it did for the bellies of those in need. There were times when the price of wheat soared to levels which, in today's terms, would put the price of bread beyond the reach of most of us.[18] Then the potato arrived on the scene.

As a crop that thrived where wheat would not grow, and survived in weather that ruined grain harvests, the potato was to be welcomed by governments and commodity markets alike. Not only because it was a cheap source of food for the poor; not just as a commodity to be bought and sold; nor simply as a cushion that would dampen the severity of fluctuations in grain supply. It was all of these things, but also promised to free up more grain for the markets. If people could be persuaded to grow and eat more potatoes there would be more grain to sell. Thus the potato nudged grain away from its primary significance as a staple food of the people who grew it, towards a formative role in national and world trade. In the eighteenth century there was no organised grain trade as we know it today.[19] When Europe ran short, there were no Canadian, Latin American, South African, Russian or Australian supplies to call upon. That would come with the improvements in transportation that facilitated the expansion of empires. Meanwhile, the arrival of the potato hastened the process by which grain became not just a food, but also an economic contributor to the health of nations.

In other words, the potato was an integral part of developments that established the foundations of the modern economic and political order. It eased the transition by which commerce took over from food supply as the basis of national stability.

Adam Smith wrote favourably of the potato in *The Wealth of Nations* (1776), but the economic potential of the crop had been openly recognised and written about more than a century earlier. In 1664, for instance, John Forster, a London resident of independent means, published a tract entitled *England's Happiness Increased*,[20] which, as was the literary custom of the day, carried a much longer subtitle:

Or
a Sure and Easie Remedy Against all Succeeding Dear Years;
by
a Plantation of the Roots called POTATOES,
whereof (with the addition of wheat flour)
Excellent, Good and Wholesome Bread may be Made, Every Year,
Eight or Nine Months Together, for Half the Charge as formerly.
ALSO
By the planting of these roots, ten thousand men in England and
Wales, who know not how to live, or what to do to get a
maintenance for their families, may of one acre of ground make
thirty pounds per annum
Invented and published for the good of the poorer sort
by John Forster, Gent.

While publishing his tract 'for the good of the poorer sort', Forster dedicated it 'To the High and Mighty Monarch, Charles the II, by grace of God, King of Great Britain, France and Ireland, Defender of the

Faith, Etc.', and here an economic motive is revealed. Though apparently an honourable attempt to popularise the potato for the benefit of those most in need, the tract also describes how the introduction of potatoes could provide a healthy supplement to the King's income. In a section headed 'Benefits to the Kingdom', Forster declares that the 'First Utility' of the new crop would be to produce an income of some £40,000 or £50,000 a year for the king, 'willingly and freely, without any manner of compulsion'. This would be achieved, he explains, by strictly regulating the right to grow potatoes. The king should retain a monopoly and grant licences to only one householder in every hundred. At that rate, 10,000 licensees could provide all of England and Wales with potatoes, Forster explains, and if each paid £5 a year for the privilege of being the only person in his district empowered to grow and sell potatoes, then the royal coffers would be handsomely enriched.

Furthermore, Forster continues in a section entitled 'The Second Utility', when people have begun using potatoes as a food and constituent of their daily bread, they will consume less wheat. Consequently:

... [an] abundance of grain, of all sorts, may every plentiful year be spared to be transported beyond the sea into other countries which will be of great benefit both to His Majesty and to his subjects, for these reasons: First, His Majesty's revenue of Custom will be increased by the often coming-in of ships for corn with foreign goods and merchandise. Also a league and amity will be continued with those people to whom it is transported so that from them His Majesty (if need require) may have aid and help against foreign invasions or domestic disturbances.

There is no evidence of Charles having pursued the options that John Forster had put before him. Perhaps because he already knew about the potato and its potential from propositions put to the Royal Society (to which Charles had granted Royal Charters in 1661 and 1662). Indeed, the social and economic benefits of the potato were among the first subjects of discussion to be formally recorded by the Society.

The Royal Society was founded in 1660 expressly to investigate and report on topics of scientific interest. Its earliest members included such luminaries as Harvey, Hooke and Boyle; they met to discuss Harvey's enquiries into the circulation of the blood, Gilbert's work on magnetism, and the ideas of Copernicus, Kepler, Galileo and Francis Bacon; their discussions delved into the substance of matter, the puzzles of the universe and such esoterica, but there was a practical side to their enquiries too. A committee dedicated to the subject of agriculture and farming was established in 1662, with explicit instructions to investigate the use and cultivation of the potato.

On 18 March 1662 the Agricultural Committee met to consider the suggestions of Mr Buckland, a gentleman from Somerset who had written to the Society advocating the cultivation of potatoes as a protection against famine. Minutes of the meeting report that the committee agreed with Buckland's suggestions and proposed that 'all those members of ye Society, as have land, should be desired to begin planting of this root, and to persuade their friends to doe ye same.' Seed potatoes and instructions on cultivation were to be provided by Mr Buckland and Robert Boyle, a member of the Society with land holdings in Ireland on which potatoes were already being grown. Boyle was to report back on the outcome of these initiatives. John Evelyn, another committee member, was to include details of potato cultivation in a treatise he was publishing 'by order of ye Society', and finally: 'ye way and usefulness of planting [potatoes], should be published and recommended to ye Nation, in ye Diurnalls [daily newspapers], . . . and yt therein direction should be given to certain places, where they may be had for those, yt have a mind to plant ym.'[21]

It would be gratifying to report that the Society's advocacy of potatoes – with members planting the tubers and their merits championed in the dailies – was instrumental in establishing the crop as a prominent feature of field and table in late seventeenth-century England. That would be the most desirable outcome of the Agricultural Committee's deliberations, and a feather in the cap of the fledgling Society. But it was not to be. There appears to have been little or no follow-up: the potato is not even mentioned in a report on English crops and cultivation subsequently published by the Royal Society.[22] So, although the Society's advocacy doubtless advanced knowledge of the potato among the intelligentsia, and stands as an early academic reference to the potato's potential, the outcome was at best an authoritative contribution to the groundswell of opinion that would eventually establish the potato as an alternative staple food. If feather there is, it is woven into the fabric of the Royal Society's cap, not flamboyantly displayed.

But of course there was no single impetus, nor a general campaign that can be marshalled as evidence for the incentive and progress of the potato's remarkable takeover of European diets. Famine, war, the avaricious attention of the commodity markets, and advocacy all helped to advance its case to the point at which it was more often praised than defamed. Time passed, but pulpits from which the potato had been condemned did eventually ring with words of commendation. In the more recalcitrant regions of France, government officials sent fact sheets on the potato and its advantages to all priests, with instructions to read them from the pulpit.[23] In Norway, where the clergy customarily had farms attached to their livings, the 'potato-priests' (as they were nick-named) were particularly active. The vicar of Gausdal (100 kilometres north of Oslo), for instance, harvested more than 11 tonnes in 1775, and in the following year distributed seed potatoes to all the 120 farming householders in his parish.[24]

The potato came late to Norway, but was prevalent enough when Thomas Malthus travelled through the country in 1799 for his *Essay on the Principle of Population* to include the observation that: 'almost everywhere the cultivation of potatoes has succeeded and they are growing more and more into general use.'[25] It was of course Malthus who wrote so extensively on the relationship between the size of a population and its food supply. He observed that human populations were capable of growing at a much faster rate than their food supply and concluded that dire consequences would ensue if the two factors were not kept in balance.

Malthus's widely distributed essays on population and food supply engendered a veritable storm of discussion and controversy as to how the essential balance might be achieved and maintained. And there were good grounds for concern. From an estimated 140 million in 1750, the population of Europe had risen to 188 million by 1800 (and would go on to become 266 million in 1850 and 400 million in 1900).

Population had become an issue. Although infectious diseases continued to carry off as many as ever (indeed, mortality was even higher in the rapidly growing cities), people were marrying younger – which tended to increase the number of children that were born. There was also a 'startling rise in the rate of illegitimacy' during the middle to late eighteenth century,[26] and the combination of these factors led to many unwanted babies being abandoned or otherwise disposed of. In France the problem of abandoned babies had become so great by 1811 that Napoleon ordered the establishment of foundling hospitals, with a turntable device at the door, where babies could be left without the parents being recognised or subjected to embarrassing questions. The arrangement was imitated in many countries – and used everywhere. More than half the children thus abandoned were the offspring of married couples.

The institutions were soon overwhelmed. Very few of the babies could be cared for by the hospitals themselves; the majority were immediately sent on to nurses in the country, where many died of malnutrition, or neglect, or simply from the effects of a long arduous journey. The figures are well documented and truly shocking. In some of the Italian foundling hospitals, up to 80 and 90 per cent of babies died before they were one year old. In Paris, the figures indicate that foundlings comprised fully 36 per cent of *all* births in the years 1817–20; of 4,779 babies admitted to the city's Maison de la Couche in 1818 alone, 2,370 died within three months. In France overall, between 20 and 30 per cent of all children born during those three years were abandoned to their fate in the foundling hospitals.[27]

We hardly hear of the foundling hospitals now, but they were well-known at the time. Many denounced the system as legalised infanticide; one suggested that foundling hospitals should put up a sign: 'Children killed at Government expense'. Thomas Malthus visited hospitals in Moscow and St Petersburg endowed by the Russian imperial family and afterwards wrote:

> Considering the extraordinary mortality which occurs in these institutions . . . it may perhaps be truly said that, if a person wished to check population, and were not solicitous about the means, he could not propose a more effective measure than the establishment of a sufficient number of foundling hospitals, unlimited as to their reception of children.

Given the scale of the problems that rapidly growing populations imposed upon society, it is hardly surprising that the consequences attracted more attention than the cause. How did it come about? Many were content to blame the vice and lascivious behaviour said to be rife among lower classes in the cities – not realising that cities were then far from self-sustaining in terms of births; in fact, their prodigious growth was fuelled by the influx of people from the countryside. It was there, beside the fields where potatoes grew, that couples were marrying earlier, and producing more children. That was where four sons could divide the land their father had farmed and each grow enough potatoes to support a family; creating four families where a generation earlier there was but one; twelve children where there had been four. Malthus stated it plainly enough: 'more food brings more mouths'; and he blamed the introduction of the potato for the seemingly intractable problem of Europe's expanding population. Potatoes tended to depress wages and living standards, he wrote, by making possible an increase in the population far beyond the opportunities of employment.[28] But Malthus was unaware of the huge demands for cheap labour that the Industrial Revolution would exert.

While it was undeniable that the great upswing in European populations coincided with the introduction of the potato, it was always going to be difficult to prove cause and effect to the satisfaction of scholars. In the nineteenth century there were agronomists willing to assert that potatoes 'had undoubtedly produced immense effects upon Europe, in the moulding and culture of which it has probably operated more powerfully than any other material object', and there were economists who declared without qualification that 'the adoption of the potato had resulted in a rapid growth of population,'[29] but demographers and social scientists were more cautious. For one thing, they needed to be sure that it really was a rise in birth rates that was responsible for the upswing, not a fall in death rates resulting from improved nutrition and better standards of health. Furthermore, the clearing and drainage of additional land, and agricultural improvements, could also have played a crucial role.

So it was not until the mid twentieth century, as quantitative science became an integral part of anthropological research, that statistical data could be attached to the bold statements of earlier generations. And then, from locations such as the Swiss Alps,[30] the Himalayas,[31] Norway,[32] Russia and China, there came studies which in their specific detail validated the general contention: wherever the potato had been adopted, populations had increased. There was a direct correlation. Even a small village in central Spain[33] experienced a late eighteenth-century upsurge in population and prosperity when farmers channelled water from a stream and began growing potatoes in fields which had been good only for olives and almonds until then. Furthermore, the studies showed that people were not only more numerous in potato-producing regions – they were also healthier, and grew taller.[34] 'It can therefore be emphatically stated,' declared the historian Chris Vandenbroeke, 'that the diffusion of potato-growing meant that, for the first time in the history of Western Europe, a definitive solution had been found to the food problem.'[35]

But it was in Ireland that the influence of the potato was most dramatically seen – and felt. There were probably no more than 1–1.5 million people living in Ireland before the potato arrived in the early 1600s. By 1700 the population had risen to 2 million; a century later it reached 5 million and by 1845 had soared to 8.5 million[36] – of whom more than 90 per cent were utterly dependent on the potato. Without it they would starve, and when a terrible disease struck their crops in 1845 and 1846 – spreading from field to field like a plague, blackening leaf and stem and rotting the potatoes in the ground – many thousands died. Hundreds of thousands more survived only by emigrating to England and America.

Chapter Nine

◡‿◡

Where the praties grow

Cecil Woodham-Smith's book on the Irish potato famine, *The Great Hunger*, was published in 1962 but I did not read it until late in 1964, some time after we had settled in for what was to become an eighteen-month stay in Connemara, on the west coast of Ireland. We rented a house in Ballynew, a village just inland from Cleggan Bay. 'Ballynew' comes from the Irish 'an baile nua', meaning 'new town', but this was never a town, nor even a village in the sense that the term is customarily used. There was no cluster of houses with a shop, a church, a pub and roads radiating to a surrounding district of farming lands. No, Ballynew was a collection of houses scattered at some distance from each other along the gentle slope of a long south-facing hillside. In fact, the village was essentially a sparsely inhabited hogbacked hill of meadow, tillage and bog that rose up from the road and over to the cliffs of Ooeywalter and Ooeyandinnawarriv, where the Atlantic tides flowed into the wide inlet known as Ballynakill harbour. Five hundred acres or thereabouts, separated from neighbouring villages by boundaries – 'mearings' is the old word – that followed streams and natural drainage channels. There were five such villages within a radius of two miles.

The lands of Ballynew were occupied by just twelve households when we were there and farming consisted principally of raising young beef cattle from the two or three cows they kept for milk, looking after the sheep that grazed common land over on the north side of the hill, growing oats, making hay, cutting peat (though they always called it turf) for the house and cooking fire, and putting in a field of praties – the colloquial term for potatoes in rural Ireland – lots of praties that were stored through the winter in long earth-covered and straw-thatched clamps, and would all be eaten by next summer.

They would sell milk, wool, sheep and a heifer or bullock as the occasion arose. In the winter they would sell labour – working on the roads for a pound a day, or putting up fences for the big house at Cartron. John Coyne had learned construction skills during his time in Portland, Oregon, and would cycle over to Recess (a 20-mile round-trip), where a hotel and service station site was being developed. Joseph Heanue, down at the shore in neighbouring Bundouglas, had bought a car that brought in a few pounds by way of the chauffeuring service he offered (his was the only car in the immediate district – apart from ours and that of John James, the rate collector). Cornelius got a grant for adding a water supply (from a spring up the hill on Patrick Coyne's land), bathroom and septic tank to the property that had become his with the passing of an aged relative, and so earned a bit from us ('will twenty-five shillings the week be too much for ye?'). But all in all, there was not a lot of money in Ballynew – nor people.

The twelve households of Ballynew made up a total of perhaps fifty men, women and children. Most were headed by a son (or daughter and son-in-law) who had returned or stayed to look after ageing parents while other siblings had moved away or gone abroad. Children were few, and it was expected that they too would leave to seek their fortunes elsewhere as soon as they were old enough. So it was that, even in the 1960s, Ballynew was contributing to the unbroken fall in numbers that had marked the population statistics of Ireland for more than a century. The 1841 census had put the figure for all of Ireland at 8,175,124; in 1961 it stood at 4,243,383 (including 1,425,042 in Northern Ireland, which after partition had become part of the United Kingdom). But the greater part of that decline had occurred in the first ten years, and – as the census returns from Ballynew woefully illustrate – it was most evident in the southern counties that later became the Republic of Ireland. Ballynew's 493 acres of farmland had supported 298 people – 152 males and 146 females – in 1841. Ten years later, little more than one-third of that total was there to be counted: 113 in all, 53 males and 60 females.

The great famine began in 1845 and its effects were still being felt in 1849. Connemara was struck especially hard, but Ballynew was by no means the worst affected. The number of people living at Bundouglas, for instance, fell from 194 to 20 between the two crucial censuses; at Lettergesh from 219 to 64; at Lettershanbally from 61 to 4 . . . and so on, throughout the county, throughout the country.

The events of the 1840s, when the failure of the potato crop brought unprecedented death from starvation and malnutrition to Ireland, are movingly described in *The Great Hunger*. Reading the book after a few months of living in Connemara left me feeling very glad I had not read it before we got there. If I had, I'm not sure I would have had the nerve to impose myself upon a community which had suffered so much at the hands of the English. The book is a fierce indictment of the British government's failure to see the crisis coming, or to take swift and appropriate action once it had arrived.

The *Sunday Times* praised Cecil Woodham-Smith for having 'the courage to recount the horrifying facts'. Her account of the famine is meticulously researched and presented with such skill that her view of events seems to be incontrovertible truth, and the whole truth at that. In short, *The Great Hunger* is utterly convincing. There were occasions when I emerged from its pages to join Patrick Coyne as he checked on his sheep on the north side, or to meet Big Mike for a game of darts, wondering how they could bear to put up with yet more English interlopers. Yet Patrick was not overly concerned, and I soon learned that Big Mike was inclined to use any enquiry into the past as an opportunity to recount his adventures during the Troubles, when he found himself as gaoler of his neighbour, Tom Heanue, who was on the side of the Black and Tans. Cornelius dismissed the issue with a shake of the head. Past, he'd say, all in the past. Who's to be worrying at it now?

I never did hear anyone speak of the Famine as an event which they thought had shaped their lives. Perhaps I did not enquire as deeply as I would have done now, and it is quite possible that they simply avoided talking about it. Silence on a subject does not imply a lack of feeling for it. Cornelius's mother – Granny Mullen, as our children called her, and as I remember her – would speak about the hard times she had experienced in her lifetime. God love ye, she would say when I brought her a bag of winkles, and go on to speak of years when there was hardly a winkle or a mussel to be found on the shore, even on the lowest tides, simply because people collected them so assiduously. Her grandparents would have been children during the years of the Famine. They survived while thousands of other children died – but I never heard stories of those times.

It has been said that oral history is hardly more reliable than myth when it is speaking of events that occurred three or more generations ago. Cornelius would speculate at length about the stoneworks he and others had found in the bog while cutting turf on the north side: who in the world could have built that? He puzzled over the boulder of gleaming white quartz which stood on his land down by the Ballynakill lake: where had that come from, what was its purpose and who put it there? He led me along the barely discernible laid-stone track they called the Danes' road and he spoke of 'fairy darts' the old people used to find, and the lights they would see wandering across the Sheeauns at night (Sheeaun comes from the Irish 'Sidheá', meaning fairy hill) in the old days. But the story of the Mullens, just a century before? Not a word. A lengthy account of the family's movements in the early twentieth century and of their settling in Ballynew – 'now isn't that a grand house they built us here?' Stories of relatives in America – 'sure, weren't they cutting down the millionaires as had lost all and hung themselves with the Crash of '29,' and then back to gossip on the behaviour of the neighbours, and who it was that would have the hay in first.

I have to blame myself for some of the silence, for after reading Woodham-Smith I was not especially keen to raise the subject of the Famine either, but there is more to it than that. People with more dispassionate motives than I have noted that Ireland's reluctance to delve into the detail of the Famine extends beyond fireside accounts of family history. Irish historians have also tended to shy away from the subject. The journal *Irish Historical Studies*, for instance, carried only six contributions on famine-related topics during its first fifty years of publication; the *Irish Economic and Social History* carried not a single piece on the Famine from its launch in 1974 to 1993, and while the much-vaunted *Milestones in Irish History* included essays on such textbook topics as the battle of Clontarf, the Flights of the Earls and the act of Union, it contained not a word on the Famine.[1]

Yet the Irish Famine was surely the main event in modern Irish history, as important to Ireland as the French Revolution was to France, the Industrial Revolution to England, and the Civil War to America. It is probably the most widely known famine in world history, but until *The Great Hunger* was published in 1962 there had not been a whole-hearted attempt to tell the story comprehensively (a 1956 collection of essays[2] is dismissed as a 'rather bloodless, sanitized affair'[3]). The book's popular approach irritated a section of Ireland's historical establishment so much that in 1963 third-year history honours students at

University College, Dublin, were invited to write an essay on '*The Great Hunger* is a great novel'; but none argued with its author's contention that, prior to the famine, '[T]he conditions of life in Ireland and the existence of the Irish people depended on the potato entirely and exclusively.'[4]

> Oh! There's not in the wide world a race that can beat us,
> From Canada's cold hills to sultry Japan,
> While we fatten and feast on the smiling potatoes
> Of Erin's green valleys so friendly to man.[5]

Along the coast of Connemara, where waves born in the open Atlantic are brought to an abrupt halt by rocky shores and cliffs, people say the potato came to Ireland 400 years ago 'like God's gift from heaven', off ships of the Spanish Armada that Francis Drake had chivvied up the North Sea and around the Orkneys, where they were caught in an Atlantic gale and driven onto the Connemara shore. Twenty-five to thirty galleons were wrecked they say, spilling cargoes that included many barrels full of potatoes.

Some fine Arabian horses and 200 sailors also managed to save themselves. The horses galloped off into the hills, where they met the local wild ponies and founded the world-famous breed of Connemara ponies – so the story goes. The fate of the sailors is more than a story. It's a tragedy. They were taken in and cared for by the local people, to whom they taught the practice of cooking and growing potatoes. Then word arrived that the villagers should hand every Spanish sailor over to the English authorities – on pain of death. From among the captives a nobleman and his nephew were ransomed and spared; the remainder were beheaded at St Augustine's monastery in Galway in late June 1589, 'amidst the murmurs and lamentations of the people'.

The Connemara version of the potato's arrival in Ireland in 1589 is not universally accepted, however; not even in Ireland. Further south, around Cork, they say Sir Walter Raleigh was responsible. His gardener allegedly planted tubers from Virginia on the Youghal estate lands Elizabeth I had granted Raleigh in return for putting down some troublesome Irish rebellions. The introduction would have occurred sometime between 1586, when Raleigh was given the estate, and 1603, when he fell from favour and was sent to the Tower, where he remained for fourteen years.

The brave Walter Raleigh, Queen
Bess's own knight
Brought here from Virginia
The root of delight.
By him it was planted
At Youghal so gay;
An' sure Munster praties
Are famed to this day[6]

Whatever the date and circumstances of its arrival, Ireland was uniquely well-suited to the cultivation and adoption of the potato as a subsistence crop. There was soft and plentiful rain, little or no frost, and enough land for a man to sow and harvest a crop of potatoes that would feed his family for a year. Moreover, Ireland had a desperately poor rural population that a troubled history had pushed close to starvation at the best of times. For them, the potato was salvation. They took to it out of desperation at first, then quickly came to appreciate its beneficial qualities. Thus the Irish were the first in northern Europe to take advantage of the potato's exceptional productivity and nutritional benefits as an alternative to (and substitute for) the cereals which hitherto had been the staple foods that people would have preferred to eat – if given the choice. Wherever people had a choice, no matter how slight, acceptance of the potato as a staple food was delayed until changing social and economic circumstances had whittled away the options. But the Irish had no choice at all, and so there was a fatal inevitability to the unfolding history of Ireland and the potato.

'You want to know about the history of England, Ireland and the potato? Then start by thinking of Ireland as England's back door, and the English as worrying that it might have been left open.'

I could not swear that Tom O'Malley actually said that, in so many words; but it is certainly the sort of thing he would have said, as he stood back to pull another pint at the Pier Bar down in Cleggan. And as with many of the generalisations that landlords are prone to make, there was truth in what Tom had said. The English had always had an avaricious eye on that land across the Irish sea – with its green hills and gentle climate, but had never managed to capture and rule it for themselves. They tried, but could never win it over – neither by negotiation, nor by arms – though their attempts caused a good deal of pain and resentment. Then the Reformation added the fuel of religious conviction to the smouldering fires of enmity. Ireland was devoutly Catholic, a natural ally of Rome, France and Spain – the European powers with whom England was never entirely at peace either, and always suspicious of their motives. With faith in common, the risk that Ireland would form an alliance with England's continental rivals was too much to countenance. Only by occupying Ireland could the English ensure they were not invaded via the back door.

That was the way they thought of it down in Tom O'Malley's Pier Bar. The brutality of the English was fierce and cruel, they would say, but served only to strengthen and consolidate the determined resistance of the Irish. Resistance that repeatedly flared into rebellion. In 1580 the Earl of Desmond appealed to Philip of Spain for help after every town, castle, village, farmhouse had been destroyed by English forces, his lands ruined and himself left a homeless wanderer. An expedition of joint Spanish and Papal forces was dispatched – and defeated shortly after landing on Irish soil at Smerwick, on the tip of the Dingle Peninsula. The English had not the forces to convey their captives in safety across Ireland to Dublin, it is said, so they were slaughtered, stripped naked and laid out on the sands. All 600 of them. 'As gallant and goodly personages as ever were beheld,' the English commander, Lord Grey, reported to Queen Elizabeth. The Queen replied with the rare compliment of a sentence written in her own gracious hand:[7]

> The mighty hand of the Almightiest power hath showed manifestly the force of his strength . . . , to make men ashamed ever hereafter to disdain us; in which action I joy that you have been chosen the instrument of his glory.

Philip's invasion had been planned not just as aid for the Irish, but principally as the Pope's first move towards recovering lost dominions. Victory would have given Catholic forces access to England via the back door. Defeat brought yet more terrible oppression. Munster was reduced to ruin, the herds swept away, the fields left untilled, and 'famine came to devour what the sword had left.' An officer reported: 'There hath died by famine only, not so few as thirty thousand in this province in less than half a year, besides others that are hanged and killed.'[8]

Edmund Spenser, who wrote most of his *Faerie Queen* during the eighteen years he lived in Ireland, saw some of this:

Out of every quarter of the woods and glynnes, they came creeping forth upon their hands, for their leggs could not beare them; they looked like anatomies of death; they spake like ghosts crying out of their graves; they did eate the dead carrions, happy where they could find them; yea, and one another soone after . . . and if they found a plot of water-cresses or shamrocks there they flocked as to a feast for a time, yet, not able long to continue therewithall; that in a short space there were none left, and a most populous and plentiful country suddenly left voyde of man and beast. Yet sure, in all that warre, there perished not many by the sword, but all by the extremities of famine, which they themselves had wrought.[9]

Meanwhile, Connaught came under the orders of a Captain Brabazon, who ensured that 'Neither the sanctuary of the saint nor of the poet; neither the wood nor the forest valley, the town nor the bawn, was a shelter from this captain and his people till the whole territory was destroyed by him.'[10] But the far west of Connaught – Iar-Connacht or Connemara – resisted to the end. Tom O'Malley knew that. He had a nineteenth-century edition of a book written by Roderic O'Flaherty in 1684. Called *A Chorographical Description of West or H-Iar Connaught*, it was a point of reference for miles around, for anyone with a question about the early history of Cleggan, Ballynew and thereabouts. And if Tom O'Malley's book did not have the answer, opinions around the bar could serve just as well.

The O'Flahertys controlled most of Connemara, along with the Joyces and O'Hallorans (all names still common locally), and were quick to take up arms again in 1641, when England's struggle between the Crown and Parliament gave the Irish an opportunity to rebel against their despised Protestant overlords. The rebellion flared on for eleven years; half a million Irish (one-third of Ireland's population) are said to have died by the sword, plague or famine, or were banished before Cromwell felt victorious enough to impose his infamous Act of Settlement in 1652. Among its stipulations, 100,000 rebels were declared liable for execution; all rebel properties were confiscated and the power to establish settler 'plantations' in Ireland assumed. In Cromwell's own words, any who refused to accept English rule must be sent either 'to hell or to Connaught'. In Connaught itself, the inhabitants of places such as Connemara, which were known to harbour 'the enemy, and other bloody and mischievous persons', must formally submit or expect to be 'taken, slayned and destroyed as enemies and their cattle and other goods shall be taken.'[11]

All of Connemara was confiscated. The O'Flaherty lands were parcelled out and subsequently distributed among a dozen or so members of the English gentry. Edmond O'Flaherty, who had led the clan in battle, was hunted down to a small dark wood near Renvyle, where the croaking of ravens led soldiers to the shallow cave in which he and some companions were hiding. They hardly recognised the miserable and emaciated man they took captive.

And truly who had seen them would have said they had been rather ghosts than men, for pitifully looked they, pyned away from want of foode and altogether ghastly with fear.[12]

Edmond O'Flaherty was executed in Galway, but the name lived on – not least as author of the book that Tom O'Malley was so proud to own.

The Battle of the Boyne (1690) and the Treaty of Limerick (1691) finally gave the English a semblance of political and economic control over Ireland. The Protestant settlers held most of the valuable land and all of the country's social, economic and political privileges. The Catholic Irish had practically no civil rights at all, and the intensity of their discontent can be judged by the fact that the English felt they must oppress the oppressed still further. A series of draconian Penal Laws were enacted in the early 1700s, under which Irish Roman Catholics could never vote or take a seat in Parliament; nor could they ever become members of a municipal corporation, aspire to become a barrister or a judge, or act as sherriff, or hold any office under the Crown. They could not serve in the Army or the Navy. No Catholic could buy or inherit land – or even receive it as a gift from a Protestant. No lease could be held by a Catholic for more than thirty-one years. Catholics could not enter the university or teach in a school. They could not own a horse worth more than five pounds, nor have more than two apprentices (except in the linen trade). They could not marry a Protestant. Most significantly, the Penal Laws banished primogeniture among Catholics. In future, an eldest son could inherit an entire estate only if he became a Protestant; otherwise the estate must be divided among all the children[13] – thus ensuring that the viability of surviving Catholic estates would be progressively reduced.

But prohibition could not weaken the faith of committed Irish

Catholics. Despite the laws, people flocked to the ruins, barns, bogs and other out-of-the-way places where devoted priests said Mass at the risk of their own lives. Persecution only intensified the people's loyalties; national sentiments became inseparable from the religion which had been theirs for centuries. And so religion was the bulwark of a 'Hidden Ireland' in which the old customs and traditions of music and song, and the old stories, were preserved. Popular superstition, belief in fairies, veneration of holy wells, the waking of the dead and the keening at funerals persisted – despite the oppression and dire poverty under which Irish Catholics were forced to live.

Religion yes, but no rights, no education – and a set of prohibitions designed to ensure that less and less of what was of value in Ireland would belong to the Irish. It would take time for the Penal Laws to work their way through every sector of Irish Catholic society, but they threatened everyone – even those who had survived so far with their property and values intact. There are no estimates of how many took the easy route, and converted to Protestantism, but the increasing number of Irish Catholics who found themselves sliding down the social scale towards abject poverty is well documented. And in a country where agriculture continued to be the mainstay of the economy, it was in the rural areas, rather than the cities, that poverty was most evident. In 1725 less than 10 per cent of the population lived in the eight largest towns;[14] the other 90 per cent lived and made their living on the land.

Land was the central issue. Not only to feed the people living on it, but also to produce an income for the English gentry who now owned the millions of acres that had been confiscated. The pattern of landownership established in the early eighteenth century was to remain intact for nearly 200 years: an untidy patchwork of over 2,000 large estates covering most of Ireland's land surface. The majority were between 2,000 and 4,000 acres in extent, though several dozen great estates each covered more than 50,000 acres.[15]

The confiscated properties included most of Ireland's best agricultural land; the vast majority were economically viable, and at a time when trade was becoming an increasingly important determinant of prosperity – both personal and national, one might have expected landlords to make the most of their new acquisitions. Some did, instigating programmes of investment and development that contributed significantly to an upsurge in Ireland's agricultural exports during the eighteenth century. But they were rare exceptions. Most landlords were content to leave their properties in the hands of farming tenants, and take their income in the form of rents, paid twice-yearly. And many of these lived in England – the 'absentee landlords' with estates to run (and fortunes to spend) at home and no desire whatsoever to live in a backward country, among Catholics with a deep and avowed hatred of the English.

Absence bred indifference and ignorance (Jonathan Swift declared that the English knew less of Ireland than of Mexico), and a grasping class of middlemen, whose prosperity increased whenever they could widen the gap between how much the landlord was expecting and what the sub-tenants could be persuaded to pay. They were not all bad – most were Irish and Catholic themselves – but the reputation of all is tainted by a profusion of negative reports. Middlemen were 'the worst description of oppressors that the curse of Cromwell has produced in Ireland – the most cruel that has ever been afflicted on any people', wrote a contemporary observer. They were 'bloodsuckers of the poor tenantry', wrote another, 'the most oppressive species of tyrant that ever lent assistance to the destruction of a country . . . Not satisfied with screwing up the rent to the uttermost farthing, they are rapacious and relentless in the collection of it.'[16]

Middlemen liked to take on an estate for as long a lease as possible – up to thirty-one years in some cases – and sub-let it for short periods. Short leases meant that rents could be raised more frequently than would otherwise be the case – with lucrative consequences. Middlemen frequently took from their sub-tenants three times more than was due to the landlord. Furthermore, there was little or no capital or maintenance expenditure towards which a portion of the rental income would have to be set aside. In England a landlord was legally obliged to put up buildings and whatever was needed to make a farm operational; even a labourer had the right to expect some land and a cottage in return for working on the farm, but nothing like that was required in Ireland. So, if existing conditions were inadequate, a new tenant or cottier – as they were known – must either put up with them and resign himself and his family to circumstances which could only get worse, or face the certainty of being denied compensation or even credit for any improvements he made during his tenancy. No wonder that 'a farm is always left by the retreating tenant in the most impoverished state; the drains are choked; the ditches and fences destroyed, the land exhausted and overrun with weeds; the house and offices fallen, or greatly out of repair.'

If the middleman chose (and the bad sort usually did) to put the lease up for auction as it approached expiry, the current lessee was not entitled to any preference. The land would go to the highest bidder. Often, therefore, 'the old occupier, unwilling to remove, and having no place for himself and his family, through fear of losing a residence, has been bidding against himself, until he has raised the rent far beyond the value.'[17] And probably far beyond what he could afford too, with only Providence to call upon when the rent became due. But he would have been put on oath, or signed a promissory note, and so left entirely without recourse when the middleman sent the bailiff to take his cattle away, or turn the family out of whatever they had called home. There was no poor law requiring the parish and gentry to assist the destitute, such as England had introduced in the sixteenth century. The next step for a man in arrears was more debt. A smaller piece of land; a shorter lease; a commitment to work off the debt, or pay it in kind ... whatever, it was another step down the slope towards absolute poverty.

Meanwhile, though, Ireland as seen from England's Treasury and counting houses was booming. A thirty-year period of economic expansion followed the Cromwellian reconquest, largely attributable to the widening demand for Irish beef, butter and ships' biscuit that English involvement in the slave and sugar trades had generated; and access to the French market, which became the single most important source of demand for Irish butter and hides.[18] However, the demand for animal products on an international scale fed back into the Irish rural economy as a rush to convert arable land to pasture, a development which hit the small, medium and even some large but under-resourced farmers particularly hard – with consequences which would radically alter the very face of the Irish landscape.

As graziers, master-dairymen and speculators jostled for a foothold in the booming cattle trade, thousands of cottagers and entire villages were displaced. The grain that people had fed upon was replaced by grass that fed only livestock. Laments heard during the English enclosures were heard in Ireland now: 'It is but putting ourselves a degree or two above the savage Indians ... if we have only tame beasts to roam about our lands, instead of wild ones, for 'tis demonstrable that the first devour more people than the latter.'[19] But while the complaints were similar, the response was very different. The 'uprooted often seem to have gone literally up the hill', so that susceptible regions contained sharply contrasting neighbourhoods: clusters of large grazing farms, with modest numbers of permanent labourers living on the boundaries, adjacent to uplands which now carried an expanding population of smallholders scratching a living from the inferior soils. This inverse correlation – with people living most densely where the soils were poorest – was the defining characteristic of events to come: a quirk in the Irish landscape created by market forces, not landlord policy alone.[20]

The sufferings of the cottiers, the grasping landlords and middlemen, the neglect and breakdown of mutual obligations which had bound communities for centuries, the ascending importance given to money and trade – none of these developments was unique to Ireland. Time, place and intensity varied, but they had been experienced by every country in Europe as the essentially subsistence- and locally based agricultural economies of the Middle Ages were transformed into the unforgiving market-driven economies of the modern era. Everywhere, the age-old customary rights to sustenance or the means of growing it were contested, set aside or brazenly ignored, as the supply-and-demand prerogatives of the marketplace took over. There was no room for compassion; no time for pondering the options. What mattered now was money. I'll give you what you need, provided I can profit by supplying it.

The rough edges of the new ethos were smoothed down by the millions whose lives were spent as fuel for the Industrial Revolution. A new and better world emerged – surprisingly quickly in some places, but delayed in Ireland by a unique set of circumstances: the arrival of the potato; a landscape and climate ideally suited to its cultivation, and a rural population whose slide towards destitution was slowed by their adoption of the new crop.

There is no certainty as to when the potato became a dominant feature of the Irish diet. Salaman believed it was well-established by 1630, but his evidence for this has been questioned,[21] and indeed it seems more likely that although the potato was certainly being cultivated in Ireland during the early 1600s, it was only during the latter part of the century that it became a dominant part of the diet. Until then, traditional diets prevailed. In an engaging article on Irish food before the potato, the social historian Anthony Lucas finds a striking continuity of dietary tradition in documents dating from the ninth century through to the seventeenth. Diets throughout were shaped by the pastoral nature of the Irish rural economy. You have only to consider the green valleys and round-shouldered hills to know that Ireland is naturally suited to the rearing of livestock (even in modern times, permanent pasture accounts for more than 70 per cent of Irish farmland). Of Connemara, Roderic O'Flaherty reported an abundance of cattle:'the chiefest product therefore and greatest commodity is beefe, butter, tallow, hides, and of late cheese'.[22] Indeed, livestock products were mentioned so frequently in contemporary documents, and customs reflecting a pastoral and semi-nomadic society were so widespread – such as common possession of land, joint tenures and the prestige attached to owning livestock – that some historians have suggested the inhabitants of late medieval Ireland had more in common with the nomadic pastoralists of East Africa than with the farmers of western Europe.[23]

And like the Maasai and other African pastoralists, the Irish valued their livestock more for its milk than its meat. Meat was eaten infrequently (and more often pork than beef), but milk was drunk by the gallon, and gallons more consumed in sundry other fashions.'The people generally being the greatest lovers of milk I ever saw,' an observer reported in 1673, 'which they eat and drink about twenty sorts of ways and what is strangest, love it best when sourest'[24] (which is also true of the East African pastoralists today). The favourite appears to have been bonnyclabber, a phonetic rendering of the Irish *bainne clabair*, meaning thick milk. The critically inclined wrote dismissively of bonny-clabber as milk left to stand until 'the cream comes off, by taking hold of it between the fingers, like a skin of leather'; the more appreciative described it in a variety of terms: 'the bravest, freshest drink you ever tasted', a delectable drink 'of very thick milk, . . . of yellow bubbling milk, the swallowing of which needs chewing'.[25]

Milk was also used to make a stirabout – 'fair white porridge . . . the treasure that is smoothest and sweetest of all food.' Medieval sources declare that the sons of kings ate stirabout made of wheaten meal and sweetened with honey; the sons of chieftains had theirs made of barley meal and butter; while for the sons of inferior grades it consisted of plain oatmeal and stale butter. Cheese was popular too – some of it so hard that a piece allegedly served instead of a stone as the sling-shot which killed Queen Maeve, the mythical Celtic Queen of Connaught.[26]

And butter. In summer, the cows on Ireland's meadows produce milk so rich that the cream floats a hand's depth thick in the churn. In Connaught, a traveller at the end of the sixteenth century noted that 'the tranquilitie and peace . . . hath been so long and so good, that they are grown very rich in Cattaill and especially in kine [cows], which brings a most wonderfull mass of Butter.' They wrapped the butter in tree bark, 'which butter they hide in bogs, or Riuers, or in fresh water pooles'.[27] Stored thus and reputed to last indefinitely, this green butter, as it was known, achieved notoriety among early English visitors: 'too loathsome to describe', wrote one.[28] Salaman tasted some from a keg which had been buried perhaps a century before and, with eloquent understatement, reported that the butter was 'if edible, without attraction'.[29]

Grain, as in Europe generally, was the energy food of pre-potato Ireland: oats the most widely grown; wheat the most valued; rye not so common; and barley used principally for beer. Oaten bread was the most commonly eaten; wheaten bread a delicacy that the lower sections of society could never afford. The cottiers grew and harvested plenty of wheat, though, for it was always a valuable commodity. Even as arable land was converted to pasture, there were still landlords who stayed with the crop, and tenants whose only hope of being able to pay the rent was to sow a field of wheat as well as the oats they would eat themselves.

And so, as economic pressures intensified, more and more of the cottiers' grain and butter went to market rather than into their stomachs. The markets stole the sustenance base of rural Ireland – consuming what the people themselves should have been eating. Cereals by the shipload. Butter was being exported at a rate of more than 5,000 tons a year by the end of the seventeenth century.[30] And an average of 60,000 cattle were being shipped across the Irish Sea each year by 1665, along with close to 100,000 sheep. In fact, the volume of livestock exports from Ireland was so great that English graziers complained and the trade was prohibited. Smugglers at once stepped in and took over as much of the trade as they could handle, while Irish farmers turned their attention to raising sheep for wool rather than live export; before long their wool was good enough to compete with the best that England produced.[31]

This was a state of affairs that should have collapsed under the weight of its iniquities, but instead was given a new lease of life by the potato. Ironically, social and economic circumstance forced the cottiers on to a diet that was better for them, and this simple fact kept the system going far longer than it deserved. No one could have known that a bowl of boiled potatoes, mashed up with butter or milk, was healthier and far more nutritious than even the wheaten bread that people so hungered for. Furthermore, potatoes were easier to grow, less susceptible to the vagaries of the Irish climate, and up to four times more productive than grain crops. Ergo, more people could eat better from the same piece of land; their labours produced more calories and – most important of all – they had something to eat even in years when the grain harvests failed. And there was yet another advantage: potatoes could be boiled and eaten straight from the ground, whereas the miller would have to be paid, in cash or kind, for converting cereals into meal or flour.

Nonetheless, the potato remained a supplementary food and a standby against famine for the first hundred years or so after its introduction to Ireland; only by the late 1600s was a majority of cottiers beginning to depend upon the potato as a food to see them through the winter. By then the advantages of its greater productivity per acre, compared with grain crops, were abundantly clear to anyone with limited resources of land or money. Within fifty years it became the staple diet of cottiers and small farmers over the greater part of the year. A spectacular expansion of potato cultivation occurred during that half-century as the potato broke through the constraints of the garden fence and spilled across millions of acres, down the length and breadth of Ireland.

Government legislation enacted in 1742 specifically 'to encourage the reclaiming of unprofitable bogs' by allowing Roman Catholics (till then barred from occupying vacant land) to claim 50 acres of bog, together with half an acre of adjoining arable, was a significant factor in the expansion of potato cultivation. Potatoes were an ideal first crop for cottiers taking advantage of the new law, promising far better results than any cereal they might have sown. Later, as market developments brought the advance of pasture to a halt – and even reversed it – the potato was given yet more room for expansion; not least because many farmers who wanted to grow corn where cattle had grazed were short of capital, and could not afford to pay their labourers in hard cash. So instead of wages, they gave them a scrap of land on which to grow potatoes. The broad consequence of all this was that potato culture and the subdivision of land jointly became cause and effect of an increase in population: the faster the pace of population growth, the more insistent was the trend towards a diet almost exclusively of potatoes.

Plant breeders were another group of entrepreneurs contributing to the phenomenal expansion of potato cultivation. Driven perhaps more by the botanical challenge than any pecuniary incentive, their crossing and experimentation with the seed of the potato berry soon brought new varieties to the fields. An agriculturalist writing in 1730 described five, of which three were especially popular. There was a white that could be planted in January and harvested at the end of June; a yellow-fleshed variety whose tubers would keep from harvest until the next summer; and the Black – the first really outstanding variety:

> It is the Black potato (not that the pulp is black, but that the skin is very dark), that is most valued by those who know it: the pulp affords a stronger invigorating diet to the labourer: it keeps till potatoes come again . . . Since the people of this country found the peculiar goodness of this potato they will scarce cultivate any other. They will grow so large, as that some of them have measured four inches in diameter.[32]

More nourishing, more appetising and with better keeping qualities – now the potato was fit to move a few notches up the social scale, becoming an acceptable item for the dining-tables of gentry, and finding warm approval in professional circles. One reverent admirer composed a veritable hymn of praise: 'the most fruitful root we have; its fructifying quality is visible in every cabin you pass by. They produce good soldiers, good seamen, good citizens and good husbandmen.' He went on to commend its use as an encouragement to fecundity: 'Doctor Lloyd, whose eminence as a physician was very great, frequently recommended potatoes as a supper to those ladies whom providence had not blessed with children, and an heir has often been the consequence.'[33]

The population of Ireland more than doubled between 1687 and 1791, rising from 2.16 million to 4.75 million. During the fifty years from 1791 to 1841 another 3.4 million were added, taking the population to 8.15 million. Another 1.75 million emigrated to North America, Scotland, England and even Australia during the same period, which brings the total born in Ireland to nearly 10 million – almost a five-fold increase in 154 years (1687 to 1841). 'Probably in no other western country has so rapid a rate of natural increase been so long sustained,' writes the historian Kenneth H. Connell.[34]

The population growth was highest where people were poorest;[35] fertility was much higher in the countryside than in the towns, and highest of all in Connemara and Connaught generally.[36] English commentators of the day were quick to blame lax morals and depraved behaviour for the burgeoning numbers, but it was never so simple. Indeed, there is good reason to believe that the cottiers of Connemara were more genuinely moral than inhabitants of the commentators' urban neighbourhoods.

Contemporary accounts abound with stories of cottiers living in appalling conditions, surrounded by dozens of scruffy snot-nosed children, but neglect to mention that 90 per cent of the Irish population contracted marriages throughout the eighteenth century.[37] Illegitimacy was rare. This was a Catholic country, in which people stripped of civil rights and opportunities had embraced religion as the bulwark of a 'Hidden Ireland' that preserved their morality and faith in themselves. Chastity was valued.

'The moral character of the Irish women is very extraordinary,' a parliamentary Select Committee was told. 'The women appear to be more virtuous, and conjugal fidelity to be more constant than in England.' And even those who resorted to 'illicit intercourse with the view of inducing marriage' could rely on more than a man's 'honourable nature' to assure them of success. Priests invariably ordered couples to marry in such cases, and threats of more physical persuasion from family and friends would usually succeed when clerical injunctions had failed. The Committee was told that of 800 Englishmen employed on government surveys across Ireland, 'almost all married there in consequence of the chastity of the women.'

> Illicit intercourse . . . is restrained, as well as by a natural decorum, which has ever characterised the women of this country, as by a strong and reverential fear of God, constantly kept alive and strengthened by the admonitions of the priests. When it once enters into our hamlets, love seeks its object, not by degrading the person and tainting the soul, but in that holy wedlock which our Redeemer has sanctified, and his Apostle declared to be honourable in all without distinction of rich or poor.[38]

These comments reminded me of the dances that Father Quinn had organised and overseen in Letterfrack, and Father Ludden in Tullycross during the winter of 1964, when the girls were swinging their skirts, and lads most frequently seen in flat caps and wellington boots were smartly dressed and brazening out a dance their feet found hard to follow. A local band blasted out the music. Low lights, Fanta and Coke, a cigarette in the darkness outside, but Father Quinn was never far away; nor Father Ludden. They knew who it was that might be tempted. And they would have their ear at confession on Friday; and if Sunday Mass was missed, they would be at the door on Monday, demanding an explanation. The teens and twenties grumbled about constraints, and the gossip, and everyone knowing everyone else's business.

I never saw a couple kissing in public, or even holding hands – the gentle touch, the glance, was about as far as it seemed to go. And then came the weddings. Joseph Heanue married Mary; Cornelius Mullen married Margaret and in due course, there he was: striding down the road with Anne in the pram. Grinning as though he did not know how to stop; horny calloused hands gently easing back the blanket to show the tiny, so perfect face. And Granny Mullen sat at the fire, cooing over her first grandchild to be born in Ireland. 'In a moment, I'll set down the tea,' she said.

Eight more children followed Anne – in not many more years. The house was mostly a big kitchen, that the front door opened into and the back door led out of. A big open fireplace on the left wall, with a black kettle dangling over the turf fire. A small room leading off from either side of the fireplace, and another two from the opposite side of the kitchen. No bathroom. A sink in the back porch bringing water on an extension from the supply Cornelius had put into our house; a table, some chairs, a cupboard – not an overly furnished house, but buzzing with children when we returned to see them a decade later. And Cornelius sitting there at the fire, boots and cap still on, talking to them so gently, joking. He was a middle-aged husband and father, for whom marriage and children were a joy he had perhaps abandoned hope of knowing.

Material possessions meant very little to Cornelius. The land, houses and livestock were just a means of making a living – but the children, they were a precious gift. You could see it: not an overt physical display of hugs and kissing, but tenderness, and an emanation of love that simply wrapped the children to him, however far away they were. In the material world most of us occupy today, social scientists say that a subsistence society welcomed children for the support they would provide as the parents grew old. But that is not the whole story. The deeper truth is that where communities were self-sufficient, with little need of anything beyond their immediate environs, children were the most that anyone wanted, and the most precious gift they could have. To be wondered at – and loved.

Says I, 'My lovely darling, I'm tired of single life
And if you've no objections, I will make you my sweet wife.'
Says she, 'I'll ask my parents, and tomorrow you shall know
If you'll meet me in the garden where the praties grow.'

Her parents they consented, and we're blessed with children
    three,
Two girls just like their mother, and a boy the image of me.
We'll train them up in decency, the way they ought to go
And I'll ne'er forget the garden where the praties grow.

Chapter Ten

Seeds of famine

Cornelius was the last to plant his potatoes during our stay in Ballynew in 1964. Mike O'Halloran in the Sheeauns had been first, down in the garden behind the cottage, turning over the lazy-beds before even February was out. The brothers John and Patrick Coyne could never agree on much, but worked together amicably enough on a joint potato crop, and along with everyone else had their patch planted out by just after St Patrick's Day. And here it was April and still Cornelius had not even got the ground cleared. Fuchsia was bursting into leaf along the boreens; violets and primroses were relieving the monotony of celandines under the hedgerows; lambing was almost finished and there would be swallows under the eaves any day soon. Cornelius was known to be laid back, idiosyncratic and not someone who believed hard work was good for body and soul, but this lack of attention to the staple crop was unusual even for him, and had the village buzzing. The tension was more than had been known since John Coyne's cow got herself stuck chest-deep in a ditch. And Cornelius enjoyed every minute of it.

Then came the day when he moved the milch cow from the field onto which she had been turned out on good days through the winter . . . he had left the gate open too, the village's keen-eyed observers noted, and later that morning Tom King drove his tractor up the road from Cleggan and had the whole field ploughed over and ridged up in time for tea. Cornelius was setting out his potatoes the next day. Each tuber a boot's-length apart, and given a kindly sprinkling of lime before the adjacent ridge was raked over.

Come harvest, there was no sign his crop had suffered from the delayed planting. Could be the potatoes had benefited, Cornelius said, from the soil being that much warmer when he planted them. In any event, he had a more than ample harvest stored in a clamp behind the house before the frosts came. They were big oval potatoes, most of them, and floury. Call at the Mullen house midday or at teatime and Cornelius was often to be found feasting on a bowl of potatoes straight from the pot. They were boiled with the skins on, then opened up for a pinch of salt and a knob of butter (or a dash of milk) to be mashed in. Delicious. We had them like that the Sunday we were invited to dinner (a midday meal in Connemara). It was to be a grand meal his mother was doing especially for us, Cornelius had said. They had bought half a leg of mutton, and boiled it for most of the morning. Pieces of meat were set beside the potatoes on our plates, and the water in which it had boiled poured over, the mutton-fat congealing as the liquid spread to the edges of the cold plates. A memorable meal indeed; the more so for the glass of 'hard stuff' (poteen – illicit whiskey) with which Cornelius plied us after we had eaten.

Like most of Ballynew in those days, the Mullens cooked over the open fire, and did not hold with fussing too much about how it was done. Virtually everything that came into the house was set down to boil: vegetables, porridge, eggs, fish, meat – even bacon was deemed best as a boiled joint rather than as rashers. There was no stove or range; no oven except the cast-iron pot they used to set on the coals to bake soda-bread in times past, with more coals heaped on the lid. But the old lady rarely did that while we were there. No fridge; no rack of pots and pans – just a kettle hanging from the hook over the fire, always filled and simmering, and a heavy long-handled saucepan alongside. That was in the 1960s. Hardly changed from centuries before when the culinary skills of Ireland's rural population did not extend very far beyond those required for boiling potatoes.

Potatoes – the praties – with a field of potatoes you could raise a family on a sub-division of the family holding, or on a vacant stretch of bog or steep mountainside. Lazy-beds were the universally preferred method of cultivation until hiring a tractor became an option. Lazy-beds may be the name, but there had been nothing lazy about the toil of manuring the metre-wide strips, setting the seed potatoes on them, then opening trenches on either side and laying the sods of turf face-down over the potatoes. More earth from the trenches on top, then more again as the green shoots came through. That was hard work, but it was also the best way of bringing waterlogged and poor land into cultivation. And the rewards were outstanding – really good food, and lots of it.

It has been said that the potato was to the Irish what the coconut was to the South Sea islanders – an ambrosial food. Not that it brought a life of halcyon luxury; simply that by improving the quality and volume of the diet, an abundance of potatoes 'supported a population of fecund young women and sexually vigorous young men'.[1] And as an eighteenth-century traveller delicately remarked, Irish 'young couple[s] pass not their youth in celibacy for want of a nest to produce their young in.'[2]

They married young. The church encouraged it, but wretched living conditions were an incentive too. Marriage could not make thing worse, and shared wretchedness might be easier to bear. What else was there? A young man knew that no amount of effort and thrift would improve his lot. Unlike an apprentice, he had no incentive to delay marriage until he was qualified; nor, by waiting, could he hope to accumulate the capital that would secure his family's future. But now, right now, he could have potatoes, the company of a wife – and children.

Their nest might be a corner of the parental home to start with – though no great outlay of energy or funds was required to erect a new house. The cottier's dwelling had originally been comfortable and well-suited to the prevailing conditions, we are told.[3] But that was before the extortions of landlords and middlemen had stripped away both the means and the incentive to put up an adequate dwelling. The typical cottier's home of the eighteenth century consisted of four walls, commonly made of sods or mud, sometimes with a few runs of stone at the base; a roof of branches, covered with turves and straw, rushes, or potato stalks; and an earthern floor with a central hearth around which the family gathered. No window, no inside partitions.

'The manner in which the poor of this country live, I cannot help calling beastly,' a visitor reported. 'For upon the same floor, and frequently without any partition, are lodged the husband and wife, the multitudinous brood of children, all huddled together upon the straw or rushes, with the cow, the calf, the pig, and the horse, if they are rich enough to have one.' Another visitor found it hard to imagine that human beings could exist in such conditions: 'Their cabins scarcely contain an article that can be called furniture; in some families there are no such things as bedclothes, the peasants showed some fern, and a quantity of straw thrown over it, upon which they slept in their working clothes.'[4]

But so long as they had potatoes they were better fed than much of Europe. A couple of acres would produce all the potatoes a family could eat – and in even an average year there would be enough left over to feed a pig. The diet was monotonous, but never less than filling. There are dozens of accounts from the late eighteenth and early nineteenth centuries of the quantities that people consumed. A farmer from Co. Down reckoned that 14 pounds a day was little enough for a working man, and the bishop of Kildare thought that 'in 24 hours a labouring man will require at least three half-stones of potatoes, that is 21 pounds.' More modestly, the historian Kenneth H. Connell puts the average consumption for an adult Irishman at around 10 pounds of potatoes a day. And if he ate nothing else and drank only water he was not undernourished. If, as was customary, he had a cup of milk with each meal, then the biochemist – if not the gourmet – would say that his needs were admirably satisfied. Such a diet of potatoes and milk would provide 4,000 calories a day, compared with the recommended 3,000; plus all the protein, calcium and iron a man needed, and a sufficiency of the listed vitamins.[5]

The typical cottier and his family were oppressed by predatory landlords, clothed in rags and not infrequently sharing their living accommodation with pigs and chickens, but they were very well nourished – and thus able to sustain a birth rate approaching the physical maximum. Potatoes kept young couples healthy, sexually active and fertile. They married early, and their respect for Catholic prohibitions encouraged uninhibited sex. Potato mashed with buttermilk made early weaning possible, thus shortening birth intervals by reducing the contraceptive effects of breast-feeding. Potatoes fed husbands and children prodigiously; generous amounts of healthy food kept mortality at bay. Furthermore, the demands of potato cultivation locked people onto the land, where they avoided the epidemics that ravaged the cities from time to time.[6] More babies were born, fewer died before adulthood; and so succeeding generations contained a proportionately larger cohort of potential parents. Two million, 3 million, 4 million, 5, 6, 7 and 8 million: Ireland's population rise was as spectacular as the expansion of potato cultivation. The former tracked the latter; the latter fed the former – cause and effect.

Such rampant population growth could not continue indefinitely. There would have to be some redress, and a sober warning of the form it might take came in 1740–41. William Wilde's *Table of Irish Famines*, compiled in 1851, reports that an early, severe and prolonged winter destroyed the country's entire potato crop that year. The shortage of food was aggravated by the difficulty of grinding corn while watermills were rendered inoperable by frozen rivers, and by the poor summer that followed – when the corn failed to ripen and the grass to grow.

> Want and misery were in every face, the rich unable to relieve the poor, the roads spread with dead and dying; mankind of the colour of the weeds and nettles on which they feed; . . . whole villages were laid waste. If one in every house in the kingdom died, and that is very probable, the loss must have been upward of 400,000 souls.[7]

Though this estimate of fatalities is little more than a random guess, modern research shows that the severity of the 1740–41 famine is not in doubt.[8] But the tragedy served not so much to warm as to clear the way for the potato's spectacular advance during the second half of the eighteenth century. This was truly the potato's 'golden age', when it proved itself 'universally palatable, from the palace to the pig-sty', and attained:

> a perfection it had never known before, [becoming] part of the diet of the rich and the whole diet of the poor; nor was this all, [for] it became an article of commerce and was soon known and admired in every part of Europe by the name of the Irish potatoes; a name which it deservedly obtained, and maintains to this day, from the pre-eminence which the Irish nation has obtained in the method of cultivating it.[9]

Arthur Young, an English farmer and Fellow of the Royal Society who made an extensive survey of Irish agriculture during the years 1776–9, saw the best of it: the wonderful potential of Ireland as a source for the grain, meat, butter, linen and so on that England and foreign markets could not produce themselves, and the potato as a staple food of what he called 'the labouring poor'. Young was impressed by the vast acreage of potato cultivation he encountered. He was appalled by the living conditions that the cottiers endured, and not slow to blame the absentee landlords and middlemen for reducing their tenants to such poverty, but unreserved in his commendation of the potato:

> I have heard it stigmatized as being unhealthy, and not sufficiently nourishing for the support of hard labour; but this opinion is very amazing in a country, many of whose poor people are as athletic in their form, as robust, and as capable of enduring labour as any upon

earth. When I see the people of a country, in spite of political oppression, with well-formed vigorous bodies, and their cottages swarming with children; when I see their men athletic and their women beautiful, I know not how to believe them subsisting on an unwholesome food.

In Young's view, Irish cottiers were better fed than England's cottagers:

If any doubts the comparative plenty which attends the board of the poor natives of England and Ireland, let him attend to their meals; the sparingness with which our labourer eats his bread and cheese is well known; mark the Irishman's potato bowl placed on the floor, the whole family upon their hams around it, devouring a quantity almost incredible, the beggar seating himself to it with a hearty welcome, the pig taking his share as readily as the wife, the cocks, the hens, turkies, geese, the cur, the cat, and perhaps the cow – and all partaking of the same dish. No man can often have been a witness of it without being convinced of the plenty, and I will add the cheerfulness, that attends it.[10]

The balance was tuned to perfection: new tasty and productive potato varieties, plenty of land, and an agricultural workforce of robust good health and compliant demeanour. Ironically, the potato, which had enabled the cottiers to survive and cheerfully multiply under the oppression and exploitations of the landlords' feudal regime, had now set them up to be the energy base of Ireland's burgeoning contribution to international commerce. So long as cottiers could feed themselves on potatoes, landlords could require them to work more intensively on the production of commodities for export.

Grain was the most attractive proposition. Not least by virtue of 'Foster's Corn Law', which provided for a bounty to be paid on Ireland's grain exports, and a duty levied on imports. Introduced in 1784 with the intention of encouraging farmers to produce a sufficiency of grain for the country and then a surplus for export, 'in a few years, it changed the face of the land, and made Ireland to a great extent an arable instead of a pasture country.'[11] The change was swift and wide-reaching. Figures on the acreage involved are elusive, but Arthur Young remarked that Belfast, which imported grain until the year before his tour, had become an exporter; and the fact that wheat exports increased twentyfold, and oats tenfold in the fifty years after 1770 must confirm that a good deal of pasture had been converted to tillage. And not just grain kept the cottiers busy: soaring demands for linen meant that the flax (a variety of linseed, *Linum usitatissimum*, with long fibrous stems) from which it was woven had to be sown and reaped too, and weaving became a cottage industry that contributed significantly to the rise in exports of Irish linen from 12 million yards of cloth per year in the 1750s to over 40 million in the 1790s. Forty million yards – over 22,000 miles; almost enough to girdle the planet, every year.[12]

And, indeed, Irish linen did girdle the planet in the late eighteenth century – as the billowing sails of ships deployed by the European powers as they vied for control of foreign parts and lucrative trade routes. This was the age of sail, and there were young colonies to be provisioned in America, the West Indies, South Africa and Australia. Wars to be fought too, as Napoleon challenged Europe. All of this meant that Europe's farmers were being called upon to do more than simply service and feed the home countries – they were required to provision the navies, merchant fleets and distant colonies as well. And a disproportionate share of this burden fell on the Irish.

Take just one example: Ireland supplied 70 per cent of England's food imports in the early nineteenth century.[13] This was all very well for the bosses and the bankers, but what about the farm labourers who were producing the wealth? They had the potato, but its advantages were counting against them now. Because potatoes were so cheap, labour was cheap, and so output could be raised simply by employing more labour. And because the labour market was choked with cheap workers, there was no incentive to improve their terms of employment, and insufficient demand in Ireland's home market to stimulate economic change: the workers had no buying power. But as long as prices were steady or rising in response to demand from England and elsewhere, farmers, middlemen and landlords prospered; and while potatoes flourished, the labourers were healthy and hard-working. But it could not last.

Already, two or more generations had grown up on the potato, healthy and fecund. Where a single couple had married and reared a conservative five children fifty years before, there could be at least 100 mouths to feed now. Land to be sub-divided yet again; bog to be reclaimed; improbable mountain slopes to be tackled with the spade: lazy-beds, indeed! And yet there was still rent to be paid. Shoes were not a priority, even in the fiercest winter, but some clothes, tools, utensils and salt were required. There had to be money for them; something to sell. And too often now it was the supplements that had hitherto made a potato diet more adequately nutritious that were sold. The pig was a source of protein and essential fats, but had to go to market:

> [The cottier] always considered this as an article of too much value to be converted to the use of himself or his family. The butter, the poultry, and the eggs, were equally his property, and the miserable family by whose care they were produced, were equally prohibited to use them. What did these people live on? They lived on those things for which little or no money could be procured at market: potatoes constituted the chief food. The next article which he retained for his own use was one of still less value, it was that part of the milk which remained after butter had been extracted from it.[14]

The golden age of the potato had not lasted long – fifty or sixty years, perhaps. Its beginnings lay somewhere in the two decades after the Great Frost of 1740–41, and its close was confirmed by the end of the Napoleonic wars in 1815, which sent grain prices tumbling and farmers looking for other ways of paying the inflated rents they had agreed upon while the market was booming. They looked to the land. 'It is not enough to say that land is desired in Ireland,' wrote an observer; 'it is envied and coveted; it is torn to pieces, and the pieces are fiercely contested: when it cannot be occupied by fair means it is seized by crime.' In Connaught, the competition for land was especially cruel.[15]

There were consolidations of previously fragmented land, as farmers sought the economies of scale. Thousands of cottiers and their families were evicted, and left with no choice but to join the pleading crowds wherever land was still to be had. More sub-division ensued, more short leases on exorbitant rents. Cottiers would promise anything, hoping that potatoes would keep them alive, but eventually even the limit of the potato's generosity was breached. The fields were full, but the new varieties which breeders had introduced, though more productive, were less nutritious and more susceptible to disease.

The Lumper, introduced in the early 1800s, was 20–30 per cent more productive than the varieties which had fuelled Ireland's spectacular population growth – the Black, the Apple and the Cups – but its short-comings were clear. Indeed, the inquities of the Lumper ring like a funeral bell through the literature:

> The root, at its first introduction, was scarcely considered food enough for swine, it neither possesses the farinaceous qualities of the better

varieties of the plant, nor is it as palatable as any other, being wet and tasteless, and, in point of substantial nutriment, little better, as an article of human food, than a Swedish turnip. A wretched kind; of a soft watery quality . . . both unwholesome and unpalatable even crows rejected them if a Cup was to be had.

I would wish a penalty imposed on anyone who would retain the Lumper . . .; they are bad food for pigs, [and] in no country but this would they be deemed fit for human beings, much less for men engaged in hard labour, who use them through necessity.[16]

Necessity was driving thousands to emigrate, while at home the constant hunger that only a sufficiency of fats could satisfy was driving some labourers to eat their potatoes half-cooked, swallowing the raw centres whole, in the belief that the lumps would remain in the stomach to be digested after the fully cooked portion had been assimilated – thus extending the benefits of the meal. But it was a mistaken belief. Humans cannot digest raw potatoes; the nutritious components have to be broken down by cooking. So while the labourers may have kept the cravings of hunger at bay, they were depriving themselves of much-needed energy.[17]

By 1815 there were 4.7 million people in Ireland for whom the potato was the predominant item of diet, and of them 3.3 million had nothing else.[18] It was not just the fate of Napoleon that had been sealed at the battle of Waterloo. Ireland's doom was sealed there too.

Cecil Woodham-Smith reports in *The Great Hunger* that during the forty-five years immediately preceding the famine of 1845–7:

no fewer than 114 Commissions and 61 Special Committees were instructed to report on the state of Ireland, and without exception their finding prophesied disaster; Ireland was on the verge of starvation, her population rapidly increasing, three-quarters of her labourers unemployed, housing conditions appalling and the standards of living unbelievably low.[19]

The laws penalising cottiers simply for being Catholics had been repealed, but the government did nothing to avert disaster, and made no arrangements for relieving the destitute should the prophesies become reality until the 1830s, when it was decided that a version of England's recently introduced Poor Law should be applied to Ireland. It was to be a more stringent version, however, in that relief would be administered only to whole family units and only within the confines of a workhouse, and once a workhouse was full, no relief would be available for those turned away. No outdoor relief and, furthermore, it was deemed that a well-run workhouse should deter people from applying for relief and discourage inmates from staying too long.

To ensure the equitable distribution of the Poor Law workhouse facilities, Ireland was divided into 130 administrative units known as unions, each of which would have its own workhouse. Each workhouse was to be administered by an elected Board of Guardians and financed by rates – locally levied. Thus the unions were to be self-financing (though loans were provided for construction of the buildings). While the unions were being demarcated and the workhouses built, teams of commissioners were sent out to investigate local diets around the country, the idea being that whatever diets were served in the workhouses should be worse (and cheaper) than anything available outside. This proved difficult, for across a wide swathe of the country men were eating four or five pounds of potatoes at breakfast, dinner and supper, with milk or buttermilk, and the commissioners could not imagine a diet worse than that. They investigated diets in about two-thirds of the 2,500 parishes in Ireland and found that potatoes were not only the sole diet of the poor, but had also made advances into the eating patterns of better-off farmers. Oatmeal, milk, cabbage, herrings, bacon and beef had not been entirely swept from the tables of the rural middle class, but they had been converted into luxuries that were eaten just a few times during the year.[20]

The speed at which the workhouses were built and opened was impressive, and the government doubtless drew some comfort from the fact that 118 were operational by the autumn of 1845, when Ireland's potato crop began to wilt and die from a hitherto unknown disease. Crop failures had caused localised hardship before, so officials probably felt that the new arrangements would be capable of relieving any distress the 1845 failures might bring. But this was a totally new order of disease, which swept across the fields like wildfire – seemingly on the wind – and left hardly a single plant uninfected.

The country had been expecting a bumper harvest: 2.5 million acres had been planted with potatoes – 6 per cent more than in the previous year. Cottiers were 'grateful and contented'; farmers were 'in the height of good spirits'; the country was 'happy and prosperous' in anticipation 'of a bright and glorious era in the history of Ireland'. A harvest of 15 million tons was predicted – enough to meet all demands. The only ones not overjoyed with the prospects were some commercial farmers who regretted having gone to the expense of sowing potatoes when 'they promise to be so cheap and plentiful'.[21]

The disease arrived without warning in September and spread remorselessly across the country, destroying in a few days fields of potatoes which until then had been proudly resplendent in all their pomp of dark green leaf and purple bloom. Nothing but black and withered stalks were left above ground, while below ground the tubers were stained and beginning to rot. Even potatoes which had been harvested earlier and were already in store became rotten and useless within a few weeks – they were reduced to an inedible stinking mess.

Nothing like the calamity which struck Ireland had been known in Europe since the Black Death of the fourteenth century. The destitution to which the country was reduced continued through 1846 when the disease devastated crops again, and went on into 1847 and '48 because farmers had virtually given up planting potatoes (only 284,000 acres in 1847[22]), leaving survivors of the first onslaughts to struggle for other sources of sustenance. In just a few years, the population was reduced by over 2 million. At least one million died of starvation and famine-related disease, while another million emigrated.

Before the famine, western Connemara had supported around 500 people per square mile – the highest rural population density in Europe, it is said,[23] on some of the continent's poorest land. The entire region was owned by just a few long-established families, most of whom still lived on their properties – although the Ballynew lands were owned by absentee speculators who paid little attention to farming or the needs of their tenants. The adjacent 10,000 acre Ballynakill estate was also poorly managed, having been in the care of the courts for more than twenty years until Robert Graham bought it in 1839. His son later wrote that when the family took possession of the property it was 'covered in paupers; . . . the houses like Indian wigwams [with] twenty families upon five acres of ground'.[24] Many were evicted and three villages demolished as the holdings were consolidated into large farms. This made the Grahams highly unpopular, though elsewhere in Connemara relations between tenants and landlords seem to have been generally good – in evidence given to a government enquiry into land-holdings in Ireland several landlords reported that defaulting was rare.

The Connemara cottiers were lucky in some respects, out there in the remotest west of the country, at the farthest extent of government influence, where the sea provided fish both as food and to pay the rent, and seaweed as a manure for the potato beds. The majority of families were self-sufficient, living off the land, fishing, and taking day labour whenever it was to be had. They had a cow or two for milk and butter, and sheep for wool that wives knitted into socks and other garments. Most were desperately poor, but 'destitution does not prevail to any extent', the Poor Law Commissioners were told in 1840, 'and the strolling beggar is seldom to be met with.'[25]

Communications were difficult; the only town, Clifden, was better served by sea than by the rough roads that linked it to Galway city (60 miles away), Westport (50 miles) and the rest of the country (Dublin was 100 miles away). The few traders who had established businesses in the town shipped in their merchandise, and farm produce was likewise shipped out on small coastal vessels. Eight hundred tons of oats were shipped from Clifden to London and Liverpool in 1835 – a measure of Connemara's economic viability at the time: there was no destitution, there were no beggars; the region was densely populated but self-sufficient and able to produce a marketable surplus of grain.

The Poor Law Commissioners concluded that Clifden must have a workhouse capable of housing 300 inmates. It was to be the largest building in the town, but not an edifice the ratepayers were keen to see erected and in operation. They would have to pay its running costs, and since there were relatively few of them, each owning large tracts of rateable land, the contributions being demanded were felt to be unreasonably high. Delaying tactics were employed, so that although contracts were signed in January 1841 and building proceeded apace, the workhouse was not opened for use until December 1845 and received its first inmates only in March 1847. By then, destitution was rife. Thousands of people were starving, already seriously malnourished and falling prey to disease. Hundreds would die.

The potato disease had reached Connemara in the last months of 1845, destroying most of the potato crop, but creating no more of a serious shortage than had been experienced many times before. The people got through by falling back on their own provisions and resources. Roadworks again provided an income, and the Clifden stores had provisions for sale – albeit at inflated prices. But the devastations that disease wrought again in 1846 created a new order of distress. Crops were again destroyed; reserves had been exhausted the previous year and everything of value had been sold or pawned to buy food. The problem was not that food was unavailable, simply that the people most in need had no money with which to buy it.

The government had responded to the 1845 crop failures by establishing relief depots around the country which would be kept supplied with maize meal – not an ideal food, but certainly good enough to keep starvation at bay. But even maize meal was not food that could be given free to the needy (the Poor Law's prohibition of outdoor relief forbade that). It was to be sold from the government depots, and then only when market prices were deemed to have become too high. Private enterprise, and a free market, would take care of things, it was believed. But while even men 'lucky' enough to be working on the roads were earning less than it cost to feed their families, the situation could only worsen.

The iniquities were abundantly clear. 'Must the People Starve', the *Galway Vindicator's* headline asked in December 1846:

Never was the condition of the people so awful as at present – not merely the utterly destitute but every class of limited means. The prices of food have arrived at such a famine pitch that if not immediately lowered by the prompt interference of the government, will most certainly either force the people to an outbreak for the preservation of their lives or doom them in hundreds upon hundreds to premature death. We see no other alternative. There is no use in thinking that the peace of the country can be maintained while the farmers, merchants, miller, meal monger, baker, and provision huxter, seem remorselessly determined with a cupidity, an avariciousness that puts to the blush every feeling of humanity and libels the very name of Christian, to wring fortunes, if they can, out of the vitals of the poor and reap a golden harvest in the plunder, shameful open plunder of the public.[26]

Meanwhile, workhouses throughout the country were filling up, and regulations were amended to render anyone owning even a quarter-acre of land ineligible for entry. This was intended to limit the number of applicants, but it did not work, for those desperate enough to see the workhouse as relief simply gave up their last scrap of land in order to get in – and then joined the homeless begging hordes when the time came for them to be ejected (as the able-bodied eventually were). Where even the workhouse was denied, crime and thus jail were another desperate option. Magistrates sympathetic to this strategy were admonished for convicting people who had committed slight offences simply in order that they may be kept alive in jail. By January 1848, there were 564 'nearly naked and almost starving' prisoners in Galway county jail – built to accommodate 110 – of whom 157 were to be transported, and some doubtless felt they would rather be shipped to Australia than left to die in Connemara.[27]

The Clifden workhouse was full, but the coffers from which its day-to-day activities were funded were empty – even overdrawn; not least because dealers and tradesmen were taking advantage of the situation and charging exorbitant rates for the goods they supplied. Conditions in the workhouse deteriorated to an appalling degree; essential maintenance was neglected and bedding not replaced as it became unfit for use, and the dormitories were left without night buckets. 'I forbear to describe the abominations consequent to this,' an inspector reported. The ominous spread of malignant typhus fever added fear to the indignities suffered by the starved and despairing inmates. As the winter of 1847 approached, forty-five of the 300 inmates had fever and were overwhelming the totally inadequate medical facilities of the institution. Each week there were deaths; among them a doctor's assistant who caught the fever.

The workhouse was desperately short of money mainly because the ratepayers had none with which to meet their commitments. Of £22,426 due in May 1847, only £129 had been collected by August. And, of course, the landowners were defaulting simply because they were not receiving any rents from their tenants – who had no money either. But some did still have cattle or sheep, and fierce clashes occurred as agents were sent out to impound livestock in lieu of rent. Thomas Driver, a deputy agent, told how he and six men were attacked by a group of about forty as they attempted to take cattle from Tooreen, in the Ballynakill parish. Stones were thrown and Driver was told in no uncertain terms that the crowd 'would have their lives' if he and his assistants took a beast to the pound. It was the same in the Sheeauns, where they managed to seize two head of cattle but were immediately surrounded by a group of about sixty, brandishing cudgels and stones. Again, their lives were threatened and the cattle reclaimed by their owners.

It was abundantly clear that the government's grand plan for a network of self-supporting workhouses to provide relief for Ireland's poor in times of distress was simply incapable of containing a disaster of the magnitude that had struck the country. The workhouses were overwhelmed, and people were dying on the roads and in their houses. William Forster, who investigated the famine in Connemara in January 1847 for the Relief Committee of the Society of Friends (the Quakers), reported that in Bundorragha village, which is today the focus of many cameras as tourists pause to capture the beauty of Killary harbour, thirteen from a population of 240 had already died 'from want', and the remainder were walking skeletons; the men gaunt and haggard, women in the cabins too weak to stand, and the children crying in pain. Forster also visited Cleggan, where he found that:

> The distress was appalling far beyond my powers of description. I was quickly surrounded by a mob of men and women, more like famished dogs than fellow creatures, whose figures, looks and cries, all showed that they were suffering the ravening agony of hunger . . . In one [cabin] there were two emaciated men, lying at full length, on the damp floor, in their ragged clothes, too weak to move, actually worn down to skin and bone. In another a young man was dying of dysentry; his mother had pawned everything . . . to keep him alive; and I never shall forget the resigned, uncomplaining tone with which he told me that all the medicine he wanted was food . . .
>
> . . . in a most miserable cabin by the sea-side, into which we could scarcely crawl, we found this poor child yet alive, but lying on the damp clay, in the dark, unable to get up, no clothes on or covering but a ragged cloth, the roof over her open to the rain. Since her mother's death she had lived on meal and water brought to the door.[28]

Cleggan village had been on the north side of the bay at the time of the famine, huddled under the headland on which a sturdy stone signal-tower had been built during the Napoleonic wars – one of the chain erected along the west coast of Ireland to ensure that England's back door stayed shut. The ruined tower was still prominent on the skyline in the 1960s, drawing the eye across the 900 acres that a scion of the Twining tea family had bought after the famine; but little of the old Cleggan village remained. Even the name had gone across the bay to Knockbrack, where the Post Office had established a district office and called it the Cleggan Post Office, thus ensuring that Knockbrack eventually became Cleggan.

The flight of Cleggan across the bay was an episode of local history that John James McLoughlin had once mentioned when I met him where the road turns away from the shore and cuts back towards Ballynew. John James now owned the site where old Cleggan had stood, and lived across the road from it in a fine two-storey house his father had built with stone and slate retrieved from the village after buying the site, perhaps half a century before. Now old Cleggan was a few lines of broken-down walls and a roofless stable on an acre or two of meadow where John James grazed cattle. The rocks on the shoreline below were encrusted with mussels, whelks and winkles. There were always dunlins and oystercatchers picking through the shingle and kelp, and in early spring salmon struggled through the shallow estuary to lake Anillaun and their spawning beds in the Sheeauns stream above.

Grand place for a village, John James would say of the old site. South-facing and sheltered by the hill. The villagers had worked on the farm, grew potatoes and kept cattle and sheep over on the north side. They fished, and there had been a slipway and a pier for their boats. When the Twinings came they had taken the village over and built dressed-stone cottages for their workers, with slate roofs, he said. But there had been many more cottages before then – the traditional kind: thatched and small with fireplaces that filled one wall, dry-stone walls with mud plaster to keep the draughts out; lime-washed and small windows, beaten earth floors and low ceilings that kept the warmth in. And do you know the cromleac, down yonder?

I did. It was a rectangle of upright boulders with a single large slab of rock balanced on top that stood prominently above the shore a few hundred yards beyond old Cleggan. A Celtic burial mound. Long since stripped of its contents and earth covering but still a powerful reminder of Cleggan's most ancient inhabitants. A memorial. No inscription, no neat descriptive panel on a post – just a tangible piece of local history that you learned about by word of mouth.

Chapter Eleven

Woe the sons of Adam!

I know nothing more imposing than the view which the Thames offers during the ascent from the sea to London Bridge. The masses of buildings, the wharves on both sides, especially from Woolwich upwards, the countless ships along both shores, crowding ever closer and closer together, until, at last, only a narrow passage remains in the middle of the river, a passage through which hundreds of steamers shoot by one another; all this is so vast, so impressive, that a man cannot collect himself, but is lost in the marvel of England's greatness before he sets foot upon English soil.[1]

It was the late autumn of 1842 and Friedrich Engels was arriving in England for the first time. The eldest son of a German textile manufacturer, twenty-two years old, Engels was passing through London on his way to Manchester, where his father had invested in a cotton manufacturing company – Ermen and Engels. Engels senior had hoped that by sending his son to live abroad, where business responsibilities should absorb most of his time and energy, the young firebrand might abandon – or at least modify – the radical tendencies he had been developing in Germany. It was a vain hope. On his way from Germany, Engels had made a point of calling on Karl Marx (then in Cologne, editing an anti-government newspaper, the *Rheinische Zeitung*). In Manchester, veritable birthplace of the Industrial Revolution, he would be exposed to extremes of wealth, poverty and exploitation which could only harden his determination to campaign for social reform and revolution. Far from modifying Engels's views, Manchester and industrial England confirmed their urgent relevance, sealing his allegiance to a political movement that found

its defining expression in *The Communist Manifesto* – written and published by Marx and Engels in 1848.

Sixty years before Engels had set foot on English soil for the first time, England had been a country just *like* every other, he noted in 1844, a country with small towns, few and simple industries, and a thin but proportionately large agricultural population. Now it was a country altogether *unlike* any other; with a capital of 2.5 million inhabitants; with vast manufacturing cities; with an industrious and dense population, of which two-thirds were engaged in the trade and commerce generated by industries that supplied the world and produced almost everything by means of the most complex machinery. The Industrial Revolution was as important to England as the political revolution had been to France, and the philosophical revolution to Germany, he said.

England's revolution had begun with the cotton industry, which in the space of eighty years had transformed Lancashire from what Engels described as 'an obscure, ill-cultivated swamp' into a frenetic hotpot of industrial activity, multiplying its population tenfold, spawning the giant cities of Liverpool and Manchester and creating a long list of manufacturing towns – Bolton, Rochdale, Preston, Oldham and so forth – 'as if by some magic touch'. But there was nothing magical about the mechanical inventions which had set it in motion; nor in the business acumen which had orchestrated its development. Indeed, if there was anything at all magical in the rapid growth of industrial activity, it was the availability of sufficient labour to dig out the coal, cast the iron, mould the bricks, raise the factories and work the looms.

With the benefit of hindsight it seems almost as though the population growth which the potato fuelled in England and across Europe in the late eighteenth century was expressly intended to make the wheels of industry and keep them turning. Or, to put it another way, that the Industrial Revolution was expressly designed to employ the people who were now surplus to requirements on the land. The reality was cruelly different. The potato, as Redcliffe Salaman notes, 'came as a heaven-sent gift to the leaders of industry; its use was urged not only by the employers, but by many well-intentioned persons who failed to appreciate its implications.'[2]

The implications were, of course, that the potato provided cheap and plentiful food and thus enabled industrialists to keep wages down and produce goods at prices low enough to capture the vast foreign markets on which the entire enterprise depended. A heaven-sent gift indeed, ironically becoming available during the decades when the slave trade (which had enriched previous generations of entrepreneurs) was abolished, but just as surely creating another army of slaves. In fact, employers were far better off than if they were using slave labour: they could hire and dismiss labour at will, without sacrificing invested capital, and get the work done much more cheaply than would have been possible with slaves. As Adam Smith pointed out in his *Wealth of Nations*:

> The wear and tear of a slave, it has been said, is at the expense of his master, but that of a free servant is at his own expense. [Furthermore] [t]he fund for replacing or repairing, if I may say so, the wear and tear of the slave, is commonly managed by a negligent master or careless overseer. That destined for performing the same office with regard to the free man, is managed by the free man himself . . . It appears, accordingly, from the experience of all ages and nations, I believe, that the work done by freemen comes cheaper in the end than that performed by slaves.[3]

Adam Smith was writing in 1776, before the full effects of the potato on Europe's population growth rate had become evident. Friedrich Engels arrived in England just as those two factors – free labour and a burgeoning population – found common purpose in the potential and demands of the Industrial Revolution. Manchester, and Engels's status in the textile industry, gave him a first-hand view of what was likely to happen when there were more people clamouring for work than there were jobs for them to do: perversely, in such circumstances, manufacturers could employ fewer of them – simply by exploiting the labourers' competition among themselves. If a manufacturer customarily employed ten workers for nine hours daily, for instance, he could employ just nine by requiring each to work ten hours daily for the same wages. The threat of being the one thrown out of work was enough to ensure that all agreed to work for less. Costs were reduced, the workforce shrank and the pool of available labour grew larger.

Whether or not Ermen and Engels indulged in such practices, the prevailing ethics of mid-nineteenth-century industry obliged Engels himself to live a double life in Manchester: committed to his father's firm of 'capitalist exploiters' on the one hand, while simultaneously accumulating the evidence he would use to call for an end to such exploitation. It was not a combination that could be easily sustained. In fact, Engels soon left the family firm and barely two years after he had first sailed up the Thames published a compilation of facts, notes and observations entitled *The Condition of the Working-Class in England in 1844*. The book was written and published in German; tellingly, an English translation did not appear until 1892, though it is a damning indictment of English society and, more particularly, an often moving account of how a very large number of people in early Victorian England lived.

Engels describes the scenes he has witnessed on visits to England's industrial cities – the filth and horrors – then in respect of one Manchester district in particular wonders if the description is:

> black enough to convey a true impression of the filth, ruin, and uninhabitableness, the defiance of all considerations of cleanliness, ventilation, and health which characterise the construction of this single district, containing at least twenty to thirty thousand inhabitants. And such a district exists in the heart of the second city of England, the first manufacturing city of the world. If any one wishes to see in how little space a human being can move, how little air – and *such* air – he can breathe, how little civilisation he may share and yet live, it is only necessary to travel hither. [Yet] everything which here arouses horror and indignation is of recent origin, belongs to the *industrial epoch*. The couple of hundred houses, which belong to old Manchester, have been long since abandoned by their original inhabitants; the industrial epoch alone has crammed into them the swarms of workers whom they now shelter; the industrial epoch alone has built up every spot between these old houses to win a covering for the masses whom it has conjured hither . . . , the industrial epoch alone enables the owners of these cattle-sheds to rent them for high prices to human beings, to plunder the poverty of the workers, to undermine the health of thousands, in order that they *alone*, the owners, may grow rich. In the industrial epoch alone has it become possible that the worker scarcely freed from feudal servitude could be used as mere material, a mere chattel.[4]

Engels believed that the industrial epoch had inflicted more inhumanity and debasement than slavery ever did. He quotes figures on the excesses of child labour, and scoffs at the minor relief afforded by the Factory Act of 1834, which limited the working day of nine- to thirteen-year-olds to nine hours, and to twelve hours for children between fourteen and eighteen. Children 'grow up like wild weeds,' he wrote, while their parents worked unlimited hours in conditions that few survived beyond the age of forty. Indeed of 22,094 people working in the factories he surveyed, only 126 were more than forty-five years old. And their options? None. Workhouses were supposed to provide a refuge for those without a job and unable to support themselves, but operated more to deter than attract those most in need of their services. 'If God punished men for crimes as man punishes man for poverty,' a commentator quoted by Engels declares, 'then woe to the sons of Adam!'

But cost-cutting industrialists and grasping landlords were not the only factors that Engels held responsible for the plight of England's workforce. He (and many others) also blamed the Irish, thousands of whom had been leaving their homes for England every year since the potato had begun to boost Ireland's population.[5] So England was doubly afflicted by the potato-driven population boom, having to contend with a sizeable proportion of Ireland's surplus as well as with its own. 'The Irish had nothing to lose at home, and much to gain in England,' Engels declared, 'and from the time when it became known in Ireland that the east side of St George's Channel offered steady work and good pay for strong arms, every year brought armies of the Irish hither.' More than one million had immigrated already, he declared, and the influx continued at the rate of about 50,000 per year. They were not welcome. Indeed, they were despised, as Thomas Carlyle, one of the Victorian era's most influential social commentators, made clear in 1839:

Crowds of miserable Irish darken our towns. The wild Irish features, looking false ingenuity, restlessness, unreason, misery and mockery salute you on all highways and byways. The English coachman, as he whirls past, lashes the Irishman with his whip, curses him with his tongue; the Irishman is holding out his hat to beg. He is the sorest evil this country has to strive with. In his rags and laughing savagery, he is there to undertake all work that can be done by mere strength of hand and back; for wages that will purchase him potatoes. He needs only salt for condiment; he lodges to his mind in any pighutch or doghutch, roosts in outhouses; and wears a suit of tatters, the getting off and on of which is said to be a difficult operation, transacted only in festivals and the hightides of the calendar. The Saxon man if he cannot work on these terms, finds no work. He too may be ignorant; but he has not sunk from decent manhood to squalid apehood: he cannot continue there . . . the uncivilised Irishman, not by his strength, but by the opposite of strength, drives out the Saxon native, takes possession in his room. There abides he, in his squalor and unreason, in his falsity and drunken violence, as the ready-made nucleus of degradation and disorder. . . . We have quarantines against pestilence; but there is no pestilence like that; and against it what quarantine is possible? . . . The wretchedness of Ireland, slowly but inevitably, has crept over to us, and become our own wretchedness.[6]

These were views that Engels fully endorsed:

These Irishmen who migrate for fourpence to England, on the deck of a steamship on which they are often packed like cattle, insinuate themselves everywhere. The worst dwellings are good enough for them; their clothing causes them little trouble, so long as it holds together by a single thread; shoes they know not; their food consists of potatoes and potatoes only . . . The filth and comfortlessness that prevail in the houses themselves it is impossible to describe. The Irishman is unaccustomed to the presence of furniture; a heap of straw, a few rags, utterly beyond use as clothing, suffice for his nightly couch. A piece of wood, a broken chair, an old chest for a table, more he needs not . . .[7]

What hope was there for the English working man, Engels asked, when faced 'with a competitor upon the lowest plane possible in a civilised country, who for this very reason requires less wages than any other'? Wages were forced down, and the mere presence of the Irish exercised 'a strong degrading influence upon their English companions in toil':

For when, in almost every great city, a fifth or a quarter of the workers are Irish, or children of Irish parents, who have grown up among Irish filth, no one can wonder if the life, habits, intelligence, moral status – in short, the whole character of the working-class assimilates a great part of the Irish characteristics. On the contrary, it is easy to understand how the degrading position of the English workers, engendered by our modern history, and its immediate consequences, has been still more degraded by the presence of Irish competition.[8]

But the Irish were not wholly to blame for the conditions under which they lived and worked in England – nor indeed, for the circumstances which had driven them to leave Ireland. As Carlyle magnanimously affirmed:

> We English pay, even now, the bitter smart of long centuries of injustice to our neighbour Island. Injustice, doubt it not, abounds; . . . England is guilty towards Ireland; and reaps at last, in full measure, the fruit of fifteen generations of wrong-doing.

England could not expect their 'Irish brothers' to stay at home and starve, he continued.

> It is just and natural that they come hither as a curse to us. Alas, for them too it is not a luxury. It is not a straight or joyful way of avenging their sore wrongs . . . Yet a way it is, and an effectual way. The time has come when the Irish population must either be improved a little, or else exterminated.[9]

Improvement or extermination? Carlyle was stating the options crudely, but when, seven years later, failure of the potato crops brought famine and starvation to Ireland, a vociferous body of opinion was certain that Providence was in favour of the second course of action and should be left to get on with it − without the interference of sympathy and aid from England. Alfred Smee, Surgeon to the Bank of England, Fellow of the Royal Society (and inventor of the wet-cell battery), expressed the sentiment in unequivocal terms:

> If left to itself this fearful state of things would have remedied itself: for had the people the control of their own community, and had the potato crop failed to the extent to which it has this year [1846], these people . . . would have been left to their own resources, which being destroyed would have left them without food. Millions of human beings, desperate with hunger and untutored in laws, would have devastated the country; this would have aggravated the misery, and at last large numbers would have perished of starvation, and the material relations of the survivors would have been re-established.[10]

But, as Smee notes, the Irish had a 'rich and powerful' neighbour who sympathised with their distress and was 'also desirous of alleviating their suffering'. Desirous? In fact the government had no choice. After centuries of religious, military, economic, social and political dissension, the Irish problem had acquired a humanitarian dimension of unparalleled proportions. Millions were starving; thousands were dying – all of them subjects of Queen Victoria and entitled to the care and attention of her government.

Robert Peel was Prime Minister at the time, leading a Conservative government elected principally to serve the interests of a landed gentry whose instinctive sympathies probably aligned with those of Alfred Smee. There was also the opinion of the country's powerful industrial leaders to consider; as well as that of agitators clamouring for workers' rights and fair wages; and, not least, the widespread conviction that Ireland's problem was born of its own iniquities. As Redcliffe Salaman reports, when the distress of the famine moved Queen Victoria to proclaim a day of prayer and intercession, even the prayer composed for the occasion echoed this belief. In church, chapel and synagogue alike, congregations prayed 'for the removal of those heavenly judgments which our manifold sins and provocations have most justly deserved, and with which Almighty God is pleased to visit the iniquities of the land by a grievous scarcity and dearth of divers articles of sustenance and necessaries of life.'[11]

Sir Robert Peel was described by those who knew him as deliberate in manner, careful and cautious in conversation, and possessing a singularly chilly smile, 'like the silver plate on a coffin'. The diarist Charles Greville noted that he had 'no popular or ingratiating qualities', but although it may have been difficult to like the man, it was impossible not to respect him. Conscientiousness and a sense of justice were his leading qualities, which he deployed with consummate skill as politician and administrator.[12] He had a loving wife and seven children, and a circle of close friends who cared for him deeply. When he died in 1850 at the age of sixty-two, tragically, following a fall from his horse, the nation mourned – 'from the queen to the humblest labourer' – in an entirely unexpected outburst of affection. Charles Greville remarked that while he knew Peel had a great hold on the country, he had 'no idea it was so deep and strong and general as now appears'. Carlyle wrote of the nation's 'affectionate appreciation of this man which he himself was far from being sure of, or aware of, while he lived'. The Duke of Wellington, though he could hardly speak for tears, told the House of Lords of Peel's passion for truth as though it was a quality not usually encountered among politicians. Former critics surprised even themselves. 'Once I little thought I should have cried for his death,' wrote Thomas Macaulay.[13]

As a man whose father had been one of the country's first (and richest) manufacturers of cotton cloth, already employing some 15,000 people in the 1790s and paying over £40,000 annually in government duty and taxes, Robert Peel knew a great deal about the issues affecting manufacturing prosperity, while the family's elevation to the aristocracy in 1800 – with concomitant country estate – gave him more than a passing familiarity with landed interests too. Since boyhood, Peel had been accustomed to luxury. He was a wealthy man who, after his father's death in 1830, had an income of more than £40,000 a year. His entertaining was renowned for its quality and style – twenty or thirty guests waited upon by a platoon of servants in orange and purple. A biographer reports that even the irreverent Disraeli was impressed: 'the dinner was curiously sumptuous,' he reported to his sister, 'the second course of dried olives, caviare, woodcock-pie, *foie gras*, and every combination of cured herring, etc. was really remarkable.'[14]

First intimations that Ireland was threatened with starvation as a consequence of diseased potato crops reached Peel's government in August 1845, in response to an enquiry about the likely size of the year's crop that Sir James Graham, the Home Secretary, had circulated. This was customary practice, a means of assessing the country's food supply for the coming winter, but as reports came in of 'fearful destruction' and crops 'entirely destroyed' in south-east England and around London, concern was aroused. There was news of similarly disastrous outbreaks on the Isle of Wight, and in Belgium, Holland and France.

'A fatal malady has broken out among the potato crop,' the respected *Gardeners' Chronicle* declared on 23 August. 'On all sides we hear of the destruction that has overtaken this valuable product, excepting in the north of England. In Belgium the fields are said to have been entirely desolated; there is hardly a sound sample in Covent Garden Market . . .' The authorities knew that if the destruction spread to the north and farther afield the consequences would be calamitous; three weeks later their worst fears were confirmed. Printing of the *Gardeners' Chronicle* for 12 September was interrupted to insert the news: 'We stop the Press with very great regret to announce that the Potato Murrain [or Pestilence] has unequivocally declared itself in Ireland. The crops around Dublin are suddenly perishing . . . where will Ireland be, in the event of a universal potato rot?'[15] Where, indeed?

For the next week or two it was still possible to hope. The government received a number of favourable reports on the situation in Ireland, and in early October the Home Secretary felt confident enough to record his belief 'that the potato crop, tho' damaged, is not so much below the average as some of the exaggerated reports from Ireland have led us to apprehend'. Meanwhile, all officers of the Irish Constabulatory had been directed to make weekly reports on the state of crops in their districts, and their news was not good. Harvest-time came, and there were few constables who could report anything other than total loss of the potato crop.

With the Lord-Lieutenant of Ireland, Lord Heytesbury, reporting from Dublin that the situation was serious and required the government's immediate attention, Peel dispatched a scientific commission to investigate – Dr John Lindley, the botanist (and editor of the *Gardeners' Chronicle*), and two professors of chemistry, Dr Lyon Playfair and Sir Robert Kane. They lost no time; indeed, no great depth of investigation was required for them to conclude that half of Ireland's potato crop was either destroyed already or soon would be. 'The account is melancholy and it cannot be looked upon in other than a serious light,' Playfair wrote to Peel in late October. 'We are confident that the accounts are under-rated rather than exaggerated . . . I am sorry to give you so desponding a letter, but we cannot conceal from ourselves that the case is much worse than the public supposes.'[16]

Meanwhile, Peel and his Home Secretary, Sir James Graham, were exchanging views on how mass starvation in Ireland could be relieved if the potato crop was completely destroyed. Peel reviewed the options in a memorandum of 13 October 1845, concluding that corn would have to be provided and, therefore, 'The removal of impediments to import is the only effectual remedy.' On the same day, Graham advised Peel that:

Indian corn might be obtained from the United States readily, and on cheap terms, [but] if we open the ports to maize duty-free, most popular and irresistible arguments present themselves why flour and oatmeal, the staple of the food of man, should . . . be restricted in its supply by artificial means, while Heaven has withheld from an entire people its accustomed sustenance. Could we with propriety remit duties . . .? Can these duties, once remitted . . ., be ever again imposed? Ought they to be maintained with their present stringency, if the people of Ireland be reduced to the last extremity for want of food?[17]

The impediments to which Peel referred and Graham alluded were the Corn Laws which imposed a custom duty on imported grain to ensure that it could never be cheaper than the home-grown product. This kept prices artificially high and, as Graham pointed out, relaxing the duty in order to feed the starving Irish would inevitably provoke demands that England's impoverished families should enjoy the same benefits.

Corn Laws of one form or another had been in operation for centuries. They were designed to guarantee the incomes of the landowners whose substantial estates produced most of the country's wheat and other cereals (known collectively as corn). Duties were imposed on imported corn – and imports permitted only when shortages and demand had raised prices of the home product to a predetermined level. Thus imports would always be more expensive than home-grown corn; consumers were denied access to any cheaper markets; and since only exceptionally good harvests were ever enough to satisfy local demand, country gentlemen could expect handsome returns from their land-holdings so long as the Corn Laws were retained.

The founding assumption of the Corn Laws was that production of this staple food must always be a viable endeavour, so that until producers had covered their costs and were receiving enough profit to make the effort worthwhile, consumers had no right to expect a reduction in the cost of food – which may have been justifiable in previous centuries, when 90 per cent of the population worked on the land, and were largely self-supporting. A degree of protection then helped to attract investment in the development of large-scale agricultural enterprises – and the benefits doubtless percolated through the national economy. But in the nineteenth century, as industrialisation proceeded apace, as more people bought their food than grew their own, the injustice of the Corn Laws became glaringly apparent: when cheap corn could be imported from the continent, the Baltic, Canada and America, why was England's bread sold at prices that made it a luxury item?

Though potatoes had taken over from grain as the food of the poor in Ireland, and had gained favour among England's working class too, the yearning for bread – as an Englishman's right – remained strong enough to split the country on the issue of the Corn Laws. Support for them was deeply entrenched among the landowners and Conservative members of parliament, but opposition was equally strong among the country's rapidly expanding workforce, and soon their employers also began clamouring for the laws to be repealed – aware that it would not only mean cheap food and less demand for higher wages, but would also open the way to free trade generally and thus give manufacturers access to cheaper raw materials, and wider markets. The Manchester Chamber of Commerce formally petitioned Parliament and in a parallel move to consolidate opposition in a single movement, the Anti-Corn Law League was formed in 1838 under the political leadership of Richard Cobden and John Bright, both of whom were cotton manufacturers.

The League launched a strenuous campaign of agitation and publicity, but as they mobilised support around the country, Parliament – a 'fortress of traditions and vested rights' – closed ranks. The numbers against repeal were formidable. Even after the changes the Reform Bill of 1832 had made in favour of manufacturing and middle-class interests, nine out of ten seats in the House of Commons were held by representatives of the landlords, while the House of Lords consisted of nothing but powerful landowners.[18] It was stalemate. Though a majority in the country were crying out for the repeal on both humanitarian and economic grounds, even those in Parliament who privately agreed with the proposition (and there were more than a few) dared not speak out for fear of enraging their minority constituencies. Short of civil war, no issue in English history has provoked such passion as Corn Law repeal, Cecil Woodham-Smith remarked.[19] But no senior politician was willing to assume the risk of sponsoring repeal. Then, as John Bright later wrote, 'Famine itself, against which we had warred, joined us.'[20]

As yet, many politicians did not take reports of Ireland's failing potato crop seriously. But by late October 1845 Peel and Graham were in no doubt and already noting that a ruined crop one year would lead to a dearth of seed potatoes the next, and thus a continuation of the need for food relief. Peel confronted his colleagues with the dilemma at a Cabinet meeting held on Saturday, 1 November:

> Shall we maintain unaltered –
> Shall we modify –
> Shall we suspend – the operation of the Corn Laws?
> Can we vote public money for the sustenance for any consider-
> able portion of the people on account of actual or apprehended
> scarcity, and maintain in full operation the existing restrictions on
> the free import of grain?
> I am bound to say that we cannot . . .[21]

The logic was inescapable: Ireland required relief on an unprecedented scale, and for many months to come, but to spend public money on relief while protection kept prices artificially high was unfair to consumers in England, who were obliged to pay inflated prices. Peel felt this was intolerable – but his colleagues in the Conservative government felt differently. 'The Cabinet by a very considerable majority declined giving its assent to the proposals which I thus made to them. They were supported by only three members,' he wrote. But persuasive tactics were applied and at a meeting later that month all but two of the Cabinet agreed with Peel's proposal. Most importantly, the Duke of Wellington, leader of the House of Lords and one of the more conservative cabinet members, had changed his mind – not because he had been persuaded that the Corn Laws should be repealed, but because he believed the government would fall if Peel failed to get his way. Ireland's 'rotten potatoes have done it all', he confided to a friend; 'they put Peel in his damned fright', and his country gentlemen looked on aghast.[22] He prepared a more moderate memorandum for the Cabinet:

> I am one of those who think the continuance of the Corn Laws essential to the agriculture of the country in its existing state and particularly to that of Ireland ... [but a] good Government for the country is more important than Corn Laws or any other consideration; and as long as Sir Robert Peel possesses the confidence of the Queen and of the public, and he has the strength to perform the duties, his administration of the Government must be supported .. . I earnestly recommend that the Cabinet should support him, and I for one declare that I will do so.[23]

With the Cabinet on his side there was now Parliament to convince – including the many members of Peel's own party who remained implacably opposed to repeal. News of Peel's intention had been leaked to the press, provoking accusations of betrayal. In Parliament and on landed estates throughout the country, none had forgotten that less than six months before Peel had specifically opposed what he now intended to propose. The occasion had been a debate on the motion calling for total abolition of the Corn Laws that was put before Parliament each year; it was an annual event, and so certain to be defeated that senior members of the government hardly needed to attend, let alone speak. But Peel himself, the Prime Minister, had spoken out against the motion. Standing at the Despatch Box he had announced that 'Considering the great importance of the subject, and the position in which I stand, I am unwilling to give a silent vote upon the immediate question before the House,' and proceeded with a disquisition which – it must be said – was not so much in support of the Corn Laws as against the arguments for its repeal. 'I shall give my decided vote against the proposition,' he concluded. The motion was defeated by a majority of 132.[24]

That was in June 1845; now it was January 1846, and the people of Ireland were starving. Peel in effect was using the Irish crisis[25] as justification for a radical shift in policy that was as significant in its time as the Battle of Hastings or Magna Carta. Repeal of the Corn Laws ushered in the era of free trade that established the viability of England's industrial economy in the late nineteenth century; in fact, it marked a crucial point in England's transformation from a small agricultural nation into a wealthy industrial power. This was historic in its own right, but also an outstanding instance of a major political event being brought about by the potato.

Peel himself denied that 'it was the resistless hand of famine in Ireland which had brought him to his resolve that the Corn Laws ought to be abolished', claiming that 'he grew into the conviction that they were bad in principle'. Maybe so, but one of his contemporaries felt it probable that if the Irish famine had not threatened, the moment for introducing the legislation might have been indefinitely postponed,[26] and it is certainly true that Peel's eloquent speeches drew heavily on the news from Ireland as a means of persuading a reluctant Parliament to vote for abolition, culminating in a masterful outburst from the Despatch Box on 27 March 1846:

Are you to hesitate in averting famine which may come, because it possibly may not come? Are you to look to and depend upon chance in such an extremity? Or, good God! Are you to sit in cabinet, and consider and calculate how much diarrhoea, and bloody flux, and dysentery, a people can bear before it becomes necessary for you to provide them with food? The precautions may be superfluous; but what is the danger where precautions are required? Is it not better to err on the side of precaution than to neglect it utterly?[27]

The Bill abolishing the Corn Laws (with compensation for affected landowners) was passed in May 1846 by a majority of 98 – with two-thirds of the governing Conservatives voting against it and the entire opposition voting in favour. An even more remarkable turnaround was achieved in the House of Lords (which could have vetoed the Bill), where the Duke of Wellington converted a majority of the country gentlemen to his belief that the security of a good government was more important than the Corn Laws. And, in any case, if they did not pass the Repeal Bill now, he pointed out, the issue would only come up again in the next Parliament.[28]

While engaged with the political struggle, Peel had not neglected Ireland's distress. Even before his proposal to repeal the Corn Laws had been put before Parliament, Peel was making arrangements for grain to be shipped to the most distressed areas of Ireland. On his authority alone, without the approval of either his Cabinet or Parliament, Peel persuaded the banker Sir Thomas Baring to buy maize to the value of £100,000 from America secretly, for shipment to Ireland as the first consignment of the government's relief programme. The grain duly arrived, and distribution began in March 1846, two months before the Bill that would have authorised its duty-free importation was passed.

Ironically, within weeks of repeal the price of corn reached heights rarely seen in the days of the Corn Laws – simply because of the huge demand that relief for Ireland put on the markets. In all, England spent a total of £33 million on corn for Ireland, according to a contemporary writer quoted by Redcliffe Salaman.[29] Speculation was rife 'as the world's corn-bins were scraped for wheat, oats, rice and maize – any food-grain that the starving Irish would eat'. Dealers bought futures in corn from home and abroad at two and three times the price of a few months before (when the Corn Laws were still in place), draining the country's gold reserves and threatening the stability of the Bank of England – already under considerable strain from the financial demands of what even the most sober-minded commentators were calling Railway Mania.

The world's first commercial line had opened between Stockton and Darlington (a distance of 40 kilometers) in 1825 and, after a slow start, railways were carrying over 5 million passengers a year by the early 1840s. That figure was destined to rise twenty- and thirtyfold over the next decades.[30] The vision of what a nationwide mechanised transport system could do for an industrial economy had infected the country and over 60 per cent of England's gross domestic investment was tied up in railways during the mid-1840s, when Railway Mania was at its peak.[31] The stock market was driven to a frenzy by people gambling on the expectation of quick and easy returns.

After the first wave of railway construction, most of the projects inviting investment consisted of plans to build rail links between local towns and the main arterial routes – but adventurous speculators were looking further afield. 'They are throwing an iron girdle around the globe itself,' D. Morier Evans, a financial journalist, reported. 'Far off India woos them over its waters, and China even listens to the voice of the charmer. The ruined hills and broken altars of Old Greece will soon re-echo the whistle of the locomotive.' There was even a scheme for bringing the benefits of railway transport to the islands of the Caribbean, St Kitt's for instance: 'Fifteen miles long and four broad, with mountains in the middle, whence rivulets flow, and between high mountains dreadful rocks, horrid precipices, thick woods, and sulphurous springs . . .'[32]

The frenzy peaked in the autumn of 1845: 457 projects were registered in September alone, and another 363 in October, bringing the total for the year to 1,035. As the *Times* 'descanted upon the nation's madness', the impossibility of it all was becoming apparent. In all, 1,428 railway companies with a paper value of £701,243,208 had been registered by November. Three-quarters of them were worthless, the *Times* opined, but all:

> had their knaves or their dupes, . . . The luxuriant crop of absolute weeds affords an indication of the favour which merely unprofitable schemes have met with. It is the ridiculous amount of premium on worthless scrip, and the gullibility, or rather the voracity, of the multitude, which have prompted a crowd of adventurers to bait their hooks and cast out their nets for the prey. If there was not a very promising shoal of flats, you would not see so many fishermen abroad.[33]

The bubble burst, and prices began to tumble in October – precipitating panic and a rush to get out of the market.

> Right and left the infatuated dupes were cut down as grass under the mower's scythe . . . Persons who perchance had written and pledged their responsibility for 200 shares in a particular company, with the expectation of getting twenty, or ten or, as had been previously the case, not more than five shares, were without further prelude, honoured with the whole number first applied for.[34]

And obliged to pay for them. For many, bankruptcy was the only option and worthless companies faded away while the few viable survivors merged into companies that would henceforward dominate the industry.

Railways were of course being laid and brought into operation even as the speculative mania raged. Plans for 10,000 miles were sanctioned in the 1840s – 4,538 of them in 1846. By mid-1847, 3,907 miles of track were under construction in Britain, employing 256,509 workers and stimulating a massive increase in coal, iron and brick production – all very good for a developing industrial economy, but stretching the country's financial resources to within a whisker of breaking point. In 1847 the railways were spending £4.3 million of share capital and borrowed funds on average each month.[35]

Then, as the good fates would have it, there came news that Ireland's potato crop was doing well. Only about one-eighth of the area previously devoted to potatoes had been planted (with seed supplied by growers in Scotland, who had been spared the devastations of 1846). The weather conditions in Ireland were perfect throughout the growing season of 1847; the potatoes flourished – which restored peoples' faith in the potato and convinced most of them that the failures of previous years had been due to exceptionally wet, overcast and mild conditions. The corn harvests of 1847 also promised to be better than average, and prices tumbled in anticipation of bountiful supplies, just as the corn bought ahead months before at inflated rates began arriving in the ports.

Dealers who had gambled on prices remaining high now found themselves unable to recoup their investments and, with the banks themselves under pressure, were left with no alternative but bankruptcy. Twenty firms of substance were brought down in September with total liabilities approaching £10 million.[36] Another ninety-nine collapsed in October as the crisis spread, bringing down eleven country banks and three of the biggest in Liverpool. All the London banks survived, but every sort of commercial failure occurred as the effects of the crisis worked their way through the system – in corn, stockbroking, insurance-broking, silk dealing and all branches of overseas trade.

Bringing the crisis under control and restoring the efficacy of the financial markets was ultimately the responsibility of the Bank of England. In his history of the Bank published in 1944, Sir John Clapham writes eloquently and at length on the strategies which were adopted. Not all the Bank's actions were approved by the Treasury Committee that subsequently investigated the crisis, however, and it is on a defensive note that Sir John claims the Bank could be held only partially responsible for the calamitous state of business in 1844–7. The Bank's policies and failures may have been contributing factors, he admits, but the Bank was not responsible for the Railway Mania, nor in any way responsible for such Acts of God as crop failure and Ireland's potato famine, which, he declared, were the immediate 'causative factors' of the catastrophe of 1847.[37]

Part Three
The World

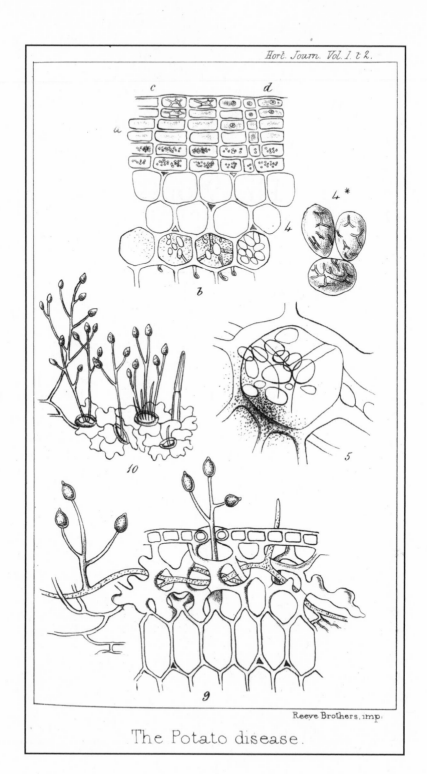

Reeve Brothers, imp.

The Potato disease.

Chapter Twelve

The fatal malady

The potato's susceptibility to disease had been a matter of concern long before the crop failures and Irish famine of 1845 and '46. A severe condition termed the 'curl' had been recorded in the 1760s and within ten years was so bad that potato cultivation through much of northern England was threatened. Similar outbreaks occurred in much of Europe. In 1770 curl caused such heavy losses in Ireland, for example, that large quantities of grain were imported to feed communities that might otherwise have starved.

Eighteenth-century farmers attributed the curl to natural degeneration, believing that any cultivated plant would inevitably revert to its wild state over a period of time, each year of propagation taking it further from the cultivated condition. But potatoes seemed to degenerate much faster than other cultivated plants – and more rapidly in some regions than in others. In the south of England, stock that produced a perfect harvest one year would be riddled with curl when its progeny was planted out the next, while farmers in the colder and more elevated regions of Scotland were untroubled by the disease. But even fresh stock from Scotland was only good for a year or so in the south. 'In 1798 I planted 6 acres with potatoes of this Scotch seed; there was scarcely a curled plant amongst them', an English farmer reported, but 'the following year, about an acre and a half was planted with the produce of these very potatoes, and at least one-sixth of the whole was curled.'[1]

We now know that curl and other similar conditions are the consequence of viral infection, the viruses having been spread through the crops by sap-feeding aphids, or greenfly. Scotch seed potatoes were free of viruses because aphids do not thrive in the colder north, but a second generation planted in the south was certain to be colonised and thus infected with a viral disease. Lacking such knowledge, eighteenth-century farmers blamed degeneration. The solution, respected authorities suggested, would be to acquire some of the wild stock from which the cultivated potato had been derived and start breeding afresh. Indeed, the Royal Horticultural Society was founded with this course of action among its priorities. On 2 April 1805 the prospective President, Thomas Knight, addressed the inaugural meeting of the society:[2]

> Were it possible to ascertain the primeval state of those vegetables which now occupy the attention of the gardener and agriculturist, . . . and could we trace out the various changes which art or accident has, in successive generations, produced in each, few inquiries would be more extensively interesting . . .
>
> We . . . know that improved flowers and fruits are the necessary produce of improved culture; and that the offspring, in a greater or less degree, inherits the character of its parent. The austere Crab of our woods has thus been converted into the Golden Pippin; and numerous varieties of the Plumb, can boast no other parent than our native sloe . . . We may therefore infer, with little danger of error, that an ample and unexplored field for future discovery and improvement lies before us, in which nature does not appear to have formed any limits to the success of our labours, if properly applied.
>
> But we possess no sources from which sufficient information to direct us in our inquiries can be derived; and are still ignorant of the native country, and existence in a wild state, of some of the most important of our plants.

The potato was foremost among the plants to which the Society directed attention, but progress on the acquisition of fresh stock was thwarted by a paucity of information on wild potatoes. It was certain that the cultivated potato had initially been brought from South America by the Spanish in the sixteenth century – but precisely *where* its wild antecedents might be acquired in the nineteenth century remained a matter of speculation.

Wild forms were said to have been seen growing in Chile; but Alexander von Humboldt, who had crossed the Andes from east to west in the course of his South American explorations (1799–1804), reported that while the cultivated potato occurred in all the temperate regions of South America,[3] the wild potato was not indigenous to Peru or any part of the tropical Cordilleras; nor had he seen or heard of it in Mexico or the south-western region of North America.[4]

Humboldt was seriously (and uncharacteristically) misleading in respect of the wild potato, for the numerous species occur throughout the region and must have been there in Humboldt's day too – we can only assume he missed them.

Meanwhile, Thomas Knight drew attention to how rapidly the potato was becoming established as the staple food of England's agricultural workforce. In 1765 their diet consisted of bread, cheese and garden produce (mainly cabbage), he reported,[5] but within ten years the potato had become dominant. An acre of potatoes could provide as much food as 8 acres of wheat or forty of pasture, Knight told a meeting of the Horticultural Society in 1810[6] – and the good news was that the potato had brought about a considerable improvement in general health; people were living longer. But there were grounds for concern here too. With chilling prescience Knight expressed alarm at the rate by which the population was expanding on the basis of the potato, especially in Ireland.

The Society's secretary, Joseph Sabine, subsequently enlarged upon these concerns, noting in 1822 that, with the exception of wheat and rice, the potato had become (on a world basis) 'the vegetable most employed as the food of Man', with a prospect of soon becoming the chief staple of life. This could lead to a great extension of the population, he told the Society,[7] though not necessarily to an increase in happiness since the potato was 'very liable to injury from casualties of season' and could not be stored for more than a few months. He warned that 'a general failure of the year's crop, whenever it shall have become the chief or sole support of a country, must inevitably lead to all the misery of famine, more dreadful in proportion to the numbers exposed to its ravages.'

Sabine urged the Society to locate and import fresh stock, with the intention of 'selecting and obtaining varieties of Potatoes, not only with superior qualities in flavour and productiveness, but which shall be less subject to injury by changes of weather when in growth, and which may possess the quality of keeping for a length of time . . .' Correspondents in the Americas were informed of the Society's quest, and several batches of wild and cultivated potatoes duly arrived from Chile, Peru and Mexico during the 1820s, '30s and '40s. They flourished in the Society's gardens, but attempts to improve Europe's cultivated potato by crossing it with wild species foundered – chiefly because the wild species being used were completely sterile.[8]

Attempts to turn the wild potatoes themselves into a cultivated form by growing them in rich soil with plenty of manure and other fertilisers were equally unsuccessful. The plants flourished well enough, forming dense bushes smothered with flowers, but tubers were few, none 'larger than the seed of kidney beans'.[9]

By then, though, the tragedy Thomas Knight had warned of more than thirty years before had become a reality and the Royal Horticultural Society's efforts to find and breed potatoes capable of withstanding the onslaughts of disease were dimmed to insignificance by the catastrophe in Ireland.

Although the potato disease had taken all Europe by surprise in 1845, it had already been ravaging the potato crops of North America for two seasons by then. The first outbreaks occurred in 1843, close to ports on the east coast of the United States, around Philadelphia and New York, and by the end of the season the disease had been reported from along 300 kilometres of coastline and to a distance of 600 kilometres inland. The following year it advanced roughly 150 kilometres on all fronts, and crossed lakes Erie and Ontario to devastate farms over the Canadian border. In 1845 it advanced another 400 kilometres west to the Mississippi, and 300 kilometres north to the Gulf of St Lawrence. In just three seasons, the disease had spread from a few farms along the east coast to infect every farm in a swathe of territory that extended 2,500 kilometres from Illinois in the west to Nova Scotia in the east, and 1,000 kilometres from Virginia in the south to Ontario in the north.[10] Then it crossed the Atlantic.

At first it was believed that if the disease had an external cause, it probably had been introduced from the west coast of South America with the guano (concentrated sea-bird droppings) that farmers in America and Europe began using as fertilisers in the 1830s. In the 1990s, however, the centre of origin and diversity of the organism responsible for the disease was traced to a valley in the highlands of central Mexico.[11] It is believed to have migrated from there to South America several centuries ago, and from South America to the United States in 1841–2 with a consignment of potatoes – the development of steam-powered ships and the use of ice to prevent deterioration having facilitated the development of an international trade in potatoes by then.

While America was suffering the first outbreaks of the new disease in 1843, farmers in West Flanders, Belgium's main area of potato production, were contending with the persistence of old foes. Their stock had become badly affected with what are now known to be viral diseases and dry rot. Harvests were poor and so, in an effort to restore the crop's vitality, the Provincial Council authorised the importation of fresh seed potatoes from America.[12] Fatefully, the shipments that crossed the Atlantic during the winter of 1843–4 included a significant number of infected tubers.

The disease was not prevalent enough to arouse concern in Europe in 1844, but a warm damp spring and early summer enabled it to build up to epidemic proportions in 1845. First reports of its devastations came from the Courtrai area of Belgium, about 100 kilometres south-west of Antwerp, towards the end of June 1845. By mid-July, it was all over Flanders, and had appeared in neighbouring parts of the Netherlands and France as well. The disease was moving fast, but its extension to the east was blocked at first by the Ardennes, and it did not appear in Luxembourg and eastward until it had flanked the mountains from north to south. First reports of its appearance in the vicinity of Paris appeared in mid-August and by then it was also present in the lower Rhineland, north-west France, the Channel Islands and southern England. By mid-September it had spread to Denmark, through England and Wales to the borders of Scotland and across the Irish Sea to the eastern counties of Ireland. By mid-October it reached Connemara and the devastation of Europe's potato crops was complete. At its maximum range, the disease had infected an area that stretched 1,600 kilometres from the western shores of Ireland to northern Italy, and 1,800 kilometres from northern Spain to the southern tips of Norway and Sweden – potato farms across more than 2 million square kilometres of land laid waste in just four months. Nothing like it had been known before. Neither the Vandal hordes nor the bubonic plague had penetrated Europe so deeply and so fast.

The disease had brought famine to Ireland, prompting a relief programme which, for its time, was truly 'the grandest attempt ever made to grapple with famine over a whole country',[13] but the failure of the potato crop had been a disaster for every farmer, market gardener and family in Europe that relied on potatoes in some way and hadn't either an alternative to turn to or some savings to fall back on. Only a few of Europe's potato-growers were unaffected. There is no way of knowing how much they contributed to the £1.5 million that public appeals raised for Irish relief, but doubtless the publicity left them feeling aggrieved at the lack of government attention to their plight. It is all very well providing relief for current distress, they might have said, but what about us, and the future of the potato? A catastrophe of these proportions calls for action on its cause as well as its consequences. What is this disease? Where had it come from? Can it be cured or eliminated, or must farmers be forever in fear of future visitations? But these were not issues the British government felt obliged to concern itself with.

For all that the potato famine and repeal of the Corn Laws had eased the importation of grain for Irish relief, a more enduring function had been to enshrine the doctrine of free trade. Despite the commercial crisis, free trade and a virtual global monopoly of manufacturing was hastening Britain's economic growth to the extent that more than scant attention to a potato disease was unlikely. Among the people whose opinions affected national policy, there was such conviction that industrialisation would be the making of a Great Britain, such determination to forge – literally – the country's future from its own coal, iron, muscle and brains, that the centuries-old link between food production and national well-being was weakening. In that era of *laissez-faire*, a new concept of self-sufficiency was spawned: what we cannot grow we will buy – in exchange for kettles, cotton cloth, locomotives and so forth. And if there was to be *laissez-faire* for the manufacturers, merchants and bankers, why not *laissez-faire* for potato diseases too – and for anyone who might feel inclined to investigate the nature of the disease, or search for a cure.

There was no ministry of agriculture, no government agency with the authority and the funds to assign a team of consultants to the problem, nor any form of government service that could study the disease and offer recommendations for its prevention, or cure. In the more paternalistic times of the 1790s there had been an official Board of Agriculture, under whose auspices Arthur Young for instance had reviewed the state of agriculture in Ireland, but that had been motivated by the personal enthusiasm of its founders, and as they became less active, so did the Board. It was dissolved in 1822, and re-established in 1889, but not until 1907 did an Act of Parliament actually authorise it to appoint technical inspectors who would monitor and report on the health of the nation's crops.[14]

It might have been possible for the Royal Agricultural Society, founded in 1840, to investigate the potato disease, but its activities were severely limited by a clause in the Society's charter which 'regulated their purposes by the strictest exclusions from their councils of every question of discussion having a political tendency'. The clause probably suited the Society's council and members rather well, since they consisted primarily of noble personages and the landed gentry, whose attitude towards farming was generally that of landlord towards respectful tenant – conservative, patronising and dictatorial[15] – and their attitude towards Ireland not overly sympathetic.

The Royal Agricultural Society did good work in the breeding of improved livestock, the use of fertilisers, and in raising the levels of agricultural productivity generally; it organised an annual agricultural show, and published papers on subjects such as land tenure and the working conditions of labourers, but its interest in crop diseases and their cure or prevention was slight. The Society offered a prize for essays on the potato disease, winning entries to be published in the *Journal of the Royal Agricultural Society*, but in truth showed little awareness of either the seriousness of the issue or the effort required to investigate and combat it.

The Royal Horticultural Society and more scientifically oriented bodies, such as the Royal and the Linnaean societies, were similarly limited in their concern for the potato disease – all of them distanced from it by rarified demeanour and the irregularity of their meetings and publications. None reached out to the people who actually worked the soil, and lived directly from it. The *Gardeners' Chronicle*, on the other hand, did just that and farmers and market gardeners looked to its pages for information on the potato disease and what could be done about it. A weekly paper launched in 1841, the *Gardeners' Chronicle* was edited by John Lindley, professor of botany and leader of the three-man commission Robert Peel sent to report on the disease when it struck Ireland in 1845.

The first announcements of the 'fatal malady' appeared in the *Gardeners' Chronicle* of 17 August 1845 and prompted many of its readers to write in with reports of the disease and requests for advice on its treatment; Lindley's reply in the next week's issue was blunt:

As to cure for this distemper – there is none. One of our correspondents is angry at our not telling the public how to stop it; but he ought to consider that man has no power to arrest the dispensations of Providence. We are visited by a great calamity; which we must bear. . . . Should we have fine weather, the disease will probably disappear; should rain and cold continue, it will spread.

Lindley was certain that the wet, cold and cheerless summer of 1845 was to blame:

During the present season . . . the Potatoes have been compelled to absorb an unusual quantity of water; the lowness of temperature has prevented their digesting it, and the absence of sunlight has rendered it impossible for them to get rid of it by perspiration. Under these circumstances it necessarily stagnated in their interior; and the inevitable result of that was rot . . . If we had had sunlight with the rain it would not have happened; and, perhaps it would not have occurred had the temperature been high, instead of low, even although the sun did not shine, and rain fell incessantly. It is the combination of untoward circumstances that has produced the mischief.[16]

Thanks to Lindley's prestige and influence, the weather theory (which had already been advanced on the continent) found widespread favour in England. The Royal Agricultural Society awarded all three of its prizes for essays on the potato disease to supporters of a meteorological cause, one prize-winner enthusiastically describing how:

The potato was not the only vegetable affected – the ash, the oak, the poplar, the hazel, the vine, the apple, the pear, and the plum, but more particularly, the walnut, the French bean, mangold wurzel, carrots and turnips suffered alike. We have a walnut tree here generally remarkable for the firmness of its fruit; yet . . . there was not one nut with the least symptom of a healthy kernel, the leaves exhibiting the same appearance as that of the potato.[17]

But while the majority of early commentators held the weather responsible, other opinions were expressed too. An eruption of pamphlets broke out all over Western Europe, written by physicians, surgeons, botanists, noblemen, chemists, geologists, excisemen, gardeners and accountants; even a country housewife added her words of wisdom. Some argued that the disease was merely another step in the progressive deterioration of the potato resulting from the repeated cultivation of the same stock. Others blamed insects or worms. Another group opted for a poisonous 'miasma' borne on the air, variously attributing it to industrial pollution, volcanic exhalations, the gases from recently introduced sulphur matches, or 'some aerial taint originating in outer space'.[18]

Meanwhile in Belgium, a churchman and keen amateur mycologist (one who studies fungi), the Abbé Edouard van den Hecke, had been examining diseased potato leaves under high magnification. On them he found a fungus whose ability to produce and disperse large numbers of microscopic spores made it likely, he concluded, to have caused the disease. The Abbé's observations were reported in a series of newspaper articles that appeared in late July and August 1845, and they were confirmed by the follow-up investigations of several reputable scientists. A defining moment came in late August, when a leading agronomist, Dr Rene Van Oye, unreservedly claimed that the one true determining cause of the potato disease was a fungus which, reproducing itself with astonishing rapidity and profuseness, had infected all the potato fields and was clearly contagious.[19] Charles Morren, a hyperactive professor of physics who had qualified as a medical doctor in his spare time and whose enthusiasm for botany was such that a new chair of botany, agriculture and forestry had been created specifically for him at Liège university, went further, declaring that a mould fungus 'having seeds finer than the dust motes in the atmosphere' was spreading amongst the potatoes and causing the rot.[20]

The Belgian findings and reports, coming so soon after the first onset of the disease in Europe, should have focused attention on the fungus as its cause, and thereby could have laid an early foundation for research that might ultimately defeat the disease. Unfortunately, however, the findings provoked controversy, stirring up the passionate divisions of an argument that had been hampering the advance of natural science for centuries: was there, or was there not, such a thing as spontaneous generation?

No authoritative figure in the 1840s believed, as the ancients had, that fireflies were the product of morning dew, that eels came from rotting seaweed and mice from moist soil, but there were still many who believed that living organisms could arise spontaneously from dead or inorganic matter. The fungus found on disease-stricken potatoes was a classic example, they said. It could only have arisen, spontaneously, from the decaying material of the plant. It was a consequence of the disease, not its cause. Alfred Smee, whose opinion of the Irish has already been mentioned, published his opinion on this issue too – the fungi never appear until some part of the potato plant is already dead, he wrote:

> then these vegetable parasites appear, their function a wonderful example of natural economy . . . as the carrion crow, the vulture and the jackal, the maggot, the beetle and the wasp may do much towards the removal of dead animal matter; yet to the vegetable parasite is

left the duty of annihilating the exhalations of putrifying vegetables.[21]

The concept of spontaneous generation was at the core of the Christian belief: life itself was a Divine creation. By the 1840s, science had
already stripped away several layers of dogma and what remained was
a very sensitive issue indeed – to be handled delicately, as Charles
Darwin himself indicated in a letter to Alfred Wallace: spontaneous
generation, he admitted tactfully, would be a 'discovery of transcendent
importance' if it really were proved.[22] Charles's grandfather, Erasmus,
had been a firm believer – even setting the concept to verse:

> Hence without parent by spontaneous birth,
> Rise the first specks of animated earth.
> From Nature's womb the plant or insect swims,
> And buds or breathes, with microscopic limbs.[23]

But Charles, as a scientist then assembling evidence for a theory of
evolution that would shake Creationist beliefs for ever, and doubtless
aware of the fury that his theory would arouse, was understandably
cautious on the issue of spontaneous generation. And almost totally
silent on the furious debate which had erupted around the question
of whether a fungus was the cause or the consequence of the potato
disease. He wrote sympathetically to a senior colleague who had sent
him several printed notices on the matter, remarking that it was, indeed,
'a painfully interesting subject' which was causing great distress among
the poor of the parish and had also rotted a good many of his own
potatoes.[24] But with an income of £1,000 a year his household could
get by without potatoes and Darwin's independence left him comfortably shielded from any need to take sides on the issue.

For those lacking such privileges, or whose position and advancement came at the whim of their superiors, there was little incentive to
argue with the majority view. A few idiosyncratic thinkers accepted
the evidence from Belgium, but the organised ranks of science and, in
particular, the learned societies (always staunch supporters of orthodox
opinion), stood firm in their distrust of novelty. By the end of 1845,
those willing to speak out in favour of a fungus having caused the
potato disease had dwindled to an insignificant few. Indeed, at the 1846
meetings of the British Association for the Advancement of Science in
Southampton, the one point on which virtually everyone agreed was

that a fungus was not responsible. 'That the fungi were the cause had now been disproved by the best chemists,' the zoologist E. Ray Lankaster declared, and the chemist on whose observations that declaration was based, Dr E. Solly, announced that the fungal theory 'had lost ground, latterly, very materially'. The notion that fungi were the cause of the disease had been abandoned by everyone who mattered, journals reported, in favour of the contention that it was the effect – as 'practical men' had known all along. In France too the argument that fungi caused the disease was 'almost completely abandoned'.[25]

But while argument faded, dedicated mycologists had continued to study the fungus, recording and exchanging information among themselves, almost as though they occupied a parallel universe. That the fungus might be instrumental in causing famine and loss of life gave their investigations added importance, but the mycologists were interested in the fungus principally for its own sake; and two of them in particular were fortunate enough to occupy positions that enabled them to pursue their passion without having to consider other opinions or demands. In France there was Jean François Camille Montagne, a surgeon in Napoleon's armies who had returned from the wars with a determination to devote the rest of his life to the peaceful labour of searching out and describing the cryptogamic (non-flowering) flora of France. And in England there was the Reverend Miles Joseph Berkeley, a country parson of retiring nature whose ministering to the few hundred souls of King's Cliffe in Northamptonshire left ample time for the pursuit of a life-long interest in the fungi.

A principal attraction of botanical science, it has to be said, is that whoever discovers and describes a plant that is new to science has the privilege of giving it a name. There is no suggestion that a race for nomenclatural precedence had drawn attention to the new and mysterious fungus which appeared on Europe's potato crops in June 1845, but the speed at which the mycologists got to work and disseminated their findings was nonetheless remarkable.

First reports of the Abbé Edouard van den Hecke's observations concerning the fungus he had seen on diseased potato leaves were published on 31 July 1845. Rene Van Oye had spoken on 18 August. The following day, the *Journal de Liège* published a letter, written on 14 August, from a cultured lady of leisure and self-taught mycologist of international repute, Anne-Marie Libert. She gave a clear and detailed description of the fungus but mistakenly believed it was identical to one already known, *Botrytis farinacea*. Nonetheless, she proposed that in view of the devastation it was causing the species name should be changed to *vastatrix* (the Latin word *vastare* means to lay waste). Charles Morren published his account on the same day and was gratified to see it distributed, translated and reprinted throughout Europe with remarkable speed – most significantly, it was published in Paris on 21 August, where it was seen by Jean Montagne.[26]

Montagne was then completing his examination of diseased potato foliage he had received three days earlier from a grower on the outskirts of Paris, and had already written to the Reverend Berkeley, enclosing specimens and a description of the fungus he would publish on 30 August, naming it *Botrytis infestans*. Montagne's letter arrived at the vicarage in King's Cliffe on the 26th. Up to that date, Berkeley had not seen the disease *in situ*, though the *Gardeners' Chronicle* had published reports of its occurrence in the south. A day or two after receiving Montagne's letter and specimens, however, the disease made a dramatic appearance in the potato fields around King's Cliffe. Berkeley lost no time, and the *Gardeners' Chronicle* of 6 September carried his report declaring that the fungus *Botrytis infestans* Mont. was responsible for the potato disease; thereby confirming Montagne's claim to the honour of naming a new species.

But John Lindley would have none of it; he published Berkeley's reports, as any responsible editor should, but he and influential botanists throughout Europe still refused to believe the fungus was the cause of the disease. The potatoes were swollen with water they could not eliminate, they said. Some putrefaction or incipient decay had set in, and *then* the fungus appeared to feed on the diseased plant. Or degeneration had become universal and predisposed the potatoes to attack in what had been an abnormal growing season. Or some unstable constituents of the plants were disturbed by electricity, or corrupted by the inclement weather . . . Something went wrong. The essence of all these contentions was that the *Botrytis* could not have established itself unless the plants were already debilitated and lacking the power to resist the agent of its decay.

The retiring Reverend Berkeley responded as any responsible scientist should: he settled down to study the fungus and prepare a thorough report. Occupying thirty-five pages, and accompanied by four plates of coloured engravings, the results were published in 1846 in the first volume of the *Journal of the Horticultural Society* (later it became the Royal Horticultural Society). Though undoubtedly worthy of full and proper consideration, Berkeley's report appeared just as support for the fungal theory sank to its lowest ebb. It attracted none of the immediate attention it deserved, though it was, in fact, the instigating work of a career that established Berkeley as the founding father of phytopathology, plant pathology – the discipline that aims to identify the organisms responsible for plant diseases and understand the manner by which they operate. Berkeley's paper on the potato disease was the beginning of what is today a huge and indispensable part of the agricultural industry.

To the naked eye, the fungus that appeared on the potato leaves looked like just a fringe of white down, spreading in a widening circle from an almost invisible spot of decay, but within that fringe Berkeley's microscope revealed a veritable forest of exceedingly fine, semi-transparent, branching filaments, with root-strands (the mycelium or spawn of the fungus) piercing the surface of the leaf (the epidermis) and going through the tightly packed 'palisade' cells that give a leaf much of its strength, and into the leaf's delicate interior – an area of thin-walled cells, separated by air-spaces which in turn are connected to the multitude of minute pores (*stomata* from the Greek for 'mouths') via which the leaf 'breathes'.

The moist and spongy interior of the leaf is where the plant manufactures its food. It is normally a clean and healthy place; bathed in air and light; absorbing the nutrients and gases the plant needs and giving off the water vapour and gaseous waste products of its living processes. Through his microscope, Berkeley watched the fungus moving in, colonising the living tissue and sending up more downy filaments as it matured. The filaments twisted and writhed their way to the stomata, emerging with spore-cases on their tips, like fruit, from which the spores or 'seeds' of the fungus were forcibly ejected: thousands from a single infection, floating on air, infinitesimally small and each capable of initiating a fresh infection. And reproduction was fast: one spore could produce 100,000 progeny in just four days.

It was clear that the fungus, weaving its tentacles through, among and between the delicate cells of a leaf's interior was lethal – it *was* the disease. If we imagine our lungs and digestive systems being destroyed by loathsome growths that sent weird and colourless seaweeds issuing from our mouth and nostrils, tipped with pustules that then burst to spread their evil infection among our neighbours, we have a crude idea of how a potato plant felt when its leaves were mouldy with *Botrytis infestans* Mont.

The Reverend Berkeley indulged in no such fancy, but his report and illustrations made it absolutely clear that the fungus derived its nourishment and grew from the living tissue of the potato plant. It was a parasite that attacked the living plant and killed it. The fungus was the *cause*, not the *consequence* of what by now was generally referred to as the potato blight (specifically late blight, to distinguish it from a similar but far less destructive disease that occurred early in the season – early blight). But although a firm believer, the Reverend was no missionary when it came to expressing his scientific convictions – his moderate tone was as likely to deter as to persuade:

> . . . after an attentive consideration of the progress of the disease and of almost everything of value that has been written on the subject, and after duly weighing the peculiar difficulties with which it is attended, I must candidly confess, that with a becoming share of philosophic doubt where such authorities are ranged upon the opposite side, I believe the fungal theory to be the true one.[27]

The 'peculiar difficulties' to which Berkeley alluded were of course the contrary opinions which he knew would greet his findings. Opponents of the fungal theory could argue – and did – that Berkeley's exemplary demonstration of the fungus's parasitic behaviour did not actually *prove* that it had caused the disease. For that he must show where the fungus had come from, and how it had managed to overcome a healthy plant's natural defences. In the absence of such evidence the majority opinion continued to believe that *Botrytis infestans* Mont. was generated, spontaneously, from the decaying effusions of an already sick potato plant. It was a judgement that Berkeley had to accept for a long time. Even ten years after the first appearance of blight in Europe he was still writing with circumspection on the subject, as his contribution to the *Cyclopedia of Agriculture* (1855) demonstrates:

> There are two theories which, in the present position of the subject, seems to us tenable . . . and although we are certainly disposed to lay the greatest stress upon the [fungal theory], . . . we acknowledge that there are great difficulties about it, and such as to make it far from becoming to speak dogmatically.[28]

Today, the experiment that resolved the difficulties seems so obvious that one wonders what took them so long. After all, the idea of taking two pots of healthy potatoes and inoculating one with the fungus and observing that it decayed while the other thrived required no sudden flash of inspiration. That sort of experiment had been done before, most famously in the 1660s, when Francesco Redi set out some cuts of meat, variously covered and uncovered, and reported that maggots appeared only where flies had been able to settle. That was one of the first blows science had dealt to the concept of spontaneous generation – proving that complex organisms did not arise spontaneously from decaying matter. Two hundred years later, the French botanist Anton de Bary would employ the same strategy in investigations of the potato blight which proved, beyond doubt, that even the simplest organisms didn't either.

Inoculating a healthy plant and observing its decay was only the final and most visible aspect of de Bary's investigations. He began where the Reverend Berkeley had left off, 'planting' blight spores in drops of water under a microscope and then watching what happened. Sometimes they merely germinated by sending out a single delicate rootlet, as was common among such organisms. But often, he was astonished to discover, they would swell up and divide into smaller portions, between six and sixteen of them, which then sprouted two propulsive hairs and swam about like tiny unicellular animals let out of a bag – not at all what anyone would have expected to find in the vegetable kingdom.

In a drop of water on a living potato leaf, these swarms of zoospores (as de Bary called them) would swim about for a while then settle down on the leaf-surface and 'grow' a protrusion, a germ tube, which pushed or dissolved its way into the leaf interior. Having thus made a small hole for entry, the zoospores squeezed their protoplasm through, leaving an empty skin behind. Once inside the leaf, the invaders rapidly absorbed the cell-juices, swelling and elongating until they reached the next cell wall, lengthening, branching and slithering along the air-spaces in between, putting a small sucker into a leaf-cell now and then for nourishment. The leaf tissue was soon completely enmeshed with these tentacle-like growths. The fungus had essentially taken over the life processes of the leaf, and when it had gathered sufficient substance and strength, it put out (through the stomata), the aerial filaments that would bear a new crop of spores. And as the fungus moved on, the plant died.

De Bary watched the process from generation to generation, certain that here was the clearest possible proof that the fungus parasitised the living tissue of healthy potato plants. It was the cause, not the conse-quence of the blight – a fact, no longer a hypothesis. He published the results in 1861, acknowledging the hitherto unobserved characteristics of the fungus with the name by which it has been known ever since: *Phytophthora infestans* (Mont.) de Bary. *Phytophthora* means 'plant destroyer'.

In 1864 the Paris Academy of Sciences awarded a prize to Louis Pasteur for experiments that finally settled the controversy over spontaneous generation. 'Life is a germ, and a germ is life,' Pasteur proclaimed, 'never will the doctrine of spontaneous generation recover from the mortal blow of this simple experiment.'[29] True, though Anton de Bary deserved credit too, for the work he had published three years before – on the potato blight.

It is sobering to note that among the comment and letters which the devastations of the potato crops in 1845 and '46 provoked, reports from Wales which gave a clue as to how a potato crop might be protected, and saved, from late blight were not followed up. On 4 September 1846, an observant gentleman by the name of Matthew Moggridge wrote to the *Gardeners' Chronicle* from his home in Swansea:

On the 31st Aug., I examined many pieces of Potatoes within the immediate influence of the copper smoke from the smelting works in this neighbourhood. There is no occasion perhaps to note the individual cases, but the general result is that the leaves, haulm, and tubers, improve as you approach the works, and that the nearest gardens, little more than 200 yards from them, are entirely free of the blight, and the crop good in quality, quantity, and flavour. The Potatoes are of different sorts. These last named gardens, as I am informed by the proprietor, entirely escaped the disease in 1845, and have borne Potatoes for 40 years.

There! '. . . copper smoke does protect the Potato crop, and effectually!' John Lindley exclaimed,[30] 'one miasma has had the power of repelling another from the Potato field.' Having thus commented on the letter from Mr Moggridge, Lindley then drew attention to evidence of potatoes having been saved by the shelter of trees or hedgerows, or as part of a mixed crop – going on to stress the role of atmospheric influence in all this, but saying no more about the ingredient which appeared to have protected crops around the Swansea smelting works: copper. Indeed, Mr Moggridge's highly pertinent observations received none of the attention that hindsight would have them deserve. Forty years would pass before anyone would investigate the use of copper as a means of controlling late blight.

The delay is puzzling. After all, a copper preparation had been protecting wheat seed from a fungus infection since the early 1800s. The Bunt or Stinking Smut of wheat was an endemic rather than an epidemic disease; it did not sweep across the countryside as the blight had done, but regularly caused heavy losses, here one year, there the next, very bad in some fields, almost totally absent in others. It was in this context that Bénédict Prévost, a professor of sciences at Montauban who had already recognised that the spores of a microscopic fungus were in some way responsible for the disease, was invited by a friend to inspect a crop of wheat which was remarkably free of bunt, unlike other fields thereabouts. Passing through the farmyard, Prévost noticed an old perforated copper vat and was told it was used for soaking the wheat seed before planting. Filled with seed, the vat was then dunked in a solution of sheep's urine and lime.

Lime was commonly used by farmers, who believed it would protect the seed – but with mixed results. Was it possible that, on his friend's farm, contact with the copper vat had made the lime solution poisonous to bunt spores? It was a long shot, but testable, and, sure enough, Prévost found that the spores he put in dishes along with a small square of polished copper died soon after germinating. He repeated the experiment with various forms of copper and found that the cheapest of them – copper sulphate – was equally effective. Even a dose of one part in a million was enough to protect seed soaked in the solution for a few hours.[31] Copper, so little poisonous to humans and animals that pumps and waterpipes were made of it, was deadly to bunt spores.

News of Prévost's discovery spread with the publication of his memoir in 1807. Fifty years later, while blight attacked potatoes, the practice of soaking wheat seed in a copper sulphate solution had become a tradition among English farmers. Dissolve one pound of copper sulphate in ten gallons of water; soak the seed; pitch it on the floor of the barn and shovel over dry slaked lime, which encrusted the seed with a protective coat and dried it in readiness for sowing. Since a copper preparation was known to protect wheat seed, in 1846 the curator of Dublin's Botanic Garden, David Moore, soaked some seed potatoes in a copper sulphate solution before planting them out.[32] The results were entirely negative. In 1847 another experimenter tested numerous preparations: from plain boiling water to sulphuric acid, coal-tar, lime and dung-water, soot, salt, potash and fat – and all were equally ineffective.[33] The problem was that the experiments were all treating the seed potatoes rather than the growing leaves and stems above ground, which in this case were the first parts of the plant to be attacked by the airborne spores of the fungus. By the time spores reached the tuber even a protective coating of copper was useless – the plant was diseased beyond saving by then.

So although Matthew Moggridge had noticed in 1846 that potato plants growing under the smoke from a copper smelting plant were blight-free, potato fields generally would remain unprotected until another fortuitous happenstance brought the lethal effect of copper on a fungus to view in 1882 – thirty-six years after his letter had been published. But this time the potential of copper to control blight on growing vegetation, as well as seed, was fully recognised and exploited.

Pierre Millardet, born in the Jura region of France in 1838, had first studied medicine but gave up a good practice to follow a deeper passion – botany. He studied under Anton de Bary, thereby gaining knowledge of fungi and their reproductive procedures which became especially useful on his appointment as professor of botany at Bordeaux University in 1876. Bordeaux and French vineyards generally were then suffering the ravages of an insect pest, *Phylloxera*, which had come to Europe on vines imported from America. Millardet is credited with having shown that European vines grafted onto resistant American rootstocks did not succumb to the pest – a strategy which quite literally saved the wine industry – but it is for work on another undesirable American import that Millardet is to be congratulated here: the downy mildew fungus, *Plasmopara viticola*. The fungus was first seen in 1878, infecting and destroying vine leaves as ferociously as late blight attacked potatoes. Though still recovering from the *Phylloxera* invasion, the French wine industry was now threatened with elimination by another deadly foreign agent. Millardet was engaged on an intense study of the organism, looking for a weakness and an agent with which to attack it when, as he later recalled, 'chance put it into my hands':

> Towards the end of October, 1882, I had occasion to traverse the vineyard of Saint-Julien en Médoc. I was not a little surprised to see, all along my way, that the vines still bore their leaves, while everywhere else they had long ago fallen. There had been some mildew

that year, and my first reaction was to attribute the persistence of the leaves along the way to some treatment that had preserved them from the malady. Examination, indeed, permitted me to confirm immediately the fact that these leaves were covered in great part on the upper surface by a thin coating of a pulverised bluish white substance.

After arriving at the Château Beaucaillon, I questioned the manager, M. Ernest David, who told me that the custom in Médoc was to cover the leaves with verdigris or with copper sulphate mixed with lime, when the grapes were ripening, in order to keep away thieves who, on seeing these leaves covered with copperish spots, would not dare to taste the fruit hidden underneath for fear of its having been blemished in the same way.[34]

Confident that the copper mixture deterred downy mildew as well as thieves, Millardet tested a variety of mixtures in his garden the following year. By the summer of 1884 he was ready to make full-scale trials 'but, by mischance, the mildew was so light in the vineyards . . . that it was impossible to judge accurately of the value of the different treatments that had been applied.'

In the meantime, though, rumours of his work had spread to scientific rivals in France's other great wine-producing region – Burgundy. There was a lot at stake here. If Millardet truly had found a treatment for mildew he could claim to have saved the vines of France, again. Furthermore, his copper preparation might be an effective treatment for potato blight and the fungus diseases that attacked tomatoes, fruit trees and even roses – all these pathogens were very similar to the vine mildew in their basic characteristics. The discovery that had eluded science and the agricultural community since late blight first devastated the potato fields forty years ago might now be his. To forestall other claimants, Millardet published his findings and a recipe for the mixture in May 1885. Eight kilograms of copper sulphate crystals should be dissolved in 100 litres of water. In a separate vessel, 15 kilograms of quicklime should be slaked and stirred up with 30 litres of water. The 'milk' of lime should then be stirred into the copper sulphate solution, producing a creamy light-blue mixture. This was the first Bordeaux Mixture, probably the world's most widely known plant and crop treatment.

The summer of 1885 was wet and the mildew very severe – which was perfect for the trials that Millardet organised on the Château Beaucaillon and adjoining estates; 150,000 vines were treated with Bordeaux Mixture and on 3 October he reported that:

> ... the treated vines show normal growth. The leaves are healthy and of a beautiful green, the grapes are black and perfectly ripe. The vines that were not treated present, on the contrary, the most wretched appearance, the majority of the leaves have fallen; the few that remain are half dried up; the grapes, still red, will not be fit for anything except sour wine.

It was a proud moment, one that encouraged the circumspect scientist to indulge in a moment of self-adulation:

> I claim the honour of having conceived the treatment with copper, that of having first experimented and, likewise, of having first proposed the practice. May I be permitted to add – for these are for us learned men our titles and our dearest souvenirs – that first, in 1878, ... I observed the presence of mildew in France. Since then I have constantly been on guard. My work gives evidence of it.[35]

The use of Bordeaux Mixture soon became common practice throughout the vineyards of France and other wine-producing regions of Europe (and the United States), but its adoption by potato-growers was slower to develop – mainly because the recipe Millardet had given for vines was not right for the more tender potato plants. A number of French farmers experimented with various mixtures at various strengths and timings, but results were indifferent and it was not until 1888 – when France's Institute of Agronomy organised the first systematic trials – that an effective recipe and spraying schedule were developed. The news spread rapidly through continental Europe and was watched closely in the United States too, where the US Department of Agriculture had established a section of Vegetable Pathology in 1886 specifically to investigate the problems of blight in vines, potatoes and other crops.

The authorities in Great Britain seem to have been ignorant of these developments. Six years passed before any of the copper mixtures were even submitted to preliminary trial on potatoes in Ireland, and it was not until 1890 that the *Journal of the Royal Agricultural Society* published any mention of the new copper preparations that were being used successfully on commercial potato crops in France and America. French journals and the US Department of Agriculture had published full details of recipes and recommended spraying schedules. Brief reports on the potato-spraying experiments in France had even appeared in *The Gardeners' Chronicle* between 1885 and 1889, but, so far as the British Government was concerned, this might all have been happening on the moon. The experimental work in France was practically finished before British farmers even knew it had begun[36] – though they were not slow to catch up once the information became available to them.

Bordeaux Mixture was the world's first agricultural application to be worthy of production on an industrial scale; to this extent, the vine and the potato were catalysts for the creation and development of the agro-chemical industry which today wields such power in the production of food crops worldwide. The invention of Bordeaux Mixture also set mechanical engineers vying to produce the most efficient and economic means of applying the mixture to crops. The world's first patented commercial spraying machine was marketed in 1883.

At last there was a reliable means of dealing with late blight, and farmers have since refined their methods of dealing with it too, for it is now known that although the airborne spores of *Phytophthora infestans* are present virtually everywhere, the conditions under which they can multiply enough to start an outbreak of late blight are very specific indeed. Typically, a period of forty-eight hours during which the temperature does not fall below 10°C and humidity remains above 75 per cent is required – and even then at least another week will pass before an outbreak occurs.[37] Farmers are thus forewarned. Meanwhile, though, the pathogen has been fighting back. New strains emerged in the early 1980s that are resistant to Bordeaux Mixture and the succession of more powerful fungicides that have been introduced since the 1930s. Moreover, this is not a mutation of the existing *P. infestans* that might be controlled with just a tweaking of existing strategies, but a new and diverse population, which is distinguished by its reproductive strategy and aggressive enough to have displaced the previous indigenous strains.[38]

Until the arrival of the new population, the farming community had believed they had late blight under control. The development of forecast systems and the discovery of systemic fungicides that cured as well as inhibited infection had made the disease far less of a problem. Now the annual skirmish threatens to become a full-scale battle. New tactics are required. Breeders strive to produce durably resistant varieties; agronomists seek better methods of crop management; botanists, biochemists and geneticists explore the form and behaviour of *Phytophthora infestans* in ever-increasing detail, searching for the weak points at which it can be attacked. Late blight is again 'the world's worst agricultural disease' and has made the potato the world's most chemically dependent crop – with the global cost of fungicides standing at more than $2 billion a year.[39]

Chapter Thirteen

Co-opting science

For all the distress that late blight had caused in the mid-1840s, there were benefits too. The disease broke the potato's hold on the economic and social structures of Europe. For Ireland, in particular, the potato famine forced the British government to confront the iniquities of land-holding practices in the country. Successive Land Acts were passed, giving tenants greater security and the right to acquire larger holdings. Meanwhile, massive emigration diminished competition for land in Ireland; rising incomes meant that enterprising farmers could afford to till their land with a plough, rather than a spade; agricultural wages doubled; and when a heavy attack of late blight struck Irish potato fields in 1890 (when the use of Bordeaux Mixture was still unknown in Ireland), there was far less absolute dependence on the crop. Pockets of severe deprivation were still to be found in the west, but 'the time when the people were entirely dependent on the potato has long gone by,' a commission of enquiry reported, 'and in every part of the west, bread, tea, stirabout, milk and sometimes salt fish and eggs form items of daily consumption'.[1]

Elsewhere, and especially in the industrial centres of Britain, Europe and America, the potato was becoming less of an arbiter between bare sufficiency and starvation and more a food that was eaten because it was liked, rather than because it was the only option.

Enter London's Baked Potato Man, and his cry: 'Baked 'taturs! baked 'taturs! All 'ot, all 'ot!'

According to the journalist Henry Mayhew, whose writings[2] on London's street traders are a fascinating record of the entrepreneurial activities that kept a significant number of the city's residents alive in Victorian times, 300 vendors of hot baked potatoes were plying their

THE BAKED POTATO MAN.

"Baked 'taturs! All 'ot, all 'ot !"

[*From a Daguerreotype by* BEARD.]

trade on the streets and in the markets of London in 1851, jostling for space and customers with equally numerous bands of fruit and vegetable sellers, fish sellers, game, poultry and dairy produce sellers, match girls, flower girls, pie-men, coffee and cocoa stalls, oyster-men – and even those specialising in the sale of nutmeg-graters, peppermint water, dog's collars and rhubarb.

Selling baked potatoes on the streets of London was a seasonal job, extending from when the new season's potatoes were of a reasonable size – which would be around the middle of August in most years, until late April, when potatoes not already consumed were already sprouting and no good for baking. This suited labourers and artisans, who were often without a job during the winter months. The potatoes were baked seventy-five or so at a time in the ovens of an amenable baker (for a charge) then sold from the potato can – essentially a large tin box on four legs, with a fire heating a water jacket that kept the potatoes hot and compartments for salt and butter at one end and charcoal at the other. The cans were painted and polished to shine 'bright as silver'; some were items of impressive craftsmanship too, and the handsomest Mayhew saw was made of brass mounted with German silver, with coloured-glass lamps attached. Engraved brass nameplates identified the proudest – including the 'Original Baked Potatoes', and the '*Old* Original Baked Potatoes'.

The Baked Potato Man's customers came from all walks of life, says Mayhew, though he found that those from the working classes bought the most. Irishmen were particularly fond of them but were a nuisance, he was told, because they always wanted the largest potato in the can. Women bought the greatest number, sometimes to eat in the street, but more often to take home; and even children with a halfpenny to spare would treat themselves to a hot baked potato. Mayhew calculated that total sales of London's baked potato vendors added up to about 10 tons per day; with each vendor selling an average of 200 or so potatoes at a halfpenny each and making an average profit of around 30 shillings per week. A vendor on Smithfield Market made at least double that, Mayhew was told, and was so busy on Fridays that he had a fresh basket of potatoes brought from the baker's every fifteen minutes.

In terms of average earnings, 30 shillings in 1851 is equivalent to a weekly income of just over £1,000 today.[3] Only for six months of the year, admittedly, and for standing out on the street all winter, but hardly to be sniffed at and an indication of how the potato had moved on from the cooking pots of the poor to become a commodity that all sorts of people have appreciated ever since – and not only for its nutritional attributes. Redcliffe Salaman remarks that if you were in central London with a lady on a cold night in the early 1900s, a potato vendor was certain to suggest you should buy one of his wares for the lady to put in her muff and keep her hands warm.[4]

Salaman does not say how much a baked potato cost in his time, but we know from Mayhew that they cost a halfpenny each in 1851, which, in terms of average earnings, is equivalent to 75 pence today. Cheaper than a McDonald's hamburger but still a sizeable portion of any child's pocket-money and an expensive option, one would imagine, for the housewife rushing to put a family meal on the table. Fresh potatoes were available too, of course, and a lot cheaper, but at the equivalent of 57 pence per pound even they were more expensive than she need pay in supermarkets today. Clearly, the potato was moving upmarket, with a helpful nudge from the most famous cookbook in the English language – *Mrs Beeton's Book of Household Management*. The book was published in 1861 and had sold nearly 2 million copies before the decade was out, so Mrs Beeton's praise for what she dubbed a 'valuable esculent' will not have passed unnoticed. 'From no other crop that can be cultivated does the public derive so much benefit,' she noted. Her recipes included one for potato rissoles, preparations in the 'French Fashion' (thin slices fried in dripping) and a 'German Method' (thick slices simmered in gravy), but mostly gave precise instructions on how potatoes should be baked, boiled, steamed or mashed. The valuable esculent had moved upmarket but was still some distance from the day when Truman Capote would declare that the only way to eat them was baked, smothered with sour cream, heaped with the freshest, biggest-grained beluga caviar, and washed down with 80-proof Russian vodka.[5]

Fortunately for the potato and its consumers, blight never again wiped out crops in Europe so completely as it had in the 1840s. Devastating local outbreaks occurred; there were severe regional shortages, but imports were always available to redress the balance (albeit at a price). In point of fact, although spores of *Phytophthora infestans* are present virtually everywhere, the conditions under which they can start an outbreak of late blight are very much dependent on the weather. Until the discovery of Bordeaux Mixture all that growers could do was to hope that the weather would be kind – or that the claims of plant-breeders offering new blight-resistant varieties of potato would turn out to be true.

'Potato-breeding' is actually a misleading description of the process by which new varieties were then produced.[6] There was as much luck as judgement to it – selection rather than deliberate breeding. In those early days, new cultivars came not from hybrid seed produced by deliberately crossing known parents, but from the seed of random crosses between a number of varieties. The trick was to select promising seedlings and their tubers for clonal propagation – and some remarkable results were achieved. In the United States, for instance, a New York preacher with interests in horticulture, the Reverend Chauncy Goodrich, picked out a cultivar with good characteristics from among the self-pollinated seedlings of tubers sent to him from South America. The selection fulfilled its promise, and was widely grown after its release as the Garnet Chile potato in 1853. Eight years later, under the nurturing hands of a gentlemen in Vermont, Garnet Chile begat Early Rose, which in its turn became very popular indeed.

That might have been the end of the line, for Early Rose was not known to produce seeds, but in 1872 a young amateur botanist by the name of Luther Burbank spotted a seed berry among his mother's crop of Early Rose on the family plot in Massachusetts. This was unusual enough for him to collect and plant its twenty-three seeds in the greenhouse. They all germinated and were grown on to produce tubers the following season. One – and only one among the twenty-three – produced significantly larger and more numerous tubers than its Early Rose parents. Burbank kept these to plant out the following year (propagating by tuber now, rather than seed) and the results confirmed that he had a viable and valuable new potato. It was a long, smooth-skinned, white-fleshed variety, high-yielding and well-adapted to long day-length; just what growers and consumers wanted. Burbank sold the rights to a seed company and used the proceeds for a move to California, where he established a nursery, greenhouse, and experimental farm that became world famous. The potato kept his name, however, and subsequently mutated into an even more valuable esculent – the Russet-Burbank, better known as the Idaho potato, superb for baking and frying, and the first choice of America's fast food chains.

The same sort of thing had been happening on the other side of the Atlantic, where growers in Belgium, the Netherlands, France and Germany were also vying to develop varieties that would find wide national approval. In Germany alone, though only five varieties were known in 1747, there were forty in 1777 and 186 by 1854.[7] Britain's favourite in the 1840s was the aptly named The Fluke – raised from the seed of an old eighteenth-century favourite variety, Pink Eye, in a cottage garden near Manchester. And The Fluke in turn produced the Victoria, Britain's most popular potato of the nineteenth century and its name a sign of converging affections – for the monarchy and the potato. The Prince Albert was another popular variety. There was also a British Queen, an Irish Queen, a Prince of Wales and, later, King Edward VII, Majestic, Red King and a Purple-Eyed King Edward. And as though to confirm that the entire nation had taken the potato to its heart, as well as to its stomach, Queen Victoria let it be known that her namesake was to be served at the royal dining table.

The Victoria had been raised in the early 1860s by William Paterson, a wealthy enthusiast from Dundee whose large-scale breeding and selection programmes became common practice among a select band of growers during the late nineteenth century. Some notable successes were achieved, but still using methods that were based more on selection than on deliberate hybridisation. These men were not guided by any science of heredity or immunity; they based their selection on yields, and on the quality and appearance of the tubers. Was it luck, or an innate affinity, that determined their success or failure? Traditional growers paid a lot of attention to the character and form of the plant, for example. They rejected tall or straggly specimens out of hand and concentrated on those with full, soft foliage which, as the season advanced, would fill out the rows. And this, science has subsequently shown, is just the sort of potato plant that does best.

And so the potato moved on to become an item of interest to science, a growing appreciation of its nutritional and economic benefits combining with the greater understanding of hereditary principles that the work of William Bateson and others was uncovering. Bateson was a pioneer of genetics (he coined the term in 1905); he was also a friend of Redcliffe Salaman, under whose direction the potato would soon be subjected to genetic investigation. But not before the Great Potato Boom of 1903 and 1904 had finally and irrecovably damaged the reputation of traditional breeding methods.

The Potato Boom was another example of the credulity and greed that had fuelled the Railway Mania fifty years before; not involving such enormous sums, it is true, but still painful to its victims. Archibald Findlay, an ambitious potato merchant turned grower, was at the root of it all. He had begun raising new varieties in the 1870s and produced several good ones, though praise was tempered by suspicion that they were merely selections from another grower's pre-existing stock – horticultural plagiarism in other words, and significant because breeders retained rights on the varieties they released and were due royalties on the sale of seed tubers. In 1891 he introduced 'Up-to-Date', which Redcliffe Salaman described as 'one the finest table varieties that has ever been grown'. Here again there were suspicions that it was derived from another named stock, but there was no denying its good qualities.

By the turn of the century Up-to-Date was a favourite with growers and consumers alike, so when Findlay whispered to some of his best customers that he now had an even better potato – Northern Star – they believed him. But stock was limited. Thomas Kime, a respected Lincolnshire merchant and grower on whose account of the Boom these paragraphs are based,[8] managed to get 12 pounds for the exorbitant sum of £6 (over £2,000 today in terms of average earnings[9]). Kime chitted the tubers and used every eye. He planted the sets a yard apart each way and gave them everything they needed to grow well. 'And grow they did', he reports, 'Splendidly . . . There was a magnificent yield of good-sized, clean-looking healthy tubers' with a market value of close to £600 (£200,000 in today's money) – not bad for a £6 investment.

A mark-up of such proportions inevitably generated excitement and the attention of speculators. Findlay hastened to bulk up his stock in anticipation of the demand and the following season was offering Northern Star seed at £25 per hundredweight – with no discount for quantity. Kime and other early customers paid £500 for a ton, and as the available stock dwindled, Findlay raised the price to £1,000 per ton. The boom was well under way now, with all and sundry speaking of the fortunes to be made from planting a field of potatoes – but with no harvest, as yet, to actually confirm Northern Star's outstanding qualities. A good moment, then, for Findlay to cap his achievements with another allegedly wonderful potato: 'Eldorado', the fortune maker! The real gold mine!! The diamond mine!!!'

As befits its name, Eldorado was even rarer than its predecessor. The few growers who managed to get some tubers (Kime was not among them – he was in bed with pneumonia) brought them on very carefully indeed – keeping the tubers warm, removing the sprouts as they appeared, potting up the sprouts in the greenhouse, then taking cuttings from the sprouts . . . and so on, until finally they had several dozen plants from each tuber for planting out. Their harvests that year were encouraging as seed material, but the small areas planted could not produce a fraction of what was required to satisfy the demand of all who had heard of this wonderful potato. Hundreds wanted them, and some growers soon realised there was probably as much to be made from selling their Eldorado seed as from planting it out. Kime reports:

> Single tubers were sold for as much as £150 each, and sprouts for as much as £5 each this first season, and holders who were in the first run began to offer for delivery in the Spring of 1904 at fabulous prices, namely, £150 to £250 per hundredweight, and buyers were plentiful, and bought as freely as they were offered at these prices; that is at the rate of £3,000 to £5,000 per ton! Think of it! ... Scores of the most substantial, level-headed, and best business men in the potato world bought these potatoes, without any doubt whatever that they would prove a splendid investment. Outsiders who knew nothing whatever about potato growing, had heard about what was being done in this potato business, and made up their minds to be in it somehow, and so make their fortunes ... What a game it was!

Even Kime himself, having missed out on Findlay's initial distributions, was obliged to place forward orders for stock on behalf of clients who insisted they should have a piece of the action too – at whatever cost. The growing crops looked good as the harvest of that first season approached, wrote Kime:

> ... and all the holders and growers of small or comparatively large lots – for there were no really large lots – were alive with interest and excitement as to how much weight of tubers their plants would give them, and of the enormous profits they were going to make, because ... many hundredweight and even tons had been sold before ever being planted at the rate of £200 per hundredweight!! £4,000 per ton!! Many farms were taken, many houses furnished, and many weddings fixed up in advance, in the full hope of the capital sums to come from this wonderful 'Eldorado'.

But the day of reckoning was at hand. 'The little rift within the lute began to appear' is how Kime put it. Experts whose examination of the growing crops had given them grounds to suspect that Eldorado was not all that Findlay had claimed, found their suspicions confirmed when the potatoes were lifted. After the first year's forced culture the crops were wretched and valueless, said Kime; in most cases they were not worth the trouble of digging up. Thousands upon thousands of pounds had been lost. Eldorado was no gold mine. In fact, it was an undistinguished variety that had fallen from favour many years before – Evergood. There were denials and calls to cover up the truth until outstanding commitments had been settled, but Thomas Kime himself was quick to blow the whistle, with advertisements announcing that '"Eldorado" is not a new Potato' and undertaking to return the deposits of customers who had placed advance orders with him. He was sued for his pains – in the High Court, for £20,000 – but the case was lost. So too was all confidence in growers and their so-called new kinds of potatoes. The trade in seed potatoes of any kind slumped to a standstill, both at home and abroad.

But the Potato Boom is notable for more than its revelations of human credulity and greed. In fact, as Redcliffe Salaman writes, 'it marks a turning point in the historic development of plant-breeding, . . . the "Eldorado" boom marked the end of one epoch and the beginning of a new and better one' – an epoch in which Salaman himself was to play a pioneering role.

Redcliffe N. Salaman was born in London in 1874, the ninth of fifteen children – eight boys and seven girls, all but one of whom survived to adulthood. The family name had been Solomon until his grandfather changed it to Salaman in the early 1800s, and it was perhaps motivation of a similar nature that persuaded the grandson, who began life as Nathan, to call himself Redcliffe N. Salaman (and no coincidence that his childhood home was situated in London's Redcliffe Gardens). The family was wealthy, Redcliffe's father, Myer, having diverged from the hat business that had sustained previous generations to make a fortune from the boas and all things feathery that ladies of fashion wore during the Victorian and Edwardian eras. Myer Salaman was one of London's leading feather merchants. Details are scant, but clearly he did well from the import and sale of ostrich feathers, egret, birds of paradise . . . Light as a feather, they say, but *Luftmensch* – a German-Yiddish expression meaning light-headed – could not be said of Myer Salaman.[10]

Grand houses in town and country, a nurse and governess, the separate worlds of nursery and 'downstairs'; private schools, classics at St Paul's, a scholarship at Trinity Hall, Cambridge, and a first in the Natural Science tripos in 1896 – the way ahead was clearly marked for Redcliffe N. Salaman. Medicine was to be his career, pathology his chosen speciality. For eight years after graduating he worked under leading pathologists in London and Germany, advancing impressively enough to be appointed Director of the Pathological Institute at the London

Hospital while still in his twenties. He might have expected to spend his thirties – that decade when energy and ambition can be so productively combined – consolidating his position, and thereafter climbing steadily to the peak of his profession. But it was not to be. In 1903 he developed tuberculosis of the lung and had to stop working. After six months in a Swiss sanatorium he bought a house in the attractive village of Barley to the south of Cambridge, where he made a full recovery over the next two years. And so, at the age of thirty-two, health restored, happily married and free of financial cares, he could have slipped easily into the role of respectable country gent, with a predilection for foxhunting, 'unconsciously graduating for the part of a Jane Austen character'.[11]

But he discovered, as he believed Jane Austen's heroes would have done 'had not their careers invariably terminated with capture and mental sterilization at the altar', that respectability and an adequate income were not enough. Returning to medicine was not an option for someone who had had tuberculosis; he had to find another field of activity on which to spend his energies and resources. With guidance from the geneticist William Bateson, he turned to the study of evolution. When a succession of experiments with butterflies, hairless mice, guinea pigs and combless chickens were all more or less complete failures, he decided that his next failure, 'if failure it was to be', would be in a field not yet attracting the attention of pioneering biologists.

Thinking that some common kitchen-garden vegetable might be just the thing, he asked his gardener, Evan Jones, for advice. Jones, who believed himself to be all but omniscient in matters of gardening, replied promptly and to the point: 'If you want to spend your time on vegetables, then you had better choose the potato, for I know more about the potato than any man living.' Jones did not. Salaman spent five years breeding a couple of Jones's varieties before discovering that the gardener had given him the wrong names for them. But no matter. When Jones steered him on to his solanaceous path, Salaman 'embarked on an enterprise which, after forty years, leaves more questions unsolved than were at that time thought to exist', he wrote later. 'Whether it was mere luck, or whether the potato and I were destined for a life partnership, I do not know, but from that moment my course was set, and I became ever more involved in problems associated directly or indirectly with a plant with which I then had no particular affinity, gustatory or romantic.' He mentioned that 'there have been not wanting those who have regarded these activities with a shake of the head and an indulgent smile, indicating that nothing, short of mental instability, could excuse a lifelong attachment to the study of so banal a subject.'

Thus happenstance brought the potato in contact with a man whose interests and personal wealth made him ideally prepared for the study of its deeper nature – at just the moment when a new approach was urgently needed. Furthermore, heredity and Mendelian genetics – the disciplines most applicable to the breeding of potato – were hot topics at the time. Eugenics, the 'science' which aimed to improve organisms (including humanity) by controlled breeding and would be used to justify the racial policies of Nazi Germany, was in the ascendant. Salaman was a member of the Eugenics Society, and a paper[12] he published on the heredity of Jewishness (his term) goes some way towards explaining his interest. Here he analysed the prevalence of physiognomic characteristics and concluded that the Jewish nose, for instance, was paternally determined and would be passed on even when the mother was Gentile. This Mendelian view of racial heredity was scathingly criticised – both for its method and for its conclusions.[13] Indeed, it was so far off the mark that one hopes it was just another of the false starts to which Salaman disarmingly confessed, even though it was published some years after his experiments with hairless mice and combless poultry, and Salaman remained a member of the Eugenics Society for some time after that.[14]

But whatever is made of Redcliffe Salaman's flirtation with eugenics and racial heredity, his motives were to promote Jewishness, not eradicate it. He supported the Zionist movement and was actively involved with Jewish issues, both at home and abroad. His studies of the potato overshadowed much of this, however, so that it seems proper – if quixotic – that the Hebrew University of Jerusalem should have acknowledged his work on its Board of Governors by proposing that his memorial at the University should be a corner of its Botanical Garden, for ever devoted to the study of the potato.

There is no way of knowing how stuck for ideas Salaman really was, following the failure of his first adventures in the field of genetic investigation, though one might suppose he was at a bit of a loose end – with the hunting season over and neither golf, tennis nor cricket holding any attraction for him – which evokes an appealing image of the potato's historic new epoch beginning with Redcliffe Salaman walking out one morning to ask his gardener for suggestions as to what he should do next. A sensible strategy in some respects: experienced gardeners are a knowledgeable lot, and there was a notable precedent – Charles Darwin had gleaned useful insights on the origin of species from his conversations with gardeners and breeders of domestic birds and animals. But Salaman's gardener, Mr Evan Jones, might have been an avid fan of leeks (his name suggests he was from Wales), turnips or cabbages. Fortunately that was not the case. The potato's new epoch was assured.

The potatoes Salaman had been given that fateful morning were a white tubered variety which Jones said was 'Ringleader', and a red he called 'Flourball'. With these, Salaman planned to conduct experiments such as Gregor Mendel had done with peas – crossing and back-crossing through a sequence of generations to discover which characteristics were dominant and which recessive – but his investigations soon took him on unexplored paths. In 1906, seeking to include wild potatoes in his experiments, he asked the authorities at Kew for a few tubers of a fairly common wild species, *Solanum maglia*. Kew's wild potato stock had been incorrectly labelled, however, and what he got was not *S. maglia* but a potato subsequently identified as *S. edinense*. And here is a wonderful example of the unforeseeable *eureka!* events that give science a helpful nudge from time to time. Because Kew sent the wrong tubers, Salaman stumbled on the hitherto unsuspected fact that a genuine resistance to late blight does, in fact, exist.

Self-fertilised seed from the *S. edinense* tubers he had grown on in the trial plots at Barley produced a family of forty plants in 1909. Late blight was particularly bad that year and the next. Because his trials were directed towards finding a potato that was blight-resistant he did not spray the plots with a Bordeaux Mixture and all the potato plants he had previously been working with were killed, both established varieties and crosses derived from them. Thirty-three of the *S. edinense* seedlings were killed too, but seven were untouched. The seven resistant seedlings were grown on in subsequent years and retained their resistance. One was grown in the kitchen garden at Barley for seventeen consecutive seasons, never showing the least sign of infection.

Convinced now that true resistance could only be found outside the domestic varieties, Salaman obtained several other wild species, including *S. demissum*, a wild potato from Mexico which also turned out to be late blight-resistant. In 1911 he began crossing *S. demissum* with domesticated stock, with the ultimate aim of combining the desirable qualities of both in single varieties – fully blight-proof and marketable. By 1914 he had a series of such hybrid families, from which the most resistant individuals were crossed again with the immune stocks previously obtained. By 1926, Salaman reported with justifiable pride: 'I was in possession of over a score of seedling varieties endowed with reasonably good economic characters which, no matter what their maturity, appeared to be immune to late blight.'[15]

It was an important breakthrough, offering real promise – after all the false starts – that it was possible to breed blight-resistant potato varieties that would spare farmers the cost of spraying and lost crops.

Meanwhile, a famine of proportions that surpassed even the tragedy of Ireland had struck the Soviet Union. But it was not the failure of a potato crop that was responsible; it was a sequence of events – the First World War, the turmoil of the 1918 revolution and its ensuing civil war – compounded by some drought and the wilful determination of the Soviets to put the survival of their new political order before that of the people.[16]

More than 35 million Soviet citizens were at risk of famine by 1921. And their plight worsened as transport networks broke down and the government ordered that all available food supplies should be sent to the cities, leaving rural communities with little or nothing – even their seed grain was requisitioned. At least 5 million people died of starvation and disease as a result,[17] many of whom would have survived if the Soviets had been willing to accept foreign aid from the moment it was first offered. They resisted, for fear of foreign influence on political developments in the country, but ultimately had to concede. At its peak the international aid programme was feeding 10 million people.

By then the Soviet elite had admitted that their state could not survive on ideology alone. The economy was ruined and its reconstruction required the expertise and knowledge of experienced engineers, scientists, industrialists and managers. But most of the country's specialists had either emigrated or perished in the aftermath of the revolution (when higher learning was deemed to be a bourgeois threat). Many had been executed for various reasons. The few who survived suddenly found themselves in demand. Among them was an agricultural botanist, Nicolay Ivanovich Vavilov (1887–1943).

As a postgraduate student before the First World War, Vavilov had worked on disease resistance in plants; he had studied in England under William Bateson, and in Germany under Ernst Haeckel (the biologist and enthusiastic proponent of evolutionary theory who – *inter alia* – had coined the term 'ecology'). Vavilov was thus uniquely prepared to address the problem of revitalising Russian agriculture. The acceptance of foreign relief had cleared the political atmosphere too, making it possible for Vavilov to visit the United States and Europe in search of fresh plant material, and keeping him in touch with advances in agricultural science – all of which doubtless contributed to the development of his theory on the centres of origin of cultivated plants.

The concept of Vavilov Centres, as they became known, has been overtaken – though not entirely discredited – by subsequent work, but in the context of the day it opened new avenues of investigation, which in turn led to valuable advances in the field of plant breeding – especially in respect of the potato.[18]

The singular beauty of the Vavilov concept was that it was discovered 'at the tip of a pen', i.e. theoretically.[19] Vavilov reasoned that since the range of cultivated plants known from acknowledged cradles of civilisation – such as the valleys of the Nile, the Tigris and Euphrates, the Indus, the Ganges and the Yangtze – was very limited, their initial domestication had probably occurred elsewhere. The origins of agriculture would be found in more isolated regions, he said, from which cultivated crops had been adopted by the expanding populations of the great valleys only at a later stage. He proposed between eight and twelve centres (the number increased with Vavilov's development of the idea) for the origin of the world's major food crops, located wherever the greatest genetic diversity of cultivated plants and their wild relatives was found: wheat in the highlands of the fertile crescent, rice in India (here Vavilov was wrong – Indonesia has the greatest genetic diversity of rice), maize in Mexico, brassicas around the Mediterranean, citrus fruits in China, walnuts in the Balkans . . . and potatoes in the Andes.

But while Vavilov clearly enjoyed exploring the intellectual landscape of his pen-tip theory, it was the practical implications that concerned him most. In 1920 he was appointed head of the Bureau of Applied Botany (later renamed the Institute of Plant Industry), charged with the task of improving the Soviet Union's food crops. The famine of 1921 served to reinforce the importance and urgency of his brief. Like the gentlemen botanists of the Royal Horticultural Society more than a century before, Vavilov felt certain that the wild relatives of cultivated plants probably possessed useful elements of disease resistance, pest immunity and environmental tolerance which had been lost in cultivated varieties. The search for varieties that would save Russia from the recurring catastrophes of drought and famine should begin with 'the primary elements, the bricks and mortar, from which the modern species and varieties were created', he said, rather than with the cultivars and hybrids that had been used hitherto.

Expanding on this theme, he reasoned that unknown useful genetic traits were likely to be found in the centres of origin he had proposed. Identifying them would call for the detailed examination of thousands of specimens from around the world; breeding them into new improved varieties would require an extensive programme of field trials.

Vavilov's proposal called for a living collection of the world's culti-vated plants and their wild relatives to be assembled at the Institute, and for the massive investment of money and manpower that would be needed to exploit the potential of that inventory. It was a revolu-tionary concept; these were revolutionary times; but even so, the scale of financial support Vavilov managed to secure from the hard-pressed Soviet treasury was staggering. That achievement alone earned him gasps of amazement and admiration (and envy) from colleagues in the West, but how had he done it? Guile, Vavilov is reputed to have explained when a British plant scientist posed the question at a diplomatic recep-tion. Apparently Vavilov had seen Leon Trotsky standing in a breadline during one of Russia's food shortages. The Party elite often queued for bread, it seems, in order to show solidarity with the proletariat. Vavilov moved into the queue at Trotsky's shoulder, struck up a conversation and, as they shuffled forward to claim their rations, explained how his programme of research and plant breeding could eliminate food short-ages and bread queues for ever. Trotsky was impressed enough to tell Lenin. Lenin was similarly impressed. Vavilov got his funding.[20]

Expeditions were arranged and dispatched to collect specimens from all parts of the Soviet Union and from sixty countries around the globe. 'Don't collect just a few specimens,' he instructed Dr S. M. Bukasov, as he prepared to set off for the Andean regions of South America, 'collect as many as you can.' Bukasov returned with thousands of speci-mens, of numerous plants – including some previously unknown species of wild and cultivated potato.

The agricultural research institute that Vavilov created was one of the largest and most active in the world, with a network of 400 research and experimental stations across the length and breadth of the Soviet Union, and close links with related establishments worldwide. By 1934, 20,000 people were working under Vavilov's overall direction. In all, more than 300,000 plant samples were available for study. No one ever had such a mass of material and data on the global distribution of culti-vated plants at their disposal. Applying it to the challenge of increasing the productivity of Russia's food crops was a relatively simple matter – but time-consuming. Satisfying the demands of his political masters was far more difficult.

With the benefit of hindsight, an ambitious and expensive research programme based on the inherent diversity of living things was certain to fail under the onslaught of uniformity which the rise of Stalin imposed on all aspects of life in the Soviet Union. As the country's food production plummeted with the collectivisation of agriculture, Vavilov was instructed to reduce the time needed to develop higher yielding and more resistant varieties from twelve to five years. His objections were countered by the claims of a rival, Trofim Denisovich Lysenko, who said he could do it in three years, with little more than five flowerpots in the corner of a greenhouse.

With a campaign of denigration and the support of Stalin, Lysenko ultimately appropriated all that Vavilov had achieved. He was more politician than scientist – when told that scientists in England had been unable to duplicate some of his results, he replied: 'I'm not surprised; they live in a bourgeois environment.'[21] With such convictions, this son of illiterate peasants was well able to ingratiate himself with the communist elite. They looked upon him as a true Soviet, and a deserving product of the communist regime – therefore his science must be better than that of anyone from a bourgeois background.

Nicolay Vavilov was arrested in August 1940 and eleven months later found guilty of belonging to a rightist conspiracy, of sabotaging Soviet agriculture and of spying for England. After a few minutes' deliberation the court sentenced him to death. The sentence was later commuted to ten years' imprisonment, but Vavilov had served little more than a year before he died in January 1943 at the age of sixty-five – slandered, disgraced, tortured and starved in the prison of the Russian city of Saratov on the Volga, centre of the famine which had been such a powerful incentive for his work.

The facts of Vavilov's whereabouts and fate were withheld from his wife and family, his students and friends as well as from the scientific community worldwide. Twenty years passed before the exact date of his death was disclosed, and many more years went by before the approximate location of his burial in the Saratov cemetery was revealed. Almost fifty years passed before his son, Dr Yuri N. Vavilov, obtained copies of the secret documents in which details of the scientist's arrest, imprisonment and death were revealed.[22]

Vavilov's name was cleared in 1955, the institute he had founded was renamed the N.I. Vavilov Institute ten years later, and a large marble memorial was erected in the Saratov cemetery. Lysenko died in his bed at the age of seventy-eight in 1976, his political acumen such that he had managed to retain high-level support even as his promises of improved crops failed to materialise. But his science was entirely discredited. In 1964 the physicist Andrei Sakharov told the General Assembly of the Soviet Academy of Sciences:

> He is responsible for the shameful backwardness of Soviet biology and of genetics in particular, for the dissemination of pseudo-scientific views, for adventurism, for the degradation of learning, and for the defamation, firing, arrest, even death, of many genuine scientists.[23]

But because Lysenko concentrated his attention on cereal crops, the work that Vavilov had initiated on potatoes went on unabated. The collections that Bukasov and his colleagues had brought back from South America became the basis of an all-embracing survey of genetic variability among wild and cultivated potatoes. Indeed, it is hardly an overstatement to say that this work, by virtue of the amazing amount of wild and primitive cultivated material collected, and the extensive and detailed tests to which it was later submitted, laid the foundations for all future work on the potato in which primitive forms were used. For the first time, primitive cultivated species and more primitive forms of *Solanum tuberosum* itself were sampled. Indeed, until these expeditions returned it was not realized that such forms of the common potato existed. No less startling discoveries came from the wild species, in some of which frost resistance and other useful traits were demonstrated.[24]

Even as Vavilov was accused of sabotaging his country's agriculture, the work he had initiated on the potato was acknowledged around the world as the first and most crucial stage in the use of its wild relatives as a means of improving the cultivated stock. He had answered the appeals Thomas Knight and Joseph Sabine had made to the Royal Horticultural Society more than a century earlier, and with its potential now fully demonstrated, the work of the Russian geneticists and plant breeders was quickly followed by collecting expeditions and investigations from Germany, Sweden, the United States and Great Britain. A new era of investigation dawned – one that would trace the characteristics of the potato down to its origins and the ordering of its genetic code. Its future as one of humanity's most valued food crops was secure. Or, to view matters from the potato's point of view, this tender, highly bred and vulnerable plant had co-opted a host of pioneering scientists on its progress to world domination.

Chapter Fourteen

Men on a mission

The British Empire Potato Collecting Expedition to South America 1938–1939 spent eight months travelling around the continent by rail, lorry, car, horse and mule, and on foot. Its team of three scientists covered a total distance of over 9,000 miles and collected over 1,100 specimens of wild and native cultivated potatoes – many of which had never been described before. The expedition was typically British in the quasi-amateur nature of its organisation: serious but not over-burdened with either participants or pretensions.

The expedition was led by Edward Balls, a professional plant collector and world traveller whose name lives on in the miniature blue iris that is seen in herbaceous borders everywhere: *Sisyrinchium* E. K. Balls. Accompanying him were Dr William 'Bill' Balfour Gourlay, an equally experienced and well-travelled botanist of independent means, and the junior member of the party, 'Jack' Hawkes,[1] fresh from graduating in botany at Cambridge – full of confidence and promise, but as yet untested. At the time Jack Hawkes was twenty-three years old and preparing to begin his research for a Ph.D. on potatoes under the supervision of Redcliffe N. Salaman at Cambridge; he knew very little about potatoes, and had no practical experience of expeditions or of collecting botanical specimens abroad. The invitation to accompany Balls and Gourlay to South America was merely one of life's 'curious coincidences', he confessed in the auto-biographical account[2] of the expedition he published in his eighty-ninth year (2003), but it was the making of the man and the scientist. The expedition smoothed the rough corners of his personality, he wrote, taught him how to deal with many of life's problems and laid the groundwork for a career that spanned six decades and saw Jack Hawkes become a leading authority on potato taxonomy and research.

The mission of the expedition was to expand upon the investigations that Vavilov had initiated in the 1920s, and provide British and Empire potato scientists and breeders with a national collection of wild and cultivated South American stock to draw upon. Of course, there already was a large collection of this kind in Russia by the late 1930s, and expeditions from Sweden, Germany and the United States had also been collecting in South America. At a scientific level, the institutions which had sponsored these efforts were co-operative – information was exchanged, findings published – but when it came to establishing a breeding programme, it was imperative that Britain should have its own collection. And the threat of war added an element of urgency to the issue.

Britain had learnt during the 1914–18 war that a nation which imports a substantial proportion of its food supply must maximise home production when incoming fleets are likely to be the target of enemy action. Government urging had encouraged Britain's allotment-holders to produce over 2 million tonnes of vegetables a year by the end of the First World War, and the experience was to be capitalised upon in the event of a Second. The generous funding that the expedition to South America received, and the extensive diplomatic arrangements made to facilitate its travels and investigations, probably reflect this. Feeding Britain and home production in the event of war had become priority issues by the late 1930s, (and imperial needs were not to be neglected). The expedition's mission was to collect:

> any varieties of economic interest, such as forms able to withstand disease, extremes of heat and cold and of drought and moisture so that all available material might be gathered to form a basis for breeding the many different varieties required for the widely differing conditions of climate in the Empire and combating the diseases which attack European potato varieties.[3]

In preparation for the expedition Hawkes was sent on an official visit to the USSR under the auspices of Britain's Imperial Agricultural Bureau. He would tour potato research stations in Leningrad (now St Petersburg) and Moscow, and have discussions with Nikolay Vavilov and other scientists. Since the Russians had already collected material in South America, and were widely regarded as world leaders in potato research, there would be much to learn from such a trip.

Hawkes had perused the potato literature, done some elementary laboratory work on potato cells and discussed his Ph.D. plans with Redcliffe N. Salaman. Whether this amounted to sufficient preparation for encounters at the cutting edge of potato science is questionable – but he need not have worried. From the moment of arrival, he was treated as a visiting dignitary and accomplished scientist. He was described in the press as 'Dr J. Hawkes, vice-director of the Imperial Bureau of Plant Genetics', though in fact he was not even employed by the Bureau and was some years away from earning his doctorate. No matter. Nikolay Vavilov himself treated the young Jack Hawkes as an honoured guest, entertaining him to extravagant lunches and dinners, taking him to the opera (reserved seats in the middle of the front row of the dress circle, Hawkes notes) and keeping him up until the early hours, talking 'as an equal' about science and potatoes.

Hawkes visited the Institute's herbaria, botanical gardens and experimental plots. Work on a rubber-producing dandelion held his attention briefly; he met the notorious Trofim Lysenko; but the greatest value of the visit undoubtedly came from discussions with Nikolay Vavilov and the scientists who had collected potatoes in South America at his instigation: S. M. Bukasov and S. W. Juzepczuk. He was urged to look for material in Bolivia and north Argentina – regions the Russians had been unable to visit – and told of places in Peru that the British expedition might otherwise have neglected. Vavilov resoundingly declared that he, personally, would be dissatisfied if Hawkes did not bring back at least twelve new species. The British expedition collected more than that and sent living samples of nearly everything the expedition had collected to Vavilov and Bukasov.

There was an ominous footnote to Hawkes's USSR visit.[4] On his last day, having said final farewells to Vavilov and his colleagues, he found two representatives of the party newspaper, *Pravda*, waiting at his hotel. At least they claimed to be from *Pravda* and wanted Hawkes to write a piece for them on his impressions of the Soviet Union and its potato research programmes. But then the conversation wandered from the requirements of a newspaper and eventually came round to the suggestion that since Hawkes viewed the USSR in such favourable light, he might like to consider a broader role: as a source of information for the Soviet state itself – as a spy, in other words. Hawkes recoiled and, as though to make the proposition more acceptable, his visitors told him that the Soviets had already recruited several people at Cambridge (now known to be Philby, Blunt, Burgess and

Maclean) and, of course, he would not be asked to inform on his fellow countrymen. It was Soviet citizens living abroad they were interested in.

After a four-week voyage from Liverpool, the expedition disembarked at Lima, Peru, on 13 January 1939. With 'an extraordinary amount of help' from British Embassy staff and the personal good wishes of the Vice-Consul and the Secretary to the Minister they were on their way to La Paz, capital of Bolivia, within days. Here again, British Embassy staff were on hand to help with obtaining the necessary clearances from the Bolivian ministries of Foreign Affairs and Agriculture. An introduction to the manager of the Bolivian Railways brought the privilege of free first-class travel throughout the network, and a meeting with the Argentinian ambassador in La Paz secured similarly generous arrangements for their excursion into his country. Clearly, these were the golden days of international travel . . .

The expedition's first wild potato was collected on the afternoon of 28 January – less than a fortnight after landing in Lima – in a valley to the south of La Paz, where a drab landscape of eroded mud and boulder pinnacles was relieved by the occasional fine flowering plant that the botanists also collected. The potato specimen, however, was found in the first village they came too. Enquiries revealed that it was called 'Quipa choque', which, they later discovered, simply means 'wild potato' in the Aymará Indian language. It was a 'weedy or more or less wild potato', Hawkes notes, which commonly grew by paths, roadsides, waste heaps and other man-made habitats. Next day they found more specimens growing in great abundance on the steep stony slopes of the river canyon, some of them in flower. With all the required botanical evidence to hand – tubers, leaves and flowers – Hawkes could now give their first wild potato a name: *Solanum sparsipilum*. *Solanum* is of course the genus, while the specific name, *sparsipilum*, acknowledges that the plant is but sparsely endowed with hairs. (Subsequently, it has been found that *S. sparsipilum* is a highly variable plant, with sufficient distinctive features on different specimens for it to have been given twelve different Latin names since its first appearance in the botanical literature.)

When the party moved across the border into Argentina, the District Officer to whom they had been directed gave them lunch and offered to show them a region where he believed wild potatoes would be found. Hawkes wrote in his diary:

234

He arrived in a very old car and took us through countryside rather like parts of Shropshire near Ludlow. The wild trees and herbs were in full flower, and the whole area seemed like a paradise in contrast to the bleak cold barren uplands we had been passing through by train. The country people all rode horses . . . the women rode side-saddle and looked very beautiful.[5]

With the District Officer's guidance, they found wild potatoes growing as weeds on a farm, and dug up lots of small tubers with the enthusiastic help of the farmer's son. Then it began to rain and they 'were invited into the farm for glasses of beer and a large bag of apples'.

A few days later they were on a train which travelled so slowly that in places they were able to get out and collect plants from beside the track. They were high in the Andes now; at Tilcara they hired mules, guides and camping equipment for a collecting expedition at even higher elevations. At about 3,600 metres they came across a veritable carpet of wild potatoes – 'this was a tremendously exciting area,' Hawkes recalled, not only for the living plants but also for the large fossil corals and pieces of Jurassic limestone lying around on the surface. A wild potato he had named *S. tilcarense* (after the Tilcara region in which it was first found) became commoner as they climbed, though varying in leaf form and in the intensity of its flower colour. The weather deteriorated in the early afternoon and by 3.30 p.m. they were ready to pitch camp for the night. 'We found a camping site at about 3,700 metres,' Hawkes wrote:[6]

A small muddy spring gave us some water of a kind, and although the ground was extremely stony we managed to get our tents up. Bill Gourlay found that he had pitched his tent on a carpet of *S. Megistacrolobum* (meaning the leaves had very large terminal lobes), which was useful because we could dig up the plants in dry and comparatively warm comfort . . . after supper we felt exhausted and went to bed early.

Hawkes recalls the next day as one of the worst he had ever experienced:

It began to rain at about 4.00 a.m. and went on steadily, turning soon into a sleety snow. The muleteers remained under a tarpaulin, whilst the mules stood around getting wet and looking as though they had seen all this before, which no doubt they had.

The men would not light a fire to make some tea or coffee or stir themselves until it stopped snowing; so Edward and I decided to explore the path higher up to keep ourselves warm. The top of the ridge did not seem to be more than 50 metres higher, but it was probably over 4,000 metres high, and at about 3,950 metres we decided to turn back, because the sleet and snow was getting worse all the time. However, the *S. acaule* (meaning 'without stem') and *S. megistacrolobum* plants seemed quite adapted to these cold snowy altitudes.

S. acaule is a highly frost-resistant and widespread wild potato that the expedition was to meet again many times. In Potosí, the town whose notorious silver mine had financed the Spanish Empire, they found it growing as a weed in gardens throughout the town, in the main square and in the railway station yard as well as between the cobblestones of the streets (being stemless, it is a very low-growing plant). There were also many specimens of *S. acaule* growing in the vicinity of the ruined ancient city of Tiahuanaco (now known as Tiwanaku), along with six of the seven known species of cultivated potato. This was important, Hawkes notes, for it clearly indicated that they had reached the Vavilov gene centre for cultivated species of potatoes – and meant they could take some time off to visit the ruins with a clear conscience:

> The most exciting part was the temple, surrounded with massive oblong stones set on end, each about five metres high. Outside this was the so-called 'Gate of the Sun', formed from one massive block and carved with curious figures supposed to be of calendaric significance. At the other end of the temple was a flight of four steps cut out of enormous blocks of stone, the top two all of one block, some six metres long and two metres wide. The whole city covered an enormous area, and had wharves which were once at the edge of Lake Titicaca.

They crossed the lake by steamer and from their accommodation in Puno took taxis out into the surrounding farmlands. They collected many wild potatoes, including *S. canasense* (named for its discovery near the Canas river), '. . . a particularly beautiful species', Hawkes noted in his diary, 'with delicate leaves and exquisite large blue-violet flowers'.[7]

Altogether, the 1939 British Empire Potato Collecting Expedition to South America collected 1,164 living specimens. After being carefully examined for disease in the Cambridge laboratories, the material was sterilised and planted out in glasshouses, to form the basis of a collection that has been harvested in the autumn and planted out again every spring since then. Today, it is known as the Commonwealth Potato Collection, and is held at the Scottish Crop Research Institute near Dundee – a precious resource which breeders and scientists are able to draw upon for their work on all aspects of the potato's nature and potential.

Hawkes himself worked on the taxonomy and genetics of the original material for his Ph.D. thesis at Cambridge (in the course of which he described thirty-one new wild species of potato, and five new cultivated species) and thereafter worked with it extensively. His scientific account of the expedition (1941) was the first of 241 papers, monographs and books on the potato and related matters that he published.

There is very little concerning the potato that Jack Hawkes did not consider and write about; some of his conclusions have turned out to be wrong – but this was inevitable as the depth of knowledge has increased and investigative methods have been refined. Of the new wild and cultivated species of potato that Hawkes described from the 1939 expedition, for instance, a number have since been subsumed into other taxa, and his conclusions concerning exactly where in the Andes the potato was originally domesticated, and which wild species were involved, are also in doubt. But these instances do not diminish the stature of Hawkes and his work in any way: they illustrate the manner by which science progresses.

No scientist can work beyond the capacity of whatever methods and technology are available. The early botanists set out a mode of botanical investigation that distinguished one plant from another on the basis of its physical structure and behaviour – the shape and structure of its flowers, its leaves and the manner of its growth. This has spawned dozens of descriptive terms – from acroscopic to xerophilous, via cuspidate, glabrescent, imparipinnatisect, rachis, stipule and tomentose,[8] to name but a few – which left ample opportunity for different botanists to put the same plant in a different taxon on the basis of naturally occurring variations in form (the specimen of *Solanum sparsipilum* that Hawkes collected in 1939 is a case in point). The microscope added the cellular characteristics of a plant to the mix, and advances in microscopy, together with the study of genetics that was introduced to botany in the early twentieth century, have brought further refinement and precision. Modern researchers are working with the potato's DNA, using techniques that not only enable them to distinguish one plant from another at the genetic level, but also to investigate their evolutionary history – from ancestral species to modern descendant.

Jack Hawkes's views on the origin and evolution of the potato were set forth in his book *The Potato: Evolution, Biodiversity and Genetic Resources*, published in 1990.[9] He was the first to acknowledge that some of his conclusions were likely to be discounted or amended by evidence as yet undiscovered, but in the meantime it is an authoritative piece of work that cannot be ignored – in fact, its mixture of hard fact and brave summary makes it probably the most frequently cited work on the potato.

The 1939 expedition had noted a concentration of modern cultivated species in the Lake Titicaca region and northern Bolivia, among which Hawkes identified some 'primitive', 'wild-looking' plants. On the basis of this and more detailed laboratory investigation, he concluded that the potato probably had been first domesticated around the southern margins of Lake Titicaca some 10,000 to 7,000 years ago by a relatively stable population of hunter-gatherers. At least four wild potato species were involved, he said, and it was from their naturally occurring hybrids that the world's first domesticated potato appeared – *solanum stenotomum* (meaning narrowly cut, in reference to its narrow leaflets). But that was only the beginning. As soon as people began attempting to cultivate and produce larger quantities of *S. stenotomum* tubers than occurred naturally, there would have been some cross-pollination between the flowers of *S. stenotomum* and other wild species. Yet more hybrids would have arisen, and it was from these, said Hawkes, that our original cultivated potato – *Solanum tuberosum* – arose.

The Hawkes scheme of things was not exclusive – it allowed for more than one instance of domestication, in more than one location – and acknowledged that there were gaps and shadowy sections which only further research could illuminate. Even so, it has stood as the standard account of the evolution of wild and cultivated potatoes, widely cited in academic papers and etched in the memory of every student who studied the subject. But it was never going to be the last word. And sure enough, in 2005 a group of geneticists published a study that overturned most of what Hawkes had proposed.

This 'groundbreaking' study aimed to obtain the genetic fingerprint of all the diverse potato species and varieties in the Commonwealth Potato Collection.[10] This would identify the wild potato species which are most similar to the cultivated ones and thus enable breeders to make better use of the Commonwealth Potato Collection in their search for the perfect potato, just as Knight and Sabine, Vavilov and Hawkes, would have advocated. A programme of such detailed genetic analysis was certain to throw light on the origin and evolutionary relationships of the cultivated potato as well. And it did:[11] 'unequivocally' identifying a single domestication event, and eliminating the progenitors Hawkes had proposed from contention. The new study broadly agreed with Hawkes on the location of the domestication event, but replaced his several progenitors with just three, one of which is the 'particularly beautiful species, with delicate leaves and exquisite large blue-violet flowers' – *Solanum canasense* – that Hawkes had collected in April 1939.

Chapter Fifteen

Global voyage

In late January 2003, in a village in the high mountains of western Papua New Guinea, So Wan Kusit and her neighbours were bewildered. Their potatoes had been flourishing, now they were dying – entire fields, every plant struck down, all in a matter of days. What had been fields of burgeoning promise were now ugly scenes of destitution, their promise transformed to a certainty of hard times ahead. Realising that there was no hope of saving their crops the villagers simply pulled up the plants and laid them in rows along the roads – like the deeply mourned victims of an unknown plague. 'They just died,' So Wan Kusit said. 'They just died. I don't know why.'

The terse newspaper reports that appeared in the capital, Port Moresby, 500 miles away, were reminiscent of the first scant reports which came from Ireland more than 150 years before – but this time information and help were more readily to hand. Dr Sergi Bang, research leader of Papua New Guinea's National Agricultural Research Institute (NARI), travelled to the remote village with a deep sense of foreboding, and a brief inspection was enough to confirm his worst fears: late blight. Hitherto, Papua New Guinea had been free of the disease. Now it was sweeping across the country, destroying crops that were to have fed the families of So Wan Kusit and many thousands like her and closing down a young but flourishing commercial potato-growing industry (already worth $11 million per year). The potato had been introduced to the highlands by aid workers in the 1970s – a latecomer which had since earned itself a vital position in the rural economy; but after nearly thirty years of untroubled expansion, the potato's reviled parasite, *Phytophthora infestans*, had breached this last redoubt.

Dr Bang could guess how it had happened. Late blight spores almost certainly had drifted into Papua New Guinea on winds from neigh-bouring Irian Jaya, where thousands of refugees from elsewhere in Indonesia were being forcibly settled on lands close to the border. Some at least must have come from regions where late blight was endemic – bringing with them infected seed, but also the planting practices and means of control that no one in Papua New Guinea had yet needed to bother with. From the parasite's point of view, Papua New Guinea and its potatoes were virgin territory – and defenceless. Dr Bang told So Wan Kusit and the villagers to bury their uprooted crops and advised them not to cultivate potatoes again for a couple of years 'to allow the late blight fungus to die'.

In a country slightly larger than California, but with less than 500 miles of paved roads and a terrain so unaccommodating that only 1.9 per cent of its land surface is suitable for growing crops of any kind, the potato had been a prized crop. Especially among the 85 per cent of a 5.4 million population that is entirely dependent upon subsistence farming for food and livelihood. The potato was particularly well-suited to the country's highlands, where altitude tempered the heat of an equatorial sun and year-round rainfall watered fertile soils. In such cool and humid conditions, farmers could grow potatoes throughout the year, and in the absence of indigenous pests and diseases they could aim for maximum productivity, never needing to bother about resist-ance. Unfortunately, though, what is good for the potato is also good for its pathogens. And once late blight had crossed the border from Irian Jaya it spread through Papua New Guinea very quickly.

By May 2003 the devastation was complete. Farmers in the moun-tains of Papua New Guinea were probably the last people on Earth to adopt the potato and enjoy its benefits for some time without having to contend with its devilish parasite. Now they too had fallen victim – but at least there was a world community of scientists and special-ists to call upon, all anxious to further the interests of people and their potatoes. While So Wan Kusit and others like her struggled to survive on alternative crops, and urban consumers bought imported potatoes at three or four times the price they had paid for local produce, the Papua New Guinea government appealed for help. Within weeks, scien-tists from Australia and the International Potato Center (CIP) in Lima visited the island to formulate a research and development project that would counter the problem.

Since increasing food security and reducing poverty in the develop-ing world were part of CIP's founding mandate, the plight of the Papua

New Guinea highlanders was of immediate concern and interest to its scientists. But such outside attention was relatively new to the mountainous interior of Papua New Guinea. Indeed, the world had no idea that the region was heavily populated until the 1930s, when Australian gold prospectors advancing up unexplored river valleys encountered groups of people no one had seen before. The men were well-built, their heads decorated with birds' wings, and strings of shell hanging from pegs that pierced their noses, one of the prospectors, Michael Leahy, wrote in his book *The Land That Time Forgot* (1937). Many were tattooed, and carried bows and arrows, and stone axes with cutting edges ground sharp as a knife. They were not welcoming. The prospectors' camps were attacked; porters were killed; Leahy himself suffered a blow from a stone axe that dented his skull and left him with a roaring in the left ear that never disappeared – but his determination was not shaken. Convinced the interior held more secrets (and gold), he made two reconnaissance flights in preparation for a major expedition to be funded by a mining syndicate. He wrote:

We saw a great, flat valley, possibly twenty miles wide and no telling how many miles long, between two high mountain ranges, with a very winding river meandering through it. . . . Below us were evidences of a fertile soil and a teeming population – a continuous patchwork of gardens, laid off in neat squares like chess-boards, with oblong grass houses, in groups of four or five, dotted thickly over the landscape. Except for the grass houses, the view below resembled the patchwork field of Belgium . . . an island of population so effectively hemmed in by mountains that the rest of the world had not even suspected its existence.

Shangri La? Not exactly, though archaeological evidence indicates that people had inhabited the region for up to 30,000 years, and ancient traces of bush clearance and drainage systems suggest that they began farming there between 9,000 and 10,000 years ago – which implies that while the inhabitants of northern Europe were still hunting mammoths, the New Guinea highlanders were already growing crops. But this was more a matter of need than choice. In fact, there was not enough animal fare to sustain them: New Guinea's native vertebrate fauna is one of the poorest in the world. It has no large mammals; no deer, no apes or monkeys; no fish of any size in the rivers. Bird life was extremely rich, with a profusion of pigeons, parrots and birds of paradise, but hardly the basis of long-term survival.

On the other hand, there was plenty of vegetable food, for the New Guinea flora is as rich as the fauna is poor, especially in the highlands. With an equatorial climate bestowing year-round high temperatures and rainfall (never more than nine days without rain in five years at one meteorological station), an extremely productive rainforest has evolved to clothe the mountains of Papua New Guinea. 650 plant species are known to have been used as food, medicine and raw materials in the highlands, all of which can still be gathered from the wild forest, although it is agriculture which has sustained people in the highlands for the past several thousand years.

The form of agriculture they practised was 'swidden' – an old Northumbrian term resurrected in the early 1950s as a substitute for the more common 'slash-and-burn', which by then had acquired a decidedly pejorative connotation. At its best, swidden agriculture is an imitation of the natural environment, transforming the natural forest into a harvestable one by substituting a diversity of edible plants for the diversity of forest plants which had previously grown there. In a classic study from the Philippines,[1] the intercropping of forty food plants on a single 3-acre plot ensured a continuous year-round supply of food. Fruit trees, bananas, vines, beans, grains, root crops, spices, sugar cane, tobacco and other non-edible items grew simultaneously, their distribution replicating not only the diversity, but also the canopy architecture of the natural forest they had replaced. The apparently random pattern of plant heights moderated the rain wash-off and weed growth that would hamper production of a single crop in an open forest clearing.

It was a version of swidden agriculture that Michael Leahy saw when he flew over those hidden highlands valleys in 1937 – though the sweet potato must already have been dominant by then. It had come from Indonesia around 300 years before – probably a good thing to begin with, but less so as it became the catalyst for cultural aberrations which placed increasing emphasis on the production of pigs as a form of wealth. Pigs (also an introduction) thrived on sweet potato vines and tubers. By the time I visited the highlands of Papua New Guinea in the early 1980s, they dominated rural life – consuming 64 per cent of the sweet potato crop and absorbing 40 per cent of agricultural labour.

'The human ecology is the highlands is very simple,' one seasoned observer told me; 'the men buy wives who work the land to produce the crops that feed the pigs which make the men wealthy in the eyes of other men.' Wealth, it should be added, that was spent solely on aggrandisement. Pe, 'big-man' of the clan with whom I stayed, told me of a recent ceremony at which he had killed twenty pigs – all raised on sweet potato his wives had grown. Asked the value of them, he quoted more than double the price per kilo that I would have paid for a prime joint of pork at Harrods. And that was not just a notional figure. I was assured that pigs actually were sold at such prices, for cash, but not to feed the family, only to meet traditional obligations.

Ominous consequences were becoming apparent to the researchers I interviewed. Women were inadequately and poorly fed for the amounts of work they were doing – especially during pregnancy; birth rates were falling; infant mortality was alarmingly high; children were malnourished . . . some redress was urgently required and it is surprising that the potato took so long to get there. The fact that its foliage is poisonous and therefore no good as pig-feed would have been a discouragement – but its advantages are indisputable. Especially the fact that while sweet potatoes take nine to twelve months to mature – which means only one crop per year – and do not store well (except in the form of pork, when fed to pigs), potatoes can produce a harvest of small but edible tubers in two months, can be grown all year round in the equatorial highland climate, and can be stored for months between harvests. There was a niche for the potato here – between crops and between seasons.

It has been estimated that less than about 200 hectares of potatoes were grown in all of Papua New Guinea[2] at the time of my visit to the highlands. I ate potatoes in the town, and saw very fine tubers on sale at the markets, but no potato plots caught my attention – only women labouring on the ubiquitous mounds of sweet potatoes. The growing prevalence of the potato since then – to the extent that it quickly became a vital component of household economies – is remarkable, and invites the conclusion that it also must have contributed significantly to the substantial rural population growth which occurred during that time. The number of people living on and from the land increased by over 70 per cent in the twenty years from 1980.[3] Surprisingly, the area of cultivated land in the highlands hardly grew at all, so only intensification or new crops could have kept food production in step with population growth,[4] which supports the contention that the potato had been responsible – just as in Europe and other parts of the world.

As with Papua New Guinea, so with other developing countries. Since the 1960s, the potato has become the fastest-spreading major food crop in the world. Today, it is grown in 148 of the 192 countries represented at the United Nations – more than can be said of any crop except maize. This fantastic global voyage began in earnest in the seventeenth century, when Europe's pioneering navigators decided that the potato would be a useful item to include among their stores – both as food for the voyage and as a crop to plant on as yet unknown shores – even while sceptical stay-at-homes were viewing it with suspicion a century after its arrival from South America. British, French, Dutch, Portuguese and Spanish fleets carried the potato to trading ports, and fishing and whaling stations, around the world.

Contemporary documents show that Dutch settlers took potatoes to the Penghu Islands in the Taiwan Strait as early as 1603. Belgian and French missionaries introduced them to Taiwan itself, where they were remarked upon by a visitor in 1650. Soon the crop had spread throughout China, where it acquired such names as 'earth bean', 'ground nut' and 'tuber with many children'. Another route to China took the potato from eastern Europe, over the Ural mountains and on to the steppes of Asia – a perfect environment, as it transpired, for potatoes. In the Near East, the potato had a champion in Sir John Malcolm, who was Britain's diplomatic representative at the Ottoman and Persian courts in the early 1800s. Fittingly, the potato is known throughout the region as 'Malcolm's plum'.

In much of Asia, the local name of the potato reflected the nationality of the colonial masters. In western Java, where the potato was introduced in 1794, it was called the 'Dutch potato'. In 1897 it arrived in Vietnam, and people called it the 'French tuber'. The British East India Company sent potatoes along its trade routes into the Himalayas, where, not surprisingly, Sherpas called them 'English potatoes'. Buddhist monks are said to have begun cultivating potatoes at their monasteries in Bhutan and Nepal in the 1700s and, just as in Europe, the new and prolific food source set the population rising dramatically. But instead of migrating abroad and to the cities as Europeans had done, sons and daughters for whom there was no room at home in the high Himalayas left to become monks and nuns. And, in turn, the potato's exceptional productivity gave talented individuals time in which to create the region's renowned buildings, paintings, weaving and sculpture.

Potatoes were being grown at the Cape of Good Hope in the 1770s (and doubtless before then) for local consumption and for the provisioning of ships en route to India and beyond, but were not known in the rest of Africa until introduced by missionaries who settled in Basutoland (now Lesotho) in the 1830s and East Africa in the 1880s.

Most reports of the potato's first arrival and adoption in a new country are sketchy, to say the least, but in the case of New Zealand they have been assembled with exceptional diligence.[5] And New Zealand's adoption of the potato is particularly interesting – first because it was the most distant point to which Europe's potatoes were carried; second because New Zealand was the last inhabitable landmass on Earth to be discovered and colonised. The first settlers were Polynesians, probably from the Marquesas islands, who arrived there in the tenth century and called themselves the Maori. They came in canoes, bringing with them little more than their sailing and fishing skills, enough people and knowledge to found viable communities, and vine cuttings of their traditional staple food – the sweet potato, which they called 'kumara'.

The Maori named their discovery Aotearoa – Land of the Long White Cloud – and by the twelfth century the favoured parts of the country supported a substantial scattering of settlements. Abel Tasman, on a Dutch East India voyage dispatched to explore the north Pacific, was the first European to see New Zealand – on 13 December 1642, less than a month after discovering Tasmania (which he named Van Dieman's Land). His encounter with the Maori on the north-western tip of the South Island was not a happy one. Four of his crew were killed as they ferried between ships. Tasman promptly weighed anchor and sailed on, naming the location 'Moordenaers Baij' – Murderer's Bay. It is now known as Golden Bay.

More than a century later, the French explorer Marc Marion du Fresne found the Maori more amenable when he sailed into the Bay of Islands on the north-eastern cost of the North Island. So much so that in March 1772 the crews were able to clear land and plant out the first European garden in New Zealand, on Moturua Island. A journal of the expedition reports:

> As the natives are extremely intelligent, we were able to make them understand that the plantations we had made . . . of wheat, maize, potatoes and various kinds of nuts, might be very useful to them . . . . All these plants had grown very well, although it was winter. The natives seemed highly pleased and informed us that they would take care of our cultivations, . . . which would be all the more valuable to them seeing that they have only the sweet potato and fern root.

Relations with the Maori deteriorated, however, when the French insisted on fishing in a part of the bay they had been told to stay away from – because it was *tapu* (a sacred place). Several hundred Maori attacked the fishing party, killing du Fresne and the twenty-six seamen accompanying him. On learning of this, the expedition's deputy commander ordered retaliatory action in which a Maori village was destroyed and 250 men, women and children massacred. The French named the bay 'Ance des Assassinats' (Assassination Cove).

Captain James Cook had sailed around New Zealand in 1769, on his first voyage to the Pacific, and had already left England on his second when the French and Maori clashed. What he knew of the French expedition and events in the Bay of Plenty can only be guessed at, but it is certain that he took a stock of potatoes on board at the Cape of Good Hope with the intention of planting them in New Zealand. Anchored in Queen Charlotte's Sound on the north island in May 1773, he instructed his crews to plant potatoes along with other European vegetables and grains at several locations along the shore. He returned to the Sound four years later and was dismayed to find that 'not a vestige of the gardens remained' and (referring to potatoes) that 'though the New Zealanders are fond of this root, it was evident that they had not taken the trouble to plant a single one.'

Cook's conclusion is disputed, however, by the Maori, who have traditionally credited him with introducing the potato to New Zealand, and by a report from 1807 indicating that potatoes by then were not only a valued food, but also a trade commodity:

> Though the natives are exceedingly fond of this root, they eat them but sparingly, on account of their great value in procuring iron by barter from European ships that touch at this part of the coast. The utility of this metal is found to be so great that they would rather suffer almost any privation, or inconvenience, for the possession of it particularly when wrought into axes, adzes or small hatchets: the potatoes are consequently preserved with great care against the arrival of a vessel.[6]

The vessels the Maori were trading with need not have come only from Europe. American whalers were also sailing in their waters and could even have been another means of the potato's introduction to New Zealand, for some traditional Maori varieties have a striking resemblance to some Peruvian native potatoes: knobbly, deep eyes, speckled, dark skins and purple flesh. American whalers are known to have regularly reprovisioned at Callao in Peru. That they might have brought Peruvian potatoes to New Zealand (and had Afro-Americans among their crews) is implied by the Maori name given to an elongated variety with a dark purple skin: *Urenika*, meaning Nigger's dick.

But from whatever source, the Maori adopted the potato widely and with alacrity. In the early nineteenth century, an area of 50 hectares devoted to potatoes was not uncommon. By the 1850s more than 3,000 acres of potatoes were reported in just two localities, and the enterprising Maori were growing large quantities of potatoes for sale to the rapidly expanding European populations of Auckland and Wellington. In 1834 a naval officer saw a store of 4,000 bags (weight estimated at 100 tons) in a coastal village. In 1835, nearly 80 tons of seed potatoes were included among the provisions of Maori families who colonised the uninhabited Chatham Islands, and within twenty years they were producing 'hundreds of tons', much of which was exported to Australia.[7]

The potato's advantage in New Zealand was that it fitted so easily into the Maoris' existing agricultural system, gave higher yields and could be stored for longer than their traditional kumara (sweet potato). The same implements could be used and the same ceremonial rituals of planting and harvest were applicable. Furthermore, it was not only palatable, but also produced a reliable surplus and could be cultivated wherever people had chosen to settle. It thrived at all altitudes, and was particularly welcome in the southern regions of the South Island, where kumara would not grow. But such widespread and enthusiastic adoption of a new and superior staple food could not fail to have a significant impact on Maori society, as the anthropologist Raymond Firth declared in 1929:

> The results of the introduction of the potato bring out with clarity, the manner in which new culture items affected the economic life and even the environment of the native. The potato is of such hardy nature that it can be grown in all districts and moreover it is prolific, yielding a plentiful return for the labour expended. Hence it was speedily introduced into districts which ... had formerly possessed no cultivated foods and also tended to replace the kumara among other tribes.[8]

Firth believed that, because potatoes required less time and attention than traditional crops, people had more time for other pursuits, and an authority writing in 1996 goes even further, suggesting the so-called 'Musket Wars' that Maori tribes fought among themselves in the early 1800s might be more accurately named the 'Potato Wars'. The areas planted with potatoes were substantial by then, he pointed out. Potatoes were exchanged for muskets, and since growing them required less labour than traditional crops, more warriors were available to take part in warfare expeditions. An army marched on its stomach, as Napoleon noted, and the potato probably was as important in Maori warfare as the musket.

The potato had a significant impact on the size of the Maori population too – just as it had in South America and throughout Europe. Captain Cook estimated the Maori population at around 100,000 in 1769. This was almost certainly an underestimate (Cook did not see what were probably more densely populated regions inland), but that hardly dents the significance of there having been some 200,000 Maori in New Zealand when Britain claimed sovereignty in 1840,[9] seventy years later. Maori numbers tumbled after that, under the impact of colonial settlement, land wars, economic marginalisation, disease and massive social disruption.

But why did Maori fertility not decline earlier, demographers ask, when the Maori had been exposed for so long to the influences and diseases that pitched other newly encountered populations into precipitous decline? The potato was a factor here. Though there are no census or baptismal records to confirm a spurt in population growth such as occurred in Europe and elsewhere, the circumstantial evidence indicates that Maori birth rates rose following the potato's introduction, to levels that compensated for losses caused by foreign influence.

Maori potatoes, with their distinctive appearance and characteristics, survive today alongside 'modern' varieties as a speciality – not simply a source of food, but something precious; a gift of the ancestors. The Maori speak of a responsibility to maintain them. Some families have been growing the same cultivars, year after year, for eight or nine generations. The Maori potato is a token of continuity and communal identity that a host would be proud to offer his guests, they say. Those who grow enough to sell have no problem disposing of all they can produce at markets and on roadside stalls (usually for considerably more than is paid for 'modern' potatoes) but production is relatively small-scale and localised – a feature which helped the old traditional varieties to survive the arrival of late blight in 1905, when New Zealand's large-scale commercial potato production was totally destroyed.

Ironically, with the European potato temporarily wiped out, New Zealand quickly turned back to the Maori's traditional food, kumara – the sweet potato. High-yielding varieties were imported from America for distribution to farmers as a crop that would reduce the country's reliance on potatoes – but only until varieties less susceptible to blight had been introduced[10] and New Zealand had caught up with the management and spraying strategies devised by blight-stricken potato-growers in Europe and America. Having once proved its worth, the potato is never willingly abandoned. The benefits it has to offer outweigh the disadvantages of production every time, and everywhere.

Today, New Zealand produces over 500,000 tonnes of potatoes per year; most of it for domestic consumption, but a significant amount for export too. In fact, the potato is New Zealand's highest-value export crop. The international market is critically important to a country whose economy is based largely on agriculture. New Zealand wants to produce top-quality high-value potatoes and invests heavily in maintaining standards – most recently by contributing to the funding of a $36 million international consortium that aims to sequence the entire genome of the potato by 2010.[11] The investment will give New Zealand early access to information that can be used to breed new improved varieties and add value to the product – a strategy typical of the developed world: hi-tech and hugely expensive.

Meanwhile, large amounts of money and resources are also being applied to the search for strategies that will boost the value of the potato in the developing world – among the rural communities for whom it is more of a life-saver than a money-maker. Cheap and low-tech is the priority here. And so two strands of endeavour carry the interests of the potato forward in the twenty-first century: one that promotes the potato's capacity to feed people in the developing world who do not otherwise have enough to eat; and another that seeks to maximise its commercial potential in the developed world.

Chapter Sixteen

Developing worlds

The Inuit have a saying; 'gifts make slaves as whips make dogs', and this is something to bear in mind when considering the motives and effectiveness of international aid, and the reaction of people receiving it. Neither the altruism of donors nor the wholehearted gratitude of recipients is guaranteed. As the Inuit so aptly noted, the act of giving can denote an assumption of superiority on the part of the givers. Add an element of colonial guilt, and even the faintest whiff of racial prejudice, and it is not surprising that some major aid programmes have been greeted with suspicion and a paralysing lack of enthusiasm from the recipients. Misconceptions about what the people in need *actually need* are often to blame. It is easy enough to see that starving communities need food, but what exactly should be done for an active and healthy population that is producing more people than its available land area can support – such as the highlanders of Papua New Guinea and agro-pastoralist communities of the Andes? They had managed their affairs very well up to that point (not least by accepting the health care that had reduced mortality rates), and were likely to resist suggestions that they should manage them differently.

It was at this juncture that anthropologists and human ecologists began to make some useful contributions in the 1960s and '70s; especially those who were interested not simply in human society as a phenomenon in itself, but in the broader picture of people as an integral part of the environment that sustains them. By examining and quantifying food production systems in terms of energy flows and interactions, human ecologists have shown that the so-called 'primitive' agricultural systems of people in the developing world were often far more efficient than was immediately apparent and, furthermore, perfectly capable of maintaining the long-term productivity and ecological stability of the environment. Their cultural practices and social organisation were often directly related to environmental circumstance, and had evolved to ensure continuous and sustainable production. The complex religious calendar in Bali, for instance, was precisely tuned to the timing of activities that maintained rice production at optimum levels. Elsewhere, marriage practices varied according to whether land-use was extensive or intensive; and even India's sacred cow – an icon of absurd and wasteful cultural practice in Western eyes – was shown to have a positive function in ecological terms as provider of fuel (dung), milk and bullocks for tractive power.

From Pacific islands to Arctic tundra, studies in human ecology demonstrated the ability of people to develop sustainable ways of life in whatever environment they occupied. It is a talent that has taken humanity into every inhabitable niche the world has to offer – obvious at the extremes of fishing communities and nomadic herders, but also evident at every nuance of difference in between, be they Alpine pastoralists, North American Indians, Pygmies in the African rainforest or even the inhabitants of a modern city.

In the early 1980s I visited a number of locations around the world where the links between culture, social organisation and environmental circumstance had been defined, following up the academic studies with some eye-witness reporting and photography for a book on human ecology.[1] The locations included the highlands of Papua New Guinea and the potato-growing regions of the Peruvian Andes. There and everywhere else it was clear that although the communities were described in the literature as though they were closed and self-sustaining, most had subsequently become more open and were now part of much larger ecosystems. This did not matter so far as validity was concerned – it was still possible to describe a system's unique features even if it no longer functioned to perfection – but it mattered a great deal in terms of the outside world's attitude to such communities. If they were now part of a larger system they deserved a share of its resources and options – but what was the foremost need? To raise living standards with the introduction of new crops, technology and ideas; or to preserve the unique traditions and customs which those introductions would make redundant?

This dilemma has created conflicts of aspiration wherever communities wanted the benefits of integration with the wider world while at the same time continuing to follow their traditional way of life –

the two are not always compatible. The external influence of tourist agencies encouraged the highlanders of Papua New Guinea, for instance, to pursue their flamboyant traditions to extremes that would not have been reached in a closed ecosystem – with unhappy consequences; on the Queen Charlotte Islands, off Canada's north-west Pacific coast, the Haida Indians were completely divorced from their traditional ways as a means of sustenance, but claimed their identity alone gave them rights to a share of revenues from oil deposits beneath the seas they had once fished.

There was understandable sympathy for these aspirations, and even implicit agreement that traditional culture should be preserved for its own sake – whether or not it was of any practical value to the people concerned. Partly this was because no one likes to admit their intrusion can destroy the very thing they admire, partly because the spectacle of people behaving differently is always fascinating, and partly because the unique communities of the undeveloped world might know or possess something that the developed world would find useful. Reports tended to emphasise the issue of preservation as the story moved along a continuum of exactitude from peer-reviewed journals to popular magazines, television and tabloid newspapers. So, although rigorous in its science, human ecology spawned a rose-tinted view of traditional cultures and communities, creating a popular expectation that they should always be considered worthy of preservation, and adding confusion to issues of development – what was its purpose: to preserve tradition for the benefit of humanity as a whole; or to bring the benefits of the wider world to people whose traditions were no longer enough?

This was especially evident when scientists and development agencies began looking in depth at the potato-growing communities of the Andes. The anthropological and human ecology studies which attracted my attention to the region were based on research conducted in the 1960s and '70s. In the mode of the day they described an indigenous agricultural system whose benefits and resilience testified to the ingenuity of its creators. They showed how a carefully integrated pattern of agriculture and herding had evolved on the Altiplano. Herds of llamas and sheep grazed the rangelands, converting widely dispersed and otherwise worthless vegetation into easily digested and nourishing food – meat – while regularly bringing back to the compound an ample supply of concentrated nutrients and energy in the form of dung. Dung was used both as manure for the crops and as fuel for the fires and so the animals speeded up the nutrient cycle and energy flow of what was otherwise a very slow-moving system. And then of course there were the potato and the strategies that ensured continuous and sustainable production.

To science and the wider world, the nurturing of native stock in the Andes was a classic demonstration of indigenous talent. The phrase 'vertical archipelago' was coined, signalling commendation for a system that exploited the different ecological zones of an ascending landscape so fully and effectively. Admiringly, researchers watched farmers heaving on the *taclla*, as they cultivated fields on the steep mountain slopes; like innocents, they rummaged through the heaps of harvested tubers, sorting out the most colourful specimens, the most odd-shaped and peculiar, for the photographs that would illustrate the published report. All this contributed to a distorted view of Andean potato-growers. The relevance of their having been victims of oppression for centuries, who farmed the high Andes because they had been forced to, or had no other option, was not highly rated. The fact that only native potatoes grow well at high altitude was similarly discounted – even though farmers themselves would tell you that the 'improved' European-type potatoes are more productive, bigger, easier to eat and socially more acceptable than native varieties. And here is the crux of the matter: a pragmatic eye, seeing native potatoes for the first time, will soon dismiss their novel characteristics as a hindrance to wider appreciation of their nutritional virtues. If ever there was a wild thing awaiting improvement, the native potato is it.

Meanwhile, the developed world had recognised the value of native potatoes as a source of genetic material from which desirable characteristics might be bred into their commercial varieties. So, whatever the Andean potato-growers might need, there was also a powerful motive to preserve the native potato's existence and inherent diversity for the benefit of the wider world. This resonated with alarm about the rate at which all wild species – animate and floral – were becoming extinct. Genetic resources must be saved before it is too late was the cry and, since the most endangered species were located in the developing world, activities designed to alleviate poverty while also preserving resources would be doubly commendable. The International Potato Centre in Lima was founded in 1971 to do just that in respect of the potato. CIP's mandate was to preserve the genetic resources of the potato in its Andean homeland and make the potato a twenty-first-century solution to hunger in the developing world. 'The potato is the forgotten crop in a world with a grain mentality,' CIP's director, Richard Sawyer, told me in 1982. 'It was never seriously considered as part of the solution to world hunger. Our goal is to make the potato available and inexpensive for everyone by the year 2000.'

When the year 2000 arrived, the realisation of Richard Sawyer's dream was still a good way off. Sawyer had moved on too. During his twenty years at CIP he had assembled a dedicated team of scientists and researchers, and the Center was helping farmers worldwide to improve the quality and yield of their crops, but one of his greatest accomplishments, he said, was the creation of CIP's World Potato Collection, which ensured that the potato's genetic material was gathered, maintained and made available to breeders around the world.[2]

In September 2000, the largest gathering of world leaders in history assembled in New York for the United Nations Millennium Summit. It was a momentous occasion, convened to commemorate the beginning of a new millennium with a commitment to eradicate poverty and end human misery around the world. The summit's final declaration was signed by the leaders or designates of 189 countries, thereby committing the international community to a specific agenda of eight Millennium Development Goals which not only identified what had to be done, but also set targets for measuring and monitoring the improvements in people's lives as the programme progressed. Primary education, gender equality and empowerment, child mortality, maternal health, HIV/AIDS, malaria and other diseases, environmental sustainability and development strategies were all identified as specific goals and assessed in terms of need and targets, but Goal One – top of the agenda – was the eradication of extreme poverty and hunger.

Here the nations of the world explicitly undertook to halve by 2015 the proportion of people who had been living on less than one dollar a day in 1990, or had suffered from hunger. Achieving that goal would still leave many millions hungry and in poverty, but the architects of the Millennium Development Goals had spurned idealistic dreams of a perfect world in favour of more realistic ambitions: aiming to do what they believed could be done. Even so, the challenges were daunting.

At the time of the Millennium Summit in 2000, over 800 million people were suffering from hunger – one-seventh of the world's population. Every day, starvation killed 24,000 people, with children the most vulnerable. One child was dying every seven seconds from the effects of insufficient food, undernourishment and associated diseases. And that despite some remarkable progress having been made in the previous half-century. The production of food worldwide had tripled since 1950, and the quantity and quality of global food supplies generally had improved, raising the nutritional status of many populations. In fact, between 1970 and 1998 alone, the daily per capita dietary intake of people in developing countries rose from 2,140 to 2,716 calories on average, and the number of malnourished people declined from a billion to 800 million. These advances were impressive . . . but not enough.

As one of fifteen international agricultural research centres which together had a total of more than 8,500 scientists and scientific staff working in 100 countries around the world under the coordinating umbrella of the Consultative Group on International Agricultural Research (CGIAR), CIP was party to the Millennium Development Goals and set about identifying which goals and which regions of the world would benefit most from its expertise and experience with potatoes.[3] The results of this targeting exercise confirmed a major result of the assessment CIP had conducted five years before, namely that wherever potatoes were grown in the developing world, people were abjectly poor. Though global poverty rates and potato production figures had changed in the meantime, the conclusion remained the same: while the potato was good at keeping people alive it did not lift many of them out of poverty. This implied that increasing potato production was unlikely to improve the overall well-being of the world's poorest people. So what aspects of agricultural knowledge and technology could CIP generate and disseminate that would help the global community achieve its Millennium Development Goals?

CIP has been very good at the development of down-to-earth, hands-on strategies that assist farmers directly. The introduction of drought- and virus-resistant varieties to a potato-growing region of China, for instance, increased returns by 106 per cent over twenty years, with poor households receiving 71 per cent of the benefit. Likewise, a twenty-five-year project which introduced methods of controlling the potato tuber moth to poor farmers in Tunisia delivered a 64 per cent return. Over the course of fifteen years, rapid multiplication and late blight-resistant varieties gave Vietnamese farmers an 81 per cent return. Andean farmers will gain a 32 per cent return from the methods to control the Andean potato weevil that CIP has developed. And then there is true potato seed, the Cinderella of propagation technologies whose advantages (and problems) are substantial.

True potato seed (TPS) is seed collected from the berries of plants grown and pollinated under controlled conditions. The principal advantage of using seed is obvious: one handful of TPS is enough to fill one hectare of land, an area which would require 2 tonnes of conventional seed tubers. This offers substantial savings – especially in remote areas where transportation costs make seed tubers prohibitively expensive. The major problem TPS faces is the production of seeds that produce tubers of uniformly high quality and yield. Because the potato is genetically so variable, seeds produced from natural pollination of potato flowers in a field usually have characteristics totally unlike those of the parents. In fact, when potato plants are grown from these seeds it is difficult to find two that produce similar tubers. Even worse, many plants exhibit deleterious hidden or recessive genes that result in weak, inferior potatoes.

After more than twenty years of research to overcome the difficulties and persuade farmers to use TPS, the best that can be said for it is that plantings in remote regions of China had reached a total of 1,000 hectares by 2006. 'That might not sound like much,' said the geneticist Enrique Chujoy, who coordinated CIP's role in the initiative, 'but most of the plots making up that total are very small. There are probably several thousand households involved.' And for them TPS is a godsend. Labour-intensive and time-consuming? Yes, since producing edible potatoes from TPS is a two-stage, two-season affair. First plants are grown from seed to produce seedling tubers; and second those tubers are planted out to produce a mature crop. But double effort has a double advantage: at the first stage farmers can produce seed tubers for sale, as well as for themselves; at the second they are assured of a good crop.

'The great thing about TPS is that it can help disadvantaged sections of society in regions where mainstream advances in agricultural technology simply aren't applicable,' said Chujoy. 'It will never replace clonal crops totally – the economics of time and labour work against it – but a kilo of TPS in the right place can feed a village ultimately – and give the villagers an income. We have to work with these farmers, and focus our efforts specifically on their needs.'[4]

And while CIP does have scientists of world repute working in hi-tech laboratories at the forefront of potato research – on DNA fingerprinting, for example, and other sophisticated scientific investigations – there are also CIP plant breeders out in the field striving, year on year, to produce the variety that will spare farmers from the depredations of late blight, and save them the cost of spraying their crops. Ever since the first epidemic struck Europe in 1845, late blight has been the major evil that potato-growers face, and breeding resistant varieties is still a preferred means of dealing with it. High levels of resistance have been attained, but durability is elusive – the pathogen always manages to find a way through whatever barrier the plant-breeders have introduced. Accepting that total resistance is probably unattainable, CIP's plant breeders are among those pursuing an alternative approach.

'Resistance breaks down because it was due to either a single major gene on the one hand, or to several minor genes on the other,' Juan Landeo, head of CIP's breeding programme, explained. 'In the case of major gene resistance, it's as though there was one big padlock with one big key keeping the pathogen out. It worked very well for a while, but eventually the pathogen broke the lock. And that's it: no more resistance.'

Landeo was speaking from personal experience. He had bred Canchan, one of Peru's most popular and widely grown varieties in the 1990s, renowned for its resistance to late blight and saving farmers over $70 per hectare in fungicides. But not any more. Since the dawn of the new millennium, Canchan's ability to withstand the disease has gradually broken down. Landeo was phlegmatic. 'Only one padlock,' he said. 'A strong one, but not durable.'

It was with this in mind that Landeo began another breeding programme in the early 1990s that was designed to develop varieties which would be protected by numerous small padlocks (minor genes), and be free of major genes (single big ones). 'In effect, each partially resistant variety has a number of small padlocks,' Landeo explained, 'and I wanted to incorporate as many as possible into breeding populations from which varieties would emerge with a string of padlocks to keep the pathogen out. The plant wouldn't be totally immune to infection, but if there were enough padlocks it would survive long enough to produce tubers.'

Working with thousands of 'pure blood' native Andean potato plants, Landeo found that although they all died when exposed to normal levels of late blight infection, specimens from sixty clones survived at lower levels. Crossing these clones and repeating the selection and crossing procedures through five cycles over a period of thirteen years, he found 150 clones which survived to maturity when exposed to severe levels of late blight. 'You could almost see the plants laughing at it,' said Landeo.

An opportunity to test resistance in the field arose when the Quechua-speaking farmers of Chacllabamba, a remote village in the high Andes, appealed to CIP (via their local government agricultural advisory service) for help. Their crops of native potatoes had been almost totally destroyed by an enemy previously unknown to them. At more than 4,000 metres above sea level, harsh climate conditions had kept *Phytophthora infestans* away from Chacllabamba until then. But the increased rain and temperatures associated with global climate change had allowed late blight to creep up the mountainside, taking hold in areas where it was not previously a threat.

'When we got news of their plight I selected twenty clones from among the resistant breeding populations we were working with,' said Landeo, 'and sent 100 tubers of each up to Chacllabamba.'

In May 2004, when the Chacllabamba potato fields were due for harvesting, a team including scientists from CIP went to see how the new clones had fared and to hear what the villagers thought of them – in terms of their agronomic and culinary characteristics. Getting to Chacllabamba from the nearest large urban centre, Cuzco, was in itself a challenge: six hours by vehicle to the roadhead, then another six hours on horseback (or on foot) across the Altiplano to the village. But the journey was worthwhile. The new clones had produced better harvests than the traditional highland varieties, and seven of them scored particularly high marks in the villagers' overall estimation. They had not succumbed to late blight or frost, they produced a good crop, their tubers were well-formed and the right colour; they cooked well, had the right texture and tasted very good.

This was good news, but a special case that must be multiplied many times over if it is to make a significant contribution to the achievement of the Millennium Development Goals. The problem is that most of what CIP has done with the potato has been science- (and scientist-) led. The research has been driven by high levels of intellectual enthusiasm and technical expertise, but applying the results has almost always required the direct input of its initiators. Furthermore, farmers receiving help from CIP have inevitably become dependent upon the continuing support of external influences – for new varieties, when the first introductions lose their resistance (as they will) or for a supply of pesticides. The villagers in the highlands of Papua New Guinea are a good example of this. Their potato crops had been wiped out by late blight, which had not been known in Papua New Guinea until then. With commendable despatch, a team of scientists from Australia and CIP flew in to assess the problem and formulate an extended research and development project to help the country deal with it.

And what did they propose? Seed tubers from ten of CIP's late blight-resistant cultivars would be produced under quarantine conditions in Lima for shipment to Papua New Guinea, where they would be multiplied over several seasons and assessed in the field for their adaptation and late blight resistance. When acceptably resistant varieties had been identified, they would be distributed as replacements for the susceptible variety previously grown in Papua New Guinea. The country's small but hitherto flourishing commercial potato-growing industry would derive considerable benefit from the project – eventually. Meanwhile, the villagers could either abandon potatoes altogether, or spray their crops – which is an expensive option for people who are probably living on less than a dollar a day. Even in high latitudes, where climates allow only one harvest per year, farmers might consider it advisable to spray their crops a dozen times. In tropical regions like Papua New Guinea, where potatoes can be grown continuously, crops may need spraying every few days – thirty or more times a year.

Unavoidably, the introduction of potatoes to poor and largely self-sufficient farming communities obliges them to participate in a wider network of economic interactions – which is fine where people have some money and the network is comprehensive and robust enough to support the additional participants, but decidedly unhelpful where communications, services, administrative policies and institutions are poor. Indeed, in such circumstances aid can be distinctly unhelpful, for communities persuaded to move on from self-sufficiency might find it impossible to get back should the support upon which they had become dependent cease to be available.

So, while agriculture is central to food security, economic development and environmental stability in the developing world, halving poverty and hunger by 2015 will require a good deal more than late blight-resistant potatoes and the means of controlling tuber moth and the Andean potato weevil – though the value of these developments is not in doubt – and already there are signs that the targets will not be reached.

A World Bank review published in 2004[5] found that while the total number of undernourished people in the developing world had declined quite significantly since 1990, most of the improvement was due to strong growth in China and India, while undernourishment overall had fallen by only 3 per cent. On current trends, the proportion of people who suffer from hunger will not have been halved by 2015, the review concluded. Similarly, although the proportion living on less than a dollar a day had fallen from 28.3 per cent in 1990 to 21.6 per cent in 1999, and overall chances of meeting the 2015 target were good, this was no cause for celebration. The dollar-a-day measure had meanwhile become seriously out of date, and if the poverty line was drawn at a more realistic $2 a day, there was no chance whatsoever of meeting the target. An estimated 2.7 billion people were caught in the poverty trap at this higher level, the World Bank reported, more than half the entire population of the developing world. By 2015, the poverty rate measured at $2 a day would still be more than 60 per cent of its 1990 level.

In terms of overall costs, the World Bank estimates that $40–60 billion of additional foreign aid per year will be required to reach the Millennium Development Goals by 2015. But even sums of this order cannot guarantee that the targets will be reached, for money is not the only requirement, nor even the most important. A country must also have the infrastructure, policies and institutions that will enable it to use the aid effectively – and this limits the amount that a country can absorb. Even the developing world's best-equipped countries reach 'saturation point' when aid is around 30 per cent of their gross domestic product (GDP), after which the growth impact of additional aid is zero. The saturation point for those with extremely weak infrastructure, policies and institutions is around just 6 per cent of GDP.[6]

So the Millennium Development Goals begin to seem a little unrealistic, and more of an idealistic dream, after all. And the potato clearly is a mixed blessing to the millions whom the world community has pledged to raise out of hunger and poverty by 2015. It is very good at feeding hungry people but not so good at improving their economic status. Indeed, as happened in Ireland and during the Industrial Revolution, reliance on the potato as a staple food ensnares more people in poverty than it lifts out of it. It is enterprising individuals with the resources needed to grow substantial quantities for sale that the potato enriches. For villagers in the highlands of Papua New Guinea and similar locations in the developing world to make the most of the potato's potential, or even be assured of an adequate return from the land and labour devoted to the crop, they must spend hard cash on sprays to keep late blight under control. This is not easy for people who live on less than a dollar a day and depend on what they grow for food. It is a lot for the developing world as a whole, too. CIP has calculated that, altogether, resource-poor farmers in the developing world spend more than $750 million per year on fungicides to protect their potatoes from late blight. And that is not the only cost. Even while in effect spraying potatoes with dollars its farmers can ill afford, the developing world loses another $2.5 billion that it would have earned if average yields were closer to the potato's potential.

Potato yields in the developing world were never high – but then did not need to be for a crop that could comfortably feed a family on an acre of land. Even with the inclusion of its commercial industry, Papua New Guinea's yield averaged only 7.4 tonnes per hectare in 1981, and has fallen since then – probably as a result of disaffection among the country's small farmers as the problems (and cost) of maintaining the crop's productivity became evident. In 2005, Papua New Guinea's farmers harvested an average of just 4.5 tonnes per hectare, one of the lowest yields in the world. Meanwhile, New Zealand's average yield had risen, from 27.4 tonnes per hectare in 1981 to 45.5 tonnes per hectare in 2005.[7] In other words, while Papua New Guinea's average potato yield had fallen by 39.3 per cent over twenty-five years, New Zealand's had risen by 66.05 per cent. Ironic that while serious disadvantages limit the potato's potential for improving the well-being of poor and hungry people in undeveloped regions, it booms in the developed world – where there is money to be made from exploiting its potential to the full.

Chapter Seventeen

For the price of apples

China's population is growing at a rate of about fifteen per minute. In June 2006 just under 1,314,000,000 Chinese were waking up to greet the day. By June 2007 the total reached 1,322,000,000. China had to accommodate and feed over 8 million more people than just twelve months before. Adding 8 million a year to a population of 1.3 billion represents a growth rate of 0.6 per cent – commendably low when compared to some countries in Africa, for instance, where population growth rates have exceeded 4 per cent (at which a population doubles every eighteen years), but daunting when the statistics are set aside and the implications of the figures are considered.

The number of extra people that China must contend with each year is significantly greater than the entire population of Papua New Guinea (5.8 million), and double the number of people currently living in New Zealand (4.076 million). And no matter how equitably the additional numbers are spread across the country, every one of them needs shelter, food and water, and clothing and will grow up to expect a job, and some fulfilment of the hopes and joys that all people aspire to. Every nation confronts these issues in some respects, if not in terms of a growing population, then certainly in terms of peoples' broadening expectations – but China has to contend with both as its population grows and becomes more affluent at the same time. How is the country coping?

'If you want to understand China's economy, think of it as a potato,' a Forbes business analyst declared in 2006.[1] Why? Because China's potatoes are increasingly consumed in the more expensive form of convenience foods, which means that growth in demand reflects growth in

consumer income, as well as expansion of the national economy, much more accurately than the figures for rice and wheat – which the government regards as strategically important foodstuffs and sets production and price levels accordingly. So, while analysts might view the jumble of official economic and financial data from Beijing with a degree of caution, the potato is seen as one of the more illustrative and reliable barometers for the state of the Chinese economy.

French fries have accounted for most of the rise in potato consumption, as affluence has inspired a taste for convenience foods, and it can be no surprise that two fast food giants from the United States, McDonald's and Kentucky Fried Chicken, have been the principal suppliers. When McDonald's opened an outlet on Beijing's Tiananmen Square in 1992, it was mobbed by 40,000 customers hungry for a taste of the hamburgers and french fries they had heard so much about. Ten years later McDonald's had more than 500 outlets in China and confidently expected to pass the 1,000 mark in time for the Beijing Olympic Games in 2008. The country's largest restaurant chain, however, was Kentucky Fried Chicken, with nearly 1,700 outlets in 2007, all endeavouring to satisfy the country's booming demand, and earning the company a robust 26 per cent growth in profits, compared with just 1 per cent in the United States.

Potato consumption in China rose more than 40 per cent in the five years to 2007 (compared with a 2.45 per cent global rise during the same period). Domestic production has kept pace, so that China is now the world's largest producer and the world's largest consumer of potatoes. But, even so, the Chinese eat an average of only 30 kilograms each per year, compared with more than 66 kilograms in the United States.[2] Clearly, there is room for expansion as affluence percolates through the population, which in turn increases demand and opens up yet more areas of opportunity. For several years after they began operations in China, McDonald's and Kentucky Fried Chicken were obliged to import 70 per cent of the french fries they sold in China, simply because local potato suppliers could not meet their exacting quality standards. Then other large US food companies moved in to begin filling the gap – first J. R. Simplot, then McCain Foods.

Simplot is one of the world's largest agribusiness companies, and potatoes account for about half of the company's $3.3 billion annual revenues. The company grew from the 120 acres John Simplot began farming after dropping out of school and running away from his home in Boise, Idaho, at the age of fourteen. The farmer owning the land he had leased 'taught me how to grow good potatoes', he said. That was in the 1920s. By the 1940s, his business had expanded to the extent that the privately owned J. R. Simplot Company was America's largest supplier of fresh potatoes and had also moved into potato processing. In the 1990s, the company (still owned by the Simplot family) began exporting its expertise to China. The strategy they adopted was not dissimilar to that which the company had been founded upon: Simplot taught Chinese farmers how to grow good potatoes, and helped them to improve their infrastructure and farming techniques. Under contracts that provided an assured income, farmers used designated seed tubers and fertilisers, as well as standardised irrigation equipment and farming methods, to produce exactly the potatoes Simplot required for the joint-venture processing facility the company had established on the outskirts of Beijing. China's first commercial frozen french fry was produced there in April 1993, and the facility continues to supply McDonald's in China and other East Asian customers with international standard french fries and hash browns.

Meanwhile, McCain Foods, the world's largest manufacturer of frozen french fries, had also established a processing plant in China and like Simplot was working with farmers to raise the quality of their potatoes to the required standards.

One might criticise the domineering approach of these international companies; one might even deplore China's growing fondness for french fries; but one cannot ignore the extent to which these developments have boosted both the quantity and quality of potatoes grown in China, while simultaneously raising farm incomes. More than 5,000 farmers are contracted to Simplot alone, supplying the company with over 30,000 tonnes of potatoes each year from a total of 2,000 hectares. And the really significant point about these figures is that they involve so many individual farmers. In Europe and the United States, 2,000 hectares would be worked by just a handful of farmers and their yields would be much greater, but in China the benefits that the potato brings to the national economy are spread more widely. Furthermore, the demand for frozen french fries and other forms of processed potato have inspired the construction of the roads and other infrastructure that will bring even the remotest regions, and the poorest farmers, into the supply chain.

Inner Mongolia, on China's north-western borders, for instance, has become one of the country's foremost potato-growing regions. This is a land of mountains and high plateaux, arid and remote, that the United

Nations once classified among the world's least habitable regions. Nonetheless, it is home to 1.5 million people, of whom nearly 90 per cent are farmers, and its disadvantages became advantages as China's insatiable demand for potatoes prompted the improvement of access to the region. The region's loess soils were ideal for the crop; with irrigation, its location and climate offered the potential of year-round production; its altitude minimised the problems of disease; and its 1.35 million farmers were poor and keen to make more of their lives. In 2005, those growing potatoes harvested a total of some 2 million tonnes from the 100,000 hectares they had planted – a respectable yield of 20 tonnes per hectare – and the predictions are that by 2010 the region will have 200,000 hectares devoted to potatoes and an annual harvest of 4.5 million tonnes.

Few of Inner Mongolia's potatoes will end up as french fries served up with hamburgers on Tiananmen Square. But that is not the only outlet: 36 per cent of China's potato production is eaten fresh; 31 per cent is exported; 22 per cent is processed into starch; 5 per cent is reserved for seed; and the remainder goes to sundry other uses. Guyuan, the administrative centre for Inner Mongolia's Xihaigu province, already has more than 2,000 potato handling companies, wholesale markets and a potato-shipping association that delivers fresh potatoes to numerous provinces and municipalities as well as to Hong Kong, Macao, Taiwan and even some European countries.[3]

There have to be some reservations about the rapid expansion of potato production in China; it cannot be all good news, as the promotional material would have us believe; there must be some failed hopes and local catastrophes that are less enthusiastically publicised. The mechanisation of production, and an increasing dependence on irrigation, chemical fertilisers and disease control are all cause for concern. But since these are all features of potato production that were developed by growers in Europe and the United States, where yields and quality are high and virtually guaranteed, it would be hypocritical to suggest that China should not follow the same route. After all, it is not so long ago that the potato was just a subsistence crop in Europe, doing a good job of feeding the poor, but enslaving them too. Only as it became a valued commodity did it contribute to the economic and social developments that freed millions from poverty. Then everyone enjoyed it, and you could say that the potato had fulfilled its mission – in the developed world, at least. Now China wants to do the same for the Chinese, and as testimony to the progress made so far, here is

Ma Quanhu, a farmer from the Xiji country of Inner Mongolia, who harvested 6,000 kilograms of potatoes from one small field in 2005. That harvest earned him 3,000 Yuan (about $360). 'It's unbelievable,' he said, 'that potatoes are sold at the same price as apples.'[4]

The China Modernisation Report 2006, drawn up by the country's leading research institute, the Chinese Academy of Sciences, claims that by 2050 China will have eradicated poverty, relocated 500 million peasants to cities, rehoused 600 million city-dwellers in hi-tech suburban homes and established itself as a world power in science and technology. Even in a country renowned for its grandiose plans, these are ambitious targets. On the other hand, 817,000 science and engineering students graduated in 2003 (about eight times the US total), and China reduced the proportion of its population living in poverty from 30 per cent in 1978 to less than 3 per cent at the end of 2005. Admittedly, this reduction was according to the Chinese government's assessment of poverty, which sets the line at 668 Yuan (about $86) per year, but even when measured against the UN's dollar-a-day benchmark, China's poverty fell from 33 per cent in 1990 to 14 per cent in 2002 – a reduction of more than half, reached well ahead of the Millennium Development Goal's 2015 target.

It would be a bold advocate who suggested that China's achievements would have been significantly less without the potato but, although its contribution may be impossible to measure precisely, its role as an enabling commodity is beyond doubt. The potato and China have been mutually supportive, echoing the tuber's role in the histories of South America and Europe. The difference is, though, that China has adopted the potato more quickly, more wholeheartedly and on a far larger scale than had ever happened before. Thirty years is all it took for the world's most populous nation to advance from insignificant grower to world's leading producer. Furthermore, those thirty years have also seen huge advances in potato science – which China has not been slow to adopt. And so, the story of the potato in China encapsulates the major advances of potato science and agronomy in recent times. But, as ever with the potato, the story has an historical and political context.

China's Communist Party had won power in 1949 'on the backs of peasants driven to revolt by hunger'. With a population of 563 million, predominantly rural, whose basic needs had been sorely neglected by previous regimes, the new People's Republic of China faced a massive burden of nutritional deficiency and disease. Local famines were frequent;

average life expectancy was thirty-five years. The imperatives were stark and clear: provide food and services; improve health care and education. But Mao Zedong was motivated more by political ideals than social realities. He believed the country's plight was due to the 'inherently capitalistic' behaviour of its peasant farmers. Scattered individual production had condemned China to perpetual poverty, he said, and only by abolishing small peasant landholdings could China begin to escape from its past and move on to become the modern industrial giant he envisaged. Collectivisation, as applied in the Soviet Union, would solve the problem. And so 400 million people were dragooned into joining 752,000 collectives across the country. A revolution fought on the backs of poor peasants became their relentless foe.[5]

By the 1950s, it was widely known that Soviet collectivisation had been a calamitous failure. Stalin's successor, Nikita Khrushchev, had seen the consequences at first hand while he was First Secretary of the Ukraine, and personally warned Mao against making the same mistakes that Stalin had made. Several of Mao's political colleagues had learned of Stalin's failure while studying in the Soviet Union. But Mao believed his genius and leadership would guarantee Chinese success where the Soviet Union had failed. His communes and 'agro-cities' would be larger and more communistic because they would abolish all private plots and all private possessions – something not even Stalin had dared to attempt.

Critics were silenced, and, with what has been aptly described as 'a metaphysical disregard for reality',[6] Mao demanded that his grand schemes should be put into operation and achieve results in no more time than he deemed necessary. Thus, the Great Leap Forward that he announced in 1957 should require only five years' hard work to produce 1,000 years of happiness. Such promises. Meat at every meal; monkey brains and swallows' nests for all; silks and woollen suits; overcoats lined with fox furs. Mao's dreams intoxicated the country as officials took the fantasy of fine living to every village. For people inured to drudgery and hunger, the promises alone were a nourishing novelty. When would it come about? Soon, very soon. How would it be achieved? With revolutionary optimism, revolutionary heroism, and a full measure of Stalinist science.

Although Mao was neither farmer nor scientist, he believed that science could make his dreams come true. He and his colleagues studied the propaganda material from Moscow which praised the achievements of Soviet science, and were particularly taken with the work of Trofim

Lysenko, who had determined the course of Soviet agriculture during the Stalin era. Any man whose alleged achievements included the doubling of grain yields, cows that produced only cream, lemon trees that bore fruit in Siberia and potatoes that survived heavy frost was a disciple Mao would unquestioningly follow. The Lysenko doctrines were imposed on collectives throughout China and within months loyal minions were delivering the news that Mao wanted to hear. The country's annual grain harvest was reported to have jumped from 185 million tonnes to 430 million tonnes. Peasants were said to be growing cabbages that each weighed 500 pounds and harvesting potatoes at the rate of more than 1,000 tonnes per hectare. One local official reported that farmers in his area had successfully crossed cotton and tomato plants. The result? Red cotton.[7]

The entire country was ensnared in the madness of Mao's dream – especially when he announced that as a reward for such spectacular success, peasants should eat as much as they wanted, plant a little less and work only half-days, using their spare time for culture, study and recreation. But there was little hope of that, for while being told to enjoy the fruits of their proclaimed success, the collectives were also required to deliver a large proportion of their harvests as taxes to central government. The consequences were inevitable. In a typical example, a county which had harvested only 88,392 tonnes but reported a harvest of 239,280 tonnes had to meet a tax assessment of around 30 per cent on the fictitious figure. The amount due was set at 75,500 tonnes, and when officials were unable to collect more than 62,500 tonnes (four-fifths of the actual harvest), they launched a brutal 'anti-hiding campaign'.[8]

Mao refused to believe that his dream had become a nightmare. He dismissed talk of food shortages as wild exaggeration; or if there was hunger, it was only the 'tuition fees that must be paid to gain experience',[9] he said. China had experienced famine before, many times, as dynastic records reveal, but these had always been local, or the result of civil war or invasion. In 1959, China was at peace, unified and ruled by a government of ethnic Chinese, entirely independent of the foreign influences which had plagued their history for centuries. Now the blatant exaggerations of the previous year's harvest were multiplied again, while the national grain harvest actually fell from 185 million tonnes to 30 million tonnes, and officials became more ruthless as they searched for hidden grain to meet their quotas.

In Ireland, little more than a century before, the worst famine the

Western world had ever known threatened 8 million people with starvation. In the winter of 1959–60, famine threatened 500 million people in China: 500 million – more than lived in all of North, Central and South America combined at the time. And every part of China was affected; there was no question of surpluses from one area being transported to relieve shortages in another. There were no surpluses. People were starving on good and poor land alike. Starving, and terrorised by officials desperate to fulfil demands from the level of authority above; no recourse to justice or assistance was available; people were living from day to day, surviving by guile or good fortune.

It was winter, and bitterly cold, [a survivor recalled], but . . . everyone was dressed only in thin and filthy rags tied together with bits of grass and stuffed with straw. Some of the survivors looked healthy, their faces puffed up and their limbs swollen by oedema, but the rest were as thin as skeletons. Sometimes she saw her neighbours and relatives simply fall down as they shuffled through the village and die without a sound. Others were dead on their earthen *kang* beds when she awoke in the morning. The dead were left where they died because she said that no one had the strength to bury them.

She remembered, too, the unnatural silence. The village oxen had died, the dogs had been eaten and the chickens and ducks had long ago been confiscated by the Communist Party in lieu of grain taxes. There were no birds left in the trees, and the trees themselves had been stripped of their leaves and bark. At night there was no longer even the scratching of rats and mice, for they too had been eaten or had starved to death . . .[10]

At least 30 million people died as a direct consequence of the Great Leap Forward.[11] Some estimates put the figure higher (up to 80 million), but none puts it lower. The most telling insight is a chart issued by China's own Population Research and Information Center, on which the green line denoting births plummets across an ugly black spike of rising deaths. Birth rates halved and death rates tripled during the Great Leap Forward.[12] But aside from the sheer scale of the disaster, what sets Mao's famine apart from all others is that it was entirely avoidable. It had not been caused by invasion or civil war; no floods had washed away the crops or droughts dried up the fields. No blight had destroyed the harvest, and the world would have shipped in emergency supplies if only China had asked.

But far from appealing for help, China kept the largest famine in history a secret from the outside world. Within the country the scale of the disaster – and its cause – was acknowledged among the higher echelons of government. Some brave souls even made efforts to relieve the distress, but Mao silenced the rumblings of discontent by unleashing the Cultural Revolution in 1966. All academics and intellectuals were sent to work on the land in distant villages, while Mao's Red Guards hunted down 'Party persons in power taking the capitalist road', among them Deng Xiaoping, who was condemned as 'the number two capitalist roader' and banished to the countryside but survived. The 'number one capitalist roader', Lui Shaoqi, former President of the Republic, was arrested, tortured and left to die in a cellar. Many other dissidents suffered similar fates.

The Cultural Revolution inflicted ten years of chaos and stagnation on a country which had just endured famine on a scale the world had never known. Mao remained obsessed with justifying his policies, but none of his dreams and grand promises were fulfilled. Living standards did not rise; food production declined. In short, the Great Leap Forward had been a huge slide backwards.

After Mao's death in 1976, it was Deng Xiaoping who emerged from the prolonged political machinations as the man in control of China. A pragmatist who put people's livelihoods ahead of ideology, he initiated the dismantling of the remaining collectives and instigated a programme of rural reforms that reinstated China's peasants as small farmers once again. Under Mao, China had spurned the improved farming inputs and methods developed elsewhere, but after Deng's reforms the peasants exploited these innovations enthusiastically. The amount of fertiliser applied in China tripled between 1977 and 1986. The national grain harvest rose from 286 million tonnes in the year Mao died, to 407 million tonnes in 1984. Peasants no longer merely survived on what they could grow, but could afford to buy cooking oil and meat, fish, vegetables and fruit.[13]

Mao's government had chosen to neglect the contribution that potatoes could have made to the Great Leap Forward. They did not consider them important enough to be included among the priority crops such as wheat, rice, maize, soybean and cotton, for which government targets were set each year. Potatoes were not listed among farm products the government accepted as agricultural tax; nor could they be grown for sale once local markets had been abolished. But lack of official and commercial incentive did not discourage farmers from exploiting the potato's value as a subsistence crop. They continued to plant potatoes – though allowed to do so after the commune's work on its annual crop quotas was sufficiently advanced.[14] Accordingly, production was localised; productivity was low; most of the crop was eaten close to where it was grown – but the potato persisted wherever it could be grown in China, once again proving its worth to people who had been left with few options.

From the potato's point of view, the Mao era was a period of marking time. Its potential was severely restrained by outbreaks of late blight and viral infections that swept across large areas of China in the 1950s. Like Ireland's crop in the 1840s, China's disease-struck potatoes were left untreated – not because the knowledge and wherewithal to protect them was lacking, but because Mao believed Lysenko knew best, and Lysenko had said that such diseases were caused by 'environmental' factors to which the progeny of any surviving tubers would be immune. They never were, of course. And while the recommendations of Chinese scientists who had been working on potato diseases for years were ignored, potato output during the Mao era is believed to have been only a fraction of its potential if the diseases had been correctly identified and treated.[15]

Though ineffectiveness gradually eroded enthusiasm for the Lysenko doctrine, China continued to rely on the Soviet bloc for its potato stock. Only after Mao's death and the reforms that Deng Xiaoping introduced in 1978 did the country's farmers begin to see more of what the potato had to offer. The depth of their ignorance surprised scientists from the International Potato Center (CIP), who were among the first foreign experts invited in to help the Chinese revitalise their food production programmes. On being asked what they had learned from the field school they had just attended, farmers from a remote village gave a most unexpected reply: 'That there is more than one kind of potato.' Until that day they had known only one variety, Mira, a bulky East German tuber that had been introduced in the 1950s and subsequently became so prevalent that the farmers believed it consti-tuted the entire species.[16]

It is not difficult to understand why Mira became so popular. With its northern European origins, Mira was a trusty 'rustic' potato of the kind that had fuelled peasant economies everywhere. It gave good yields, was a useful thickener of soups and stews, tasted good and filled the stomach – especially when there was not much else to eat. But the farmers' lack of alternatives had led to a dangerous dependence. The narrow genetic base of their potato fields heightened the risk of crop failure when disease or pests were about. Mira had withstood the onslaughts of late blight to begin with, farmers told the CIP scientists, but its resistance had broken down. When blight struck, yields were very poor. Viral infection of seed tubers was also a problem.

Such then was the parlous state of potato production in which Mao had left China. The situation improved steadily after the introduction of Deng Xiaoping's enabling social and economic reforms in 1978. When the government approved the potato as a commodity that could make a significant contribution to the economic development of the country, farmers were quick to take advantage of the advice and material assistance that government and international agencies were offering. Working with seed provided by CIP, plant-breeders at the Crop Research Institute in Kunming, Yunnan Province, developed a variety they named Cooperation 88 to reflect the importance of partnership in its development. The new variety delivered a massive yield gain over Mira, producing up to 60 tons per hectare. Within a few years, Cooperation 88 covered nearly one-quarter of the area devoted to potato in Yunnan, and had also spilled over into neighbouring provinces. Furthermore, Cooperation 88 seed tubers were being traded over China's borders, into Vietnam and Burma.

With extension programmes taking technical advice and expertise to farmers everywhere, and the incentives of new marketing opportunities, China's potato-growing area almost doubled in twenty years – from 2.45 million hectares in 1982 to 4.7 million hectares in 2002. Yields rose too, from an average of 9.7 tonnes per hectare to 16 tonnes during the same period. By 1993 China had become the world's leading producer of potatoes, and has remained the largest producer ever since. In 1961, China's output was not even one-twentieth of the world's potato crop; by 2005 it had risen to one-quarter, a total of over 73 million tonnes[17] – a large and growing proportion of which was consumed by people who had never seen a potato field and rarely handled raw potatoes: city-dwellers with a taste for fast food and snacks.

The social, economic and historical developments that took the potato from subsistence food in the Andes to industrial commodity in America and Europe stretched across three centuries. In China the process took less than three decades and brought China world dominance in potato production and consumption. During the same period, China also established itself as the workship of the world; then moved from the status of mass producer to that of mass consumer. By 2006, China had over-taken the United States as the world's leading consumer of everything from steel, copper and aluminium to mobile phones, from fertilisers to foodstuffs, and was scouring the planet for the raw materials and energy resources it needed to fuel growth and feed the nation's burgeoning appetites.

In terms of food resources alone, alarmists have predicted that China's growing population and shrinking harvests (as urban centres spread over agricultural land) will make the country dangerously reliant on imports just as the drive to produce biofuels reduces the amount of grain avail-able on world markets – thus forcing up global food prices and threat-ening to strain international relations.[18] From around the world, China already imports vast quantities of grain, soybeans, iron ore, aluminium, copper, platinum, phosphates, potash, oil and natural gas, forest prod-ucts for lumber and paper – not to mention cotton for its world-domi-nating textile industry. Such massive imports have put China at the centre of the world raw materials economy, driving up not only commodity prices but shipping rates as well.

The detrimental effects that China's emergence could have on the global environment, economic stability and balance of power in the twenty-first century are clear enough. But the prospects are not all bad. Improved standards of living also engender a sense of enlightened self-interest, and thus give the beneficiaries a vested interest in the future – in China and around the world.

In the 1990s, a typical Chinese housewife, Li Wen, shopped at her local street market and rarely spent more than £10 a week. Less than twenty years later, she is a successful businesswomen and mother of two in the booming city of Shenzhen in southern China, pushing a trolley through her local Wal-Mart, piling it high with goods that are not that much different from those a shopper in London or New York might choose; nor is the amount she spends on the weekly shop: £100. Mrs Li and her trolley epitomise the transformation of China from an inward-looking agricultural nation to an industrial behemoth in little more than the span of one generation.

In 1978, when Deng Xiaoping launched China's programme of social and economic reforms, Shenzhen was a fishing village. Today it is a free-trade zone of skyscrapers, factories and shopping malls. The city's population has surged to 12 million, average incomes are twice the national level and many residents are very rich indeed. Li Wen is one of them. Her family business, which deals in real estate and share trading, has funded the purchase of a three-storey villa, the VW Touareg she drives to the supermarket, and overseas travel at least three times a year. She also spends a lot of money on clothes. 'Compared to 10 years ago, I feel I know more about how to lead a good life,' she says.[19]

And who would begrudge her a share of the good life, after the poverty and subjugation previous generations had endured? A good life, not just for clever and entrepreneurial individuals like her, but for all.

George Bernard Shaw, the Irish author and ardent socialist, once remarked: 'If at age 20 you are not a Communist then you have no heart. If at age 30 you are not a Capitalist then you have no brains.' And it is true that while the selfless idealism of youth rarely survives the realities of adult life, the tenets of capitalism do indeed offer an acceptable compromise – with pragmatism clearing a way through the tangle of moral issues that the pursuit of personal advancement might engender, and recourse to charity salving the discomfort of having set youthful idealism aside. China, as a nation, has gone through a similar transformation; from the idealistic visions of the revolution, to the recognition of communist failings, and finally the pragmatic acceptance of capitalism as a viable means of harnessing individual energy and ambition to the common good. Mao was not wrong when he described China's peasant farmers as 'inherently capitalistic' but not only peasant farmers are inherent capitalists – we all are and now, at last, the Chinese are actively encouraged to pursue the fundamental ambition that motivates virtually all human endeavour: improvement, a better life, for individual and family; from potato field to city apartment.

And the potato has been similarly transformed, from the knobbly subsistence crop that hard-worked hands plant and harvest on the high slopes of the Andes, to the improved varieties that enhance the inherent qualities of the ancestral line – delivering tubers that are variously suited to all tastes and styles of home cooking; or ideal for the production of potato crisps, frozen french fries and starch on an industrial scale. And then there are the sleek thoroughbreds that NASA nurtures as an indispensible element of its plans for the flight to Mars; a propitious esculent indeed – feeding humanity as we have taken this generous bundle of nutrition from the Andes to the stars. It has been a long and often difficult journey, but for the potato and for us, eminently worthwhile.

Notes

Part One

1. To Mars from the Andes

1. Wheeler, 2006.
2. Wheeler et al., 2001.
3. Davies, He, Lacey and Ngo, 2003.
4. Wheeler, 2006, p. 84.
5. http://www.potato2008.org/en/potato/origins.html. See also: Ugent, Dillehay, and Ramirez, 1987; Spooner and Hetterscheid, 2005.
6. Brush, 1977. Brush, 2004.
7. Whitaker, 1941, pp. 3–4.
8. ibid., pp. 82, 12–13.
9. These paragraphs draw on sources cited in Brown, 2001.
10. Quoted in ibid., p. 494.
11. Whitaker, 1941, p. 87.
12. Cieza de Léon, 1553/1864, pp. 143, 361.
13. Whitaker, 1941, pp. 21, 26.
14. Mallon, 1983, p. 19.
15. Jacobson, 1993, p. 296.
16. Cited in ibid., p. 314.
17. Fitzgerald, 1979, p. 108.
18. de Haan, Bonierbale, Burgos and Thiele (in press).
19. ibid. http://www.geographyiq.com/ranking/ranking_Infant_ Mortality_Rate_aall.htm.
20. http://www.hrcr.org/docs/OAS_Declaration/oasrights2.html.

2. What exactly is a potato?

1. Heiser, 1969, p. 42.
2. Salaman, 1985, p. 124.
3. ibid., p. 131.
4. Hawkes, 1990, p. vii.
5. Ochoa, 1990, p. xxix.
6. Simmonds, 1995, p. 466.
7. Hijmans and Spooner, 2001.
8. Hawkes, 1990, p. 52.
9. Spooner et al., 2005.
10. ibid., p. 75.
11. ibid., p. 175.
12. Bradshaw, Bryan and Ramsey, 2006, pp. 51–2.
13. Hawkes, 2003, p. 189.
14. Lang, 2001, p. 163, quoting International Potato Center Annual Report 1993, Lima 1994, pp. 1, 12.

3. Domestication

1. Gregory, 1984.
2. Hall, 1992.
3. Papathanasiou, Mitchell and Harvey, 1998, p. 117.
4. Johns, 1989, p. 509.
5. Darwin, 1871, p. 167.
6. Ibid.
7. Sahlins, 1968.
8. Lee, 1968, p. 33.
9. Harlan, 1992, p. 14.
10. Wenke and Olszewski, 2007, p. 237.
11. Darwin, 1868, p. 325.
12. These paragraphs on the development of agriculture follow a review of the issues by Harlan, 1992, chapters 1, 2 and 3.
13. These paragraphs summarise a review of the issues given with references to original sources in Wenke and Olszewski, 2007, pp. 239–41.
14. Hawkes, 1989, pp. 482–3.
15. Johns, 1989, pp. 513–14. Johns, 1996.

4. Whence have they come?

1. Darwin, 1860, p. 303.
2. Ochoa, 2001, p. 129.
3. The quotations in the preceding paragraphs are taken from Darwin, 1860, pp. 205–6, 210–11, 213, 215.
4. Rubies, 1991, p. 225.
5. Quoted in Ford, 1998, p. 28.
6. Jefferson, 1781, p. 226.
7. Dillehay, 2000, p. 5.
8. Meltzer, 1997, p. 754.
9. Dillehay, 2000, p. xv.
10. ibid., pp. 161–5.
11. Ugent, Dillehay and Ramirez, 1987.
12. Meltzer, 1997, p. 754.
13. Fladmark, 1979.
14. Meltzer, 1997, p. 755.
15. Lee and DeVore (eds.), 1968, pp. ix, 304, 293.
16. ibid., p. 303
17. Dillehay, 2000, p. 170.
18. Earlier dates are often quoted, but their accuracy is in doubt. Indeed, material from a second occupation site at Monte Verde has been dated at 33,000 years ago, but Dillehay himself declines to accept this without more evidence or sites of comparable age elsewhere in the Americas: see Dillehay, 2000, p. 167.
19. Engel, 1970.
20. Dillehay, 2000, p. 173.
21. Lumbreras, 2001.
22. Salaman, 1985, p. 23.
23. Winterhalder, Larsen and Brooke Thomas, 1974.
24. Morris, 1999, p. 290.
25. ibid., p. 289.
26. Kolata, 1993, pp. 201, 205.
27. Morris, 1999, p. 292.
28. Protzen and Nair, 1997.
29. Wenke and Olszewski, 2007, p. 554.
30. Von Hagen, 1952.
31. Poma, 1978, p. 33.

5. A dainty dish

1. Stirling, 2005, p. 11.
2. Hemming, 1970, p. 73.
3. Lockhart, 1972, pp. 41–2.
4. ibid., pp. 330–31, 457–63.
5. Hemming, 1970, p. 106.
6. Quoted in Lockhart, 1972, pp. 57, 346–7.
7. Bath, 1963, pp. 18, 328. Vicens Vives, 1969, p. 506.
8. Braudel, 1973, vol. 1. p. 573.
9. Bakewell, 1984.
10. Hamilton, 1934, pp. 44–5.
11. Smith, 1776/1853, p. 415.
12. Super, 1988, pp. 25–6.
13. Stirling, 2005, p. 50. Hemming, 1970, p. 60.
14. Hawkes, 1966, pp. 219–20.
15. Cieza de Léon, 1553/1864, pp. 68, 255.
16. ibid., pp. 143, 361.
17. Quoted in Debenham, 1968, pp. 69–70.
18. Super, 1988, p. 42.
19. ibid., p. 15.
20. Hemming, 1970, p. 31.
21. Super, 1988, pp. 32, 35.
22. ibid., pp. 87–8.
23. Cook, 1981, p. 114.
24. Super, 1988, p. 88.

Part Two

6. The lonely impulse of delight

1. Fletcher, 1617, III, v.
2. Harbage, 1941, pp. 38, 41, 59–61.
3. Names, figures and dates are from sources quoted in Hall, 1998, p. 115.
4. W. Shakespeare, *The Merry Wives of Windsor* (1597), V, v.
5. W. Shakespeare, *Troilus and Cressida* (1603), V, ii.
6. Salaman, 1985, p. 425.
7. Fletcher, 1637, IV, iv. NB 'Eringoes' were candied sea-holly and 'cantharides' a powdered dried beetle (Spanish Fly). Both were considered to be aphrodisiacs.
8. Harrison, 1968.

9. Quoted in Salaman, 1985, p. 105.
10. Banks, 1805, p. 8.
11. For an engaging account see Arber, 1938, reissued 1986.
12. Ogilvie, 2006, p. 45.
13. Arber, 1938, reissued 1986, p. 251.
14. Ogilvie, 2006, p. 1.
15. Whittle, 1970, chapter 2.
16. Morton, 1981, p. 144.
17. Quoted in Ogilvie, 2006, p. 52.
18. Raven, 1947, p. 208.
19. Quoted in ibid., p. 207.
20. Salaman, 1985, p. 82.
21. Gerard, 1931, p. 269.
22. Salaman, 1985, p. 83.
23. Hawkes, 1966, pp. 249–62, 259.
24. The translation of Clusius from which these paragraphs are taken is in Salaman, 1985, pp. 89–91.
25. Ogilvie, 2006, p. 143.
26. ibid., p. 210.
27. Hernández, 2000, p. 111.
28. Lowood, 1995, pp. 300.
29. Ogilvie, 2006, pp. 266, 330 note 7. Ward and Lovejoy, 1999.
30. Drake, 1628/1854, pp. 97, 238.
31. Ogilvie, 2006, p. 77.
32. Hamilton, 1934, p. 196, note 2
33. Salaman, 1985, p. 143.
34. Hawkes, 1990, p. 32.
35. Hawkes and Francisco-Ortega, 1992.
36. Hawkes and Francisco-Ortega, 1993.
37. ibid., p. 3.
38. ibid., p. 5.

7. The way it was

1. Netting, 1981, p. 159.
2. McNeill, 1999.
3. Harrison, 1968, p. 276.
4. Capp, 2003, p. 6.
5. Forbes, 1979.
6. Coleman, 1974, p. 368.
7. Wrigley, 1969, p. 125. Cited in Kellum, 'Infanticide', p. 372.

8. Kellum, 1974, pp. 369–70.
9. Langer, 1974, p. 356.
10. Watts, 1984, pp. 68–9.
11. Kellum, 1974, p. 367.
12. Braudel, 1981, p. 74.
13. Tawney, 1912, p. 112. Overton, 1996, p. 172.
14. Augon, 1911, pp. 171–2, 189.
15. Frank, 1995.
16. Watts, 1984, p. 20.
17. Bath, 1963, p. 81.
18. Watts, 1984, p. 75.
19. Reader, 2004, pp. 137–8.
20. Rackham, 1986, p. 263.
21. ibid., p. 259.
22. ibid., p. 254.
23. Kowaleski, 2000.
24. Kowaleski, 1995, p. 245.
25. ibid., p. 88.
26. Dyer, 1998, pp. 7, 32–3, 49.
27. Overton, 1996, pp. 168–9.
28. Mark 14:7.
29. Watts, 1984, pp. 228–9.
30. Braudel, 1981, p. 143.
31. Watts, 1984, p. 251.
32. Tawney, 1912.
33. Overton, 1996, pp. 88, 15.
34. Bath, 1963, p. 184.
35. Quoted in Overton, 1996, p. 92.
36. Overton, 1996, p. 8.
37. Bath, 1963, pp. 164–5.
38. Overton, 1996, p. 41.
39. ibid., p. 68.
40. Drummond and Wilbraham, 1957, p. 100.
41. ibid., p. 35.
42. Harrison, 1968, p. 126.
43. Burnett, 1969, p. 80.
44. Dyer, 1998, p. 55.
45. Appleby, 1979, p. 115.
46. Quoted in Appleby, 1979, p. 115.

8. The demoralising esculent

1. Wilson, 1993, p. 13.
2. See Salaman, 1985, p. 599.
3. McNeill, 1999, p. 79.
4. Drummond and Wilbraham, 1957, p. 22.
5. Previous and following paragraphs summarise Vandenbroeke, 1971.
6. Translated by Hugh Jones from the French quoted in Vandenbroeke, 1971, p. 21.
7. The contentions of this and the following paragraphs follow McNeill, 1999, pp. 71–2.
8. ibid., p. 72.
9. See Vandenbroeke, 1971, pp. 34–5.
10. Quoted in Bruford, 1935, pp. 116–17.
11. Quoted in Kaplan, 1984, p. 47.
12. Kahn, 1984, p. 78.
13. Langer, 1975, p. 55.
14. Kahn, 1984.
15. Salaman, 1985, pp. 451–3.
16. ibid., p. 454.
17. Rickman, 1980, p. 2.
18. Hobhouse, 1999, p. 268.
19. ibid., p. 256.
20. This and the following references to Forster's tract are taken from the version printed in Forster, 1664/2001.
21. Quoted in Salaman, 1985, p. 447.
22. Lennard, 1932, p. 23.
23. Vandenbroeke, 1971, p. 30.
24. Drake, 1969, pp. 64, 54.
25. Malthus, 1914, p. 162; quoted in Drake, 1969, p. 63.
26. Langer, 1963, p. 8.
27. ibid.
28. See ibid., pp. 11, 13.
29. See ibid., p. 17.
30. Netting, 1981, chapter 7.
31. Fürer-Haimendorf, 1964, p. 10.
32. Drake, 1969, chapter 3 and p. 157.
33. Brandes, 1975, p. 180.
34. Baten and Murray, 2000.
35. Vandenbroeke, 1971, p. 39.
36. Clarkson and Margaret Crawford, 2001, p. 9.

9. Where the praties grow

1. O Gráda, 1993, pp. 98–9.
2. Edwards and Williams (eds.), 1956.
3. O Gráda, 1992, p. 19.
4. Woodham-Smith, 1962, p. 30.
5. A verse by the Reverend John Graham, who died in 1844, quoted in Kahn, 1984, p. 56.
6. Quoted in Salaman, 1985, p. 153.
7. Froude, 1893, pp. 584, 590.
8. ibid., p. 603.
9. From Wilde 1851/1989, p. 9.
10. Froude, 1893, p. 602.
11. Berresford-Ellis, 1975.
12. O'Flaherty, 1684/1846, p. 408.
13. Maxwell, 1954, pp. 125–6.
14. Cullen, 1987, p. 84.
15. Dickson, 2000, p. 117.
16. Connell, 1950, pp. 66–7.
17. Connell, 1950, pp. 73–4.
18. Dickson, 2000, pp. 114–15.
19. Connell, 1950, p. 91.
20. Dickson, 2000, p. 124.
21. Connell, 1950, p. 126.
22. Quoted in Clarkson and Crawford, 2001, p. 16. O'Flaherty, 1684/1846.
23. Clarkson and Crawford, 2001, p. 25.
24. Lucas, 1960, p. 21.
25. ibid., p. 22.
26. ibid., p. 25.
27. Quoted in Clarkson and Crawford, 2001, p. 19.
28. Quoted in Froude, 1893, p. 600.
29. Salaman, 1985, p. 217.
30. Clarkson and Crawford, 2001, p. 20.
31. Trow-Smith, 1957, pp. 229–30.
32. Quoted in Salaman, 1985, p. 161.
33. Quoted in Bourke, 1993, p. 17.
34. Connell, 1962, p. 60.
35. O Gráda, 1993, pp. 6–8.
36. Connell, 1950, p. 34.

37. Clarkson and Crawford, 2001, p. 134.
38. Connell, 1950, p. 48–9.

10. Seeds of famine

1. Clarkson and Crawford, 2001, p. 232.
2. Young, 1892, vol. 2, p. 120.
3. Salaman, 1985, pp. 199–200.
4. Quoted in Connell, 1950, p. 58.
5. Connell, 1962, pp. 59–60.
6. Clarkson and Crawford, 2001, p. 233.
7. From Wilde, 1851/1989, p. 14.
8. O Gráda, 1993, p. 3. Dickson, 1998.
9. Quotes from Bourke, 1993, p. 18–19.
10. Young, 1892, vol. 2, pp. 43, 45.
11. Quoted in Connell, 1950, p. 109.
12. Connell, 1950, p. 98, Appendix III.
13. Overton, 1996, p. 88.
14. Quoted in Clarkson and Crawford, 2001, p. 86.
15. Quoted in Connell, 1950, p. 70.
16. Bourke, 1993, pp. 36–7.
17. Clarkson and Crawford, 2001, p. 184.
18. Bourke, 1993, p. 52. NB Bourke gives no date for his figures, but they accord with an estimate for 1815 based on Connell, 1950, p. 25.
19. Woodham-Smith, 1962, p. 31.
20. Connell, 1950, pp. 158–9. Clarkson and Crawford, 2001, p. 70.
21. Bourke, 1993, p. 90.
22. Turner, 1996, pp. 228–30, 245–7.
23. Michael Gibbons, personal communication 2004, Clifden.
24. Quoted in Villiers-Tuthill, 1997, p. 4.
25. Villiers-Tuthill, 1997, pp. 7, 11.
26. Quoted in ibid., p. 45.
27. Villiers-Tuthill, 1997, pp. 64, 122, 125, 130.
28. Society of Friends, *Distress in Ireland 1846–'47*.

11. 'Woe the sons of Adam!'

1. Engels, 1892, p. 23.
2. Salaman, 1985, p. 342.
3. Smith, 1853/1776, section 8, p. 36.
4. Engels, 1892, pp. 51, 53–4.

5. ibid., p. 90.
6. Carlyle, 1899, vol. IV, pp. 138–9, 140.
7. Engels, 1892, p. 92.
8. ibid., pp. 93–4.
9. Carlyle, 1899, vol. IV, pp. 138–9.
10. Smee, 1846, p. 160.
11. Salaman, 1985, p. 314.
12. Woodham-Smith, 1962, p. 37.
13. Gash, 1976, p. 309.
14. ibid., p. 189.
15. *Gardeners' Chronicle*, 12 September 1845, editorial.
16. Woodham-Smith, 1962, pp. 35–6, 39–40.
17. McLean and Bustani, p. 820.
18. McCarthy, 1879, vol. 1, p. 349.
19. Woodham-Smith, 1962, p. 45.
20. Quoted in Stakman, 1958, p. 17.
21. McLean and Bustani, 1999, p. 821.
22. Greville, 1927, vol. 2, p. 179.
23. Quoted in McLean and Bustani, 1999, p. 822.
24. Peel, 1853, vol. 4, pp. 528–30.
25. For an illuminating discussion of this issue see Lusztig, 1995.
26. McCarthy, 1879, vol. 1, pp. 366, 359.
27. Peel, 1853, vol. 4, p. 639.
28. McLean and Bustani, 1999, p. 825.
29. Salaman, 1985, p. 299.
30. Vance, 1986, p. 216.
31. Boot, 1984, pp. 7 and 4.
32. Evans, 1849, p. 9.
33. Quoted in ibid., p. 23.
34. Evans, 1849, pp. 11, 28.
35. Boot, 1984, pp. 7–8.
36. Evans, 1849, p. 75.
37. Clapham, 1944, vol. 2, p. 213.

Part Three

12. The fatal malady

1. Glendinning, 1983, p. 48.
2. Knight, 1805. NB for the sake of clarity, these extracts from Knight's address are in an order that differs from the published account.

3. *Sturtevant's Notes on Edible Plants*, p. 545.
4. Humboldt, 1811, vol. 2, pp. 484, 489.
5. Quoted in Glendinning, 1983, pp. 486–7.
6. Knight, 1810.
7. Joseph Sabine, 1822, pp. 257–8.
8. Hawkes, 1958, p. 257.
9. Lindley, 1848, p. 67.
10. Bourke, 1964.
11. Niederhauser, 1991.
12. Andrivon, 1996.
13. Trevelyan, 1880, p. 65.
14. National Archives at http://www.nationalarchives.gov.uk. Salaman, 1985, p. 172.
15. Large, 1940, p. 141.
16. Lindley, 1845.
17. Cox, 1846, p. 486.
18. Bourke, 1991, p. 15.
19. ibid., pp. 15–16.
20. Large, 1940, p. 27.
21. Smee, 1846, p. 77.
22. Quoted in Desmond and Moore, 1991, p. 595.
23. Darwin, 1803, lines 247–50.
24. Charles Darwin to J. S. Henslow, 28 October 1845.
25. Bourke, 1991, p. 21.
26. ibid., p. 15.
27. Berkeley, 1846/1948.
28. Bourke, 1991, p. 22.
29. Quoted in Curtis and Barnes, 1989, p. 86.
30. Lindley, 1846, p. 643.
31. Large, 1940, p. 78–9.
32. Moore, 1846.
33. Thompson, 1848.
34. Millardet, 1933, p. 7.
35. Millardet, ibid., pp. 9, 25.
36. Large, 1940, p. 237.
37. Burton, 1989, p. 221.
38. Fry and Smart, 1999.
39. International Potato Center Annual Report, Lima, 1994, pp. 1, 12.

13. Co-opting science

1. Quoted in Salaman, 1985, p. 330.
2. Mayhew, 1861–2/1968, vol. 1, pp. 173–5.
3. www.measuringworth.com.
4. Salaman, 1985, p. 597.
5. Quoted in Kahn, 1984, p. 71.
6. The following paragraphs on potato breeding draw variously on Salaman, 1985, pp. 164–9; Burton, 1989, pp. 57–61; Lang, 2001, p. 45.
7. Burton, 1989, p. 36.
8. Kime, c. 1906.
9. www.measuringworth.com.
10. Royal Society, 1955. Mintz, 2002, p. 4.
11. These paragraphs draw on the preface to Salaman, 1985.
12. Salaman, 1911.
13. Laski, 1912.
14. http://www.eugenics-watch.com/briteugen/eug_sasl.html.
15. Salaman, 1985, p. 177.
16. Edmondson, 1977.
17. Furet, 1999.
18. A full discussion of Vavilov's work and influence can be found in the proceedings of a commemorative Centenary Symposium held in 1987 and published as *Biological Journal* of the Linnaean Society, vol. 39 (1990), part 1.
19. Vavilov, 1997, p. xxiii.
20. Hawkes, 2003, p. 15.
21. Hawkes, 2003, p. 17.
22. Vavilov, 1997, p. xvii.
23. www.learntoquestion.com/seevak/groups/2003/sites/sakharov/AS/biography/dissent.html.
24. Hawkes, 1958, p. 258.

14. Men on a mission

1. Throughout his life, John Gregory Hawkes (1915–2007) was known to friends and colleagues as 'Jack'.
2. Hawkes, 2003, p. 9.
3. ibid., p. 151.
4. ibid., p. 20.
5. ibid., p. 39.

6. ibid., p. 39.
7. ibid., pp. 64, 74.
8. For an explanation of these terms see the Glossary in Hawkes, 1990.
9. Hawkes, 1990.
10. Bryan et al., 2006.
11. Spooner et al., 2005.

15. Global voyage

1. Conklin, 1957.
2. http:/www.Ianra.uga.edu/potato/asia/png.htm.
3. National Statistical Office of Papua New Guinea, at http://www.nso .gov.pg/Pop_Soc_%20Stats/popsoc.htm.
4. Bourke, 2001.
5. Harris and Ngā Poai Pakeha Niha, 1999.
6. Savage, 1807.
7. Harris and Ngā Poai Pakeha Niha, 1999, p. 25.
8. Quoted in ibid p. 18.
9. Orange, 1987, p. 7.
10. Graham Harris, at http//slowfoodfoundation.org (n.d.).
11. Trought, 2005.

16. Developing worlds

1. Reader, 1988.
2. Chauvin, 2001, p. 157.
3. Sweet potatoes and other aspects of CIP's work were also applicable to the Millennium Development Goals, but are not relevant here.
4. CIP, *Food, Livelihood and Health*, International Potato Center Annual Report 2004, Lima (2005), p. 11.
5. World Bank, 2006.
6. World Bank, 2001.
7. Figures on PNG and NZ production from http://faostat.fao.org.

17. For the price of apples

1. Forbes.com, 2006.
2. http://www.potato2008.org/en/world/china.html.
3. Mengshan, 2004.

4. *People's Daily*, 2005.
5. Becker, 1996, pp. 88, 50–51.
6. Chang, p. 293.
7. Lang, 2001, p. 147. Chang, 1993, p. 296. Becker, 1996 p. 70.
8. Becker, 1996, pp. 88, 113.
9. ibid., p. 89.
10. ibid., pp. 1–2.
11. ibid., pp. 270–74.
12. Nicolas, Platzer and Menocal, 2004.
13. Becker, 1996, p. 263.
14. Wang, 2004.
15. Becker, 1996, pp. 69–70.
16. International Potato Center, 2001.
17. http://faostat.fao.org/site/340/DesktopDefault.aspx?PageID=340.
18. Lester Brown, 2004.
19. Watts, 2005.

Bibliography

Andrivon, D., 1996. 'The origin of *Phytophthora infestans* populations present in Europe in the 1840s: a critical review of historical and scientific evidence', *Plant Pathology*, vol. 45, pp. 1027–35

Appleby, Andrew B. 1979. 'Diet in sixteenth-century England: sources, problems, possibilities', in Webster (ed.), 1979, pp. 97–116

Arber, Agnes 1938 (reissued 1986). *Herbal – Their Origin and Evolution. A Chapter in the History of Botany* (3rd edn), Cambridge, CUP

Augon, Cecile, 1911. *Social France in the XVII* Century, London, Methuen

Bakewell, Peter, 1984. *Miners of the Red Mountain. Indian Labor in Potosi, 1545–1650*, Albuquerque, University of New Mexico Press

Banks, Sir Joseph, 1805. *Transactions of the Horticultural Society*, vol. I, p. 8

Baten, Jörg, and John E. Murray, 2000. 'Heights of men and women in 19th-century Bavaria: economic, nutritional, and disease influences', *Explorations in Economic History*, vol. 37; pp. 351–69

Bath, B. H. van Slicher, 1963. *The Agrarian History of Western Europe AD 500–1850*, London, Edward Arnold

Becker, Jasper, 1996. *Hungry Ghosts. China's Secret Famine*, London, John Murray

Berkeley, the Rev. M. J., 1846. 'Observations, botanical and physiological, on the potato murrain', *Journal of the Horticultural Society of London*, vol. 1, pp. 9–34. Reprinted as Phytopathological Classics no. 8, 1948, Lansing, American Phytopathological Society

Berresford-Ellis, P., 1975. *Hell or Connaught, the Cromwellian Colonisation of Ireland 1652–62*, Hamish Hamilton, London

Boot, H. M., 1984. *The Commercial Crisis of 1847*, Hull University Press, Hull

Bourke, Austin, 1964. 'Emergence of potato blight, 1843–46', *Nature*, vol. 203, no. 4947, pp. 805–8

Bourke, Austin, 1991. 'Potato blight in Europe in 1845: the scientific controversy', Pages 12–24 in: Lucas, Shattock, Shaw and Cooke (eds.), pp. 12–24

Bourke, Austin, 1993. *'The visitation of God'? The Potato and the Great Irish Famine*, Dublin; Lilliput Press

Bourke, Michael R, 2001. Intensification of agricultural systems in Papua New Guinea', *Asia Pacific Viewpoint*, vol. 42, nos. 2/3, pp. 219–35

Bradshaw J. E., G. J. Bryan and G. Ramsey, 2006. 'Genetic resources and progress in their utilisation in potato breeding', *Potato Research*, vol. 49, pp. 49–65

Brandes, Stanley H., 1975. *Migration, Kinship and Community: Tradition and Transition in a Spanish Village*, New York, Academic Press

Braudel, Fernand (trans. Sian Reynolds), 1973. *The Mediterranean and the Mediterranean in the Age of Philip II*, 2 vols, London, Collins

—, (trans. Sian Reynolds), 1981. *Civilization and Capitalism: 15th–18th Century*, Vol. 1, *The Structures of Everyday Life: The Limits of the Possible*, London, Collins

Brown, Kendall W., 2001. 'Workers' health and colonial mercury mining at Huancavelica, Peru', *The Americas*, vol. 57 (4 April 2001), pp. 467–96

Brown, Lester, 2004. 'China's shrinking grain harvest', Earth Policy Institute, at http//www.earth-policy.org/Updates/Updates36_printable.htm

Bruford, W. H., 1935. *Germany in the Eighteenth Century*, Cambridge, CUP

Brush, S. B., 1977. *Mountain, Field and Family: The Economy and Human Ecology of an Andean Valley*, Philadelphia, University of Pennsylvania Press

Brush, S. B., 2004. *Farmers' Bounty: Locating Crop Diversity in the Contemporary World*, New Haven, Yale University Press

Bryan, G. J., et al., 2006. 'A single domestication for cultivated potato', *Annual Report 2004/2005*, Invergowrie, Scottish Crop Research Institute, pp. 16–17

Burnett, J., 1969. *A History of the Cost of Living*, Harmondsworth, Penguin Books

Burton, W. G., 1989. *The Potato* (3rd edn), Harlow, Longman Scientific and Technical

Capp, Bernard, 2003. *When Gossips Meet. Women, Family, and Neighbourhood in Early Modern England*, Oxford, OUP

Carlyle, Thomas, 1899. *Critical and Miscellaneous Essays*, 5 vols., London, Chapman and Hall

Chang, Jung, 1993. *Wild Swans. Three Daughters of China*, London, Flamingo

Chauvin, Lucien O., in Graves (ed.), 2001

Cieza de León, Pedro de, 1553 (trans. C. R. Markham, 1864). *The Travels of Pedro Cieza de Leon*, Hakluyt Society, London, 1st series, vol. 33,

Clapham, Sir John, 1944. *The Bank of England, A History*, 2 vols., Cambridge, CUP

Clarkson, L. A., and E. Margaret Crawford, 2001. *Feast and Famine. Food and Nutrition in Ireland 1500–1920*, Oxford, OUP

Coleman, Emily R., 1974. 'Infanticide dans le Haut Moyen Age', *Annales ESC*, vol. 29, pp. 315–34, cited in Kellum, 1974, pp. 36–8

Conklin, H. C., 1957. *Hanunoo Agriculture*, Rome, UN Food and Agricultural Organisation

Connell, K. H., 1950. *The Population of Ireland 1750–1845*, Oxford, Clarendon Press

—, 1962. 'The potato in Ireland', *Past and Present*, no. 23 (November 1962)

Cook, David Noble, 1981. *Demographic Collapse: Indian Peru, 1520–1620*, Cambridge, CUP

Cox, H., 1846. 'Prize essay on the potato blight', *Journal of the Royal Agricultural Society*, vol. 7, pp. 486–98

Crawford, E. Margaret (ed.), 1989. *Famine: The Irish Experience 900–1900. Subsistence Crises and Famines in Ireland*, John Donald, Edinburgh

Cullen, L. M., 1987. *An Economic History of Ireland since 1660* (2nd edn), London, Batsford

Curtis, Helena, and N. Sue Barnes, 1989. *Biology* (5th edn), New York, Worth Publishing Inc.

Darwin, C. R., 1860. *Journal of Researches into the Natural History and Geology of the Countries Visited during the Voyage of H.M.S. Beagle round the World, under the Command of Capt. Fitz Roy R.N.*, London, John Murray. Final text. Available online at: http://darwin-online.org.uk

—, 1868. *The Variation of Animals and Plants under Domestication* (1st edn, 2nd issue), vol. 1, London, John Murray

—, 1871. *The Descent of Man, and Selection in Relation to Sex* (1st edn), London, John Murray

— to J. S. Henslow, 28 October 1845. The Darwin Correspondence Online Database, at http//darwin.lib.cam.ac.uk

—, 1913. *Journal of Researches into the Natural History and Geology of the*

Countries Visited during the Voyage round the World of H.M.S. Beagle (11th edition), London, John Murray

Darwin, E. 1803. 'The temple of nature or, the origin of society: a poem', London

Davies, Fred T., Jr, Chunajiu He, Ronald E. Lacey, and Que Ngo, 2003. 'Growing plants for NASA – challenges in lunar and Martian agriculture', *Combined Proceedings International Plant Propagators' Society*, vol. 53, pp. 59–64

de Haan, Stef, Meredith Bonierbale, Gabriella Burgos and Graham Thiele, 2006. *Potato-Based Cropping and Food Systems, Huancavelica Department, Peru* (in press)

Debenham, Frank, 1968. *Discovery and Exploration. An Atlas History of Man's Journeys into the Unknown*, London, Paul Hamlyn

Desmond, Adrian, and James Moore, 1991. *Darwin*, London, Michael Joseph

Dickson, David, 1998. *Arctic Ireland: The Extraordinary Story of the Great Frost and the Forgotten Famine of 1740–41*, Belfast, White Row Press

—, 2000. *New Foundations: Ireland 1660–1800* (2nd edn), Dublin, Irish Academic Press

Dillehay, Thomas D., 2000. *The Settlement of the Americas. A New Prehistory*, New York, Basic Books

Drake, Michael, 1969. *Population and Society in Norway 1735–1865*, Cambridge, CUP

Drake, Sir Francis, 1628. *The World Encompassed*, London, Hakluyt Society (1854)

Drummond, J. C. and Wilbraham, Anne, 1957. *The Englishman's Food. A History of Five Centuries of English Diet*, London, Jonathan Cape

Dyer, Christopher, 1998. *Standards of Living in the Later Middle Ages. Social Change in England c. 1200–1520*, Cambridge, CUP

Edmondson, Charles, 1977. 'The politics of hunger: the Soviet response to the famine, 1921', *Soviet Studies*, vol. 29 (4), pp. 506–18

Edwards, R. D. and T. D. Williams (eds.), 1956. *The Great Famine: Studies in Irish History*, Dublin, Brown and Nolan

Engel, F. A., 1970. 'Explorations of the Chilca Canyon, Peru', *Current Anthropology*, vol. 11, pp. 55–8

Engels, Freidrich, 1892. *The Condition of the Working-Class in England in 1844*, London, George Allen & Unwin

Evans, D. Morier, 1849. *The Commercial Crisis, 1847–1848*, London, Letts, Son & Steer

Bibliography

Fitzgerald, E.V. K., 1979. *The Political Economy of Peru 1956–78. Economic Development and the Restructuring of Capital*, Cambridge, CUP

Fladmark, K. R., 1979. 'Routes: alternative migration corridors for early man in North America', *American Antiquity*, vol. 44, pp. 55–69

Fletcher, John, 1617. *The Loyal Subject*, London

—, 1637. *The Elder Brother*, London

Forbes, Thomas R., 1979. 'By what disease or casualty: the changing face of death in London', in Webster (ed.), 1979, pp. 117–39

Forbes.com 2006. 'China's potato economy', http://www.forbes.com/2006/10/12/china-agriculture-mcdonalds-biz_cx_jc_1012potato_print.html

Ford, Thayne R., 1998. 'Stranger in a foreign land: José de Acosta's scientific realizations in sixteenth-century Peru', *Sixteenth-Century Journal*, vol. 29, no. 1, pp. 19–33

Forster, John, 1664. 'The politics of potatoes', reprinted in *Ode to the Welsh Leek, and Other 17th-Century Tales*, 2001, Cambridge, Mass., Rhwymbooks

Frank, Robert Worth, Jr, 1995. Cited in Sweeney (ed.), 1995, p. 227

Froude, James A., 1893. *History of England*, vol. 10, London, Longmans, Green

Fry, William E., and Christine D. Smart, 1999. 'The return of *Phytophthora infestans*, a potato pathogen that just won't quit', *Potato Research*, vol. 42, pp. 279–82

Fürer-Haimendorf, C.V., 1964. *The Sherpas of Nepal*, Berkeley, University of California Press

Furet, François, 1999. *The Passing of an Illusion: the Idea of Communism in the Twentieth Century* (trans. Deborah Furet), Chicago, University of Chicago Press

Gardeners' Chronicle, 12 September 1845, editorial

Gash, Norman, 1976. *Peel*, London, Longman

Gerard, John, 1931. *Leaves from Gerard's Herball. Arranged for Garden Lovers by Marcus Woodward*, London, Gerald Howe

Glendinning, D. R., 1983. 'Potato introductions and breeding up to the early 20th century', *New Phytologist*, vol. 94, no. 3 (Jul, 1983), pp. 479–505

Graves, Christine (ed.), 2001. *The Potato, Treasure of the Andes*, Lima, International Potato Center

Gregory, P., 1984. 'Gylcoalkaloid composition of potatoes: diversity and biological implications', *American Potato Journal*, vol. 61, pp. 115–22

Greville, Charles, 1927. *The Greville Diary* (ed. vol. Philip Wilson), 2 vols., London, Heinemann

Häkkinen, Antti (ed.), 1992. *Just a Sack of Potatoes? Crisis Experiences in European Societies, Past and Present*, Helsinki, Studia Historica 44

Hall, Peter, 1998. *Cities in Civilization. Culture, Innovation, and Urban Order*, London, Weidenfeld and Nicolson

Hall, R. L., 1992. 'Toxicological burden and the shifting burden of toxicology', *Food Technology*, vol. 46, pp. 109–12

Hamilton, E. J., 1934. *American Treasure and the Price Revolution in Spain, 1501–1650*, Harvard Economic Studies, vol. 43

Harbage, A., 1941. *Shakespeare's Audience*, New York, Columbia University Press

Harlan, Jack R., 1992. *Crops and Man* (2nd edn), Madison, Wisc., American Society of Agronomy Inc.

Harris, D. R. and G. C. Hillman (eds.), 1989. *Foraging and Farming. The Evolution of Plant Exploitation*, London, Unwin Hyman

Harris, Graham, and Ngā Poai Pakeha Niha, 1999. *Riwai Māori – Māori Potatoes*, Lower Hutt, Open Polytechnic of New Zealand

Harrison, William, 1968. *The Description of England* (ed. Georges Edelen), Ithaca, NY, Cornell University Press

Hawkes, J. G., 1958. 'Significance of wild species and primitive forms for potato breeding', *Euphytica*, vol. 7, pp. 257–70

—, 1966. 'Masters Memorial Lecture. The history of the potato', 3 parts, *Journal of the Royal Horticultural Society*, vol. 92, pp. 207–24, 249–92, 288–300

—, 1989. 'The domestication of roots and tubers in the American tropics', in Harris and Hillman (eds.), 1989, pp. 481–503

—, 1990. *The Potato. Evolution, Biodiversity and Genetic Resources*, London, Belhaven Press

—, 2003. *Hunting the Wild Potato in the South American Andes*, Botanical and Experimental Garden, University of Nijmegen

Hawkes, J. G. and J. Francisco-Ortega, 1992. 'The potato in Spain during the late 16th century', *Economic Botany*, vol. 46 (1), pp. 86–97

—, 1993. 'The early history of the potato in Europe', *Euphytica*, vol. 70, pp. 1–7

Heiser, Charles B., Jr, 1969. *Nightshades, the Paradoxical Plants*, San Francisco, W. H. Freeman & Co.

Hemming, John, 1970. *The Conquest of the Incas*, London, Macmillan

Hernández, Dr Francisco (1515–87), 2000. *The Mexican Treasury. The Writings of Dr Francisco Hernández*, (trans. Rafael Chabrán, Cynthia

L. Chamberlain and Simon Varey), ed. Simon Varey, Stanford, Stanford University Press

Hijmans, R. J. and D. M. Spooner, 2001. 'Geographic distribution of wild potato species', *American Journal of Botany,* vol. 88, pp. 2101–2112

Hobhouse, Henry, 1999. *Seeds of Change. Six Plants That Transformed Mankind*, London, Macmillan

Humboldt, Alexander von, 1811. *Political Essay on the Kingdom of New Spain*, Black's edn, vol. 2

International Potato Center, 1994. *CIP Annual Report, 1994*, Lima

—, 2001. *CIP Annual Report, 2001*, Lima

—, 2000. 'Cooperation pays: CIP supports China's drive to end hunger and poverty,' *CIP Annual Report*, Lima

Jacobson, Nils, 1993. *Mirages of Transition. The Peruvian Altiplano 1780– 1930*, Berkeley, University of California Press

Jefferson, Thomas, 1781 (ed. Merrill D. Peterson, 1984). *Notes on the State of Virginia*, Library of America, Literary Classics of the United States, New York. Available online at: etext.virginia.edu/jefferson/texts

Johns, Timothy, 1989. 'A chemical-ecological model of root and tuber domestication in the Andes', in Harris and Hillman (eds.), 1989, pp. 504–19

—, 1996. *The Origins of Human Diet and Medicine – Chemical Ecology.* Tucson, University of Arizona Press

Kahn, E. J., Jr, 1984. 'The staffs of life. II. Man is what he eats', *New Yorker*, November 1984

Kaplan, Steven L., 1984. *Provisioning Paris*, Ithaca, NY, Cornell University Press

Kellum, Barbara A., 1974. 'Infanticide in England in the later Middle Ages', *History of Childhood Quarterly*, vol. 1, pp. 367–88

Kime, T., c. 1906. *The Great Potato Boom*, privately printed pamphlet, in the Royal Horticultural Society's Lindley Library, London

Knight, Thomas Andrew, 1805. 'Introductory remarks', Transactions of the Horticultural Society London, vol. 1 (1807), pp. 1–2

—, 1810. 'On potatoes', Transactions of the Horticultural Society of London, vol. 1, pp. 187–93

Kolata, A., 1993. *The Tiwanaku: Portrait of an Andean Civilization*, Oxford, Blackwell

Kowaleski, Maryanne, 1995. *Local Markets and Regional Trade in Medieval Exeter*, Cambridge, CUP

—, 2000. 'The expansion of the south-western fisheries in late medieval England', *Economic History Review*, vol. 53 (3), pp. 429–54

Kupperman, Karen O. (ed.), 1995. *America in European Consciousness, 1493–1750*, Williamsburg, University of North Carolina Press

Lang, James, 2001. *Notes of a Potato-Watcher*, College Station, Texas A & M University Press

Langer, William L., 1974. 'Infanticide: a historical survey', *History of Childhood Quarterly*, vol. 1, pp. 353–65

—, 1963. 'Europe's initial population explosion', *The American Historical Review*, vol. 69, no. 1 (October 1963), pp. 1–17

—, 1975. 'American foods and Europe's population growth 1750–1850', *Journal of the Society for History*, vol. 8 (winter), pp. 51–66

Large, E. C., 1940. *The Advance of the Fungi*, London, Jonathan Cape

Laski, H. J., 1912. 'A Mendelian view of racial heredity', *Biometrika*, vol. 8, pp. 424–30

Lee, Richard B., and I. DeVore (eds.), 1968. *Man the Hunter*, Chicago, Aldine

Lee, Richard E., 1968. 'What hunters do for a living, or, how to make out on scarce resources', in Lee and DeVore (eds.), 1968, pp. 31–48

Lennard, Reginald, 1932. 'English agriculture under Charles II', *Economic History Review*, vol. IV, p. 23

Lindley, John, 1845. *Gardeners' Chronicle*, 23 August 1845, editorial

—, 1846. *Gardeners' Chronicle*, 26 September 1846, editorial

—, 1848. 'Notes on the wild potato', *Journal of the Royal Horticultural Society*, vol. 3, pp. 65–72

Lockhart, James, 1972. *The Men of Cajamarca. A Social and Biographical Study of the First Conquerors of Peru*, Austin, University of Texas Press, pp. 41–2

Lowood, Henry, 1995. 'The New World and the European Catalog of Nature', in Kupperman (ed.), 1995, pp. 295–323

Lucas, Anthony T., 1960. 'Irish food before the potato', *Gwerin*, vol. 3, pp. 8–43

Lucas, J. A., R. C. Shattock, D. S. Shaw and L. R. Cooke (eds.), 1991. *Phytophthora*, Cambridge, CUP

Lumbreras, Luis G., in Graves (ed.), 2001, pp. 52–3

Lusztig, Michael, 1995. 'Solving Peel's puzzle. Repeal of the Corn Laws and institutional preservation', *Comparative Politics*, vol. 27 (4), pp. 393–408

Mallon, Florencia E., 1983. *The Defense of Community in Peru's Central Highlands: Peasant Struggle and Capitalist Transition, 1860–1940*, Princeton, Princeton University Press

Bibliography

Malthus, T. R. *Essay on the Principle of Population*, London, Everyman edn (1914)

Maxwell, Constantia, 1954. *The Stranger in Ireland. From the Reign of Elizabeth to the Great Famine*, London, Jonathan Cape

Mayhew, Henry, 1861–2 (1968). *London Labour and the London Poor*, 4 vols, New York, Dover Publications

McCarthy, Justin, 1879. *A History of Our Own Times*, 4 vols, London, Chatto & Windus

McLean, Ian, and Camilla Bustani, 1999. 'Irish potatoes and British politics: interests, ideology, heresthetic and the repeal of the Corn Laws', *Political Studies*, vol. 47, pp. 817–36

McNeill, William H., 1999. 'How the potato changed the world's history', *Social Research*, vol. 66, no. 1 (Spring 1999), pp. 69–83

Meltzer, David J., 1997. 'Monte Verde and the Pleistocene peopling of the Americas', *Science*, vol. 276, pp. 754–5

Mengshan, Chen, 2004. 'The present and prospect of potato industrial development in China'; paper presented at the 5th World Potato Congress (2004). Available online at http://www.potato-congress.org

Millardet, Pierre Marie Alexis, 1885. *The Discovery of Bordeaux Mixture*, 3 papers (trans. Felix John Schneiderhan). Reprinted as Phytopathological Classics number 3, 1933, Ithaca, NY, American Phytopathological Society

Mintz, Sidney, 2002. 'Heroes sung and unsung', *Nutritional Anthropology*, vol. 25 (2), pp. 3–8

Moore, David, 1846. 'Experiments on preserving potatoes conducted at the Glasnevin Botanic Garden', *The Phytologist*, vol. 2, pp. 528–37

Morris, Arthur, 1999. 'The agricultural base of the pre-Incan Andean civilizations', *Geographical Journal*, vol. 165 (3), pp. 286–95

Morton, A. G., 1981. *History of Botanical Science*, London, Academic Press

National Archives at http://www.nationalarchives.gov.uk

National Statistical Office of Papua New Guinea, at http://www.nso.gov.pg/Pop_Soc_%20Stats/popsoc.htm

Netting, Robert McC., 1981. *Balancing on an Alp. Ecological Change and Continuity in a Swiss Mountain Community*, Cambridge, CUP

Nicolas, Alexander, Brian Platzer and Prof. deMenocal, 2004. 'Population control in China', p. 2 at http://www.columbia.edu/~bcp26/

Niederhauser, J. S., 1991. '*Phytophthora infestans*: the Mexican connection', in Lucas, Shattock, Shaw and Cooke (eds.), 1991, pp. 25–45

O Gráda, Cormac, 1992. 'For Irishmen to forget? Recent research on the Great Irish Famine', in Häkkinen (ed.), 1992, pp. 17–52

—, 1993. *Ireland before and after the Famine. Explorations in Economic History, 1800–1925*, 2nd edn, Manchester, Manchester University Press

O'Flaherty, Roderic, 1684. *A Chorographical Description of West or H-Iar Connaught*, ed. James Hardiman, 1846, Dublin

Ochoa, Carlos M., 1990. *The Potatoes of South America: Bolivia* (trans. Donald Ugent), Cambridge, CUP

—, 2001, in Graves (ed.), 2001

Ogilvie, Brian W., 2006. *The Science of Describing. Natural History in Renaissance Europe*, Chicago, University of Chicago Press

Orange, Claudia, 1987. *The Treaty of Waitangi*, Wellington, Allen & Unwin

Overton, Mark, 1996. *Agricultural Revolution in England 1500–1850*, Cambridge, CUP

Papathanasiou, F., S. H. Mitchell and Barbara M.R. Harvey, 1998. 'Glycoalkaloid accumulation during early tuber development of early potato cultivars', *Potato Research*, vol. 41, pp. 117–25

Peel, Sir Robert, 1853. *The Speeches of the Late Right Honourable Sir Robert Peel, Bart. Delivered in the House of Commons. 1853*, 4 vols, London, Routledge & Co.

People's Daily, 2005. 'Farmers' income gains on robust sales of potatoes', at http://english.people.com.cn/200510/19/eng20051019_215385.html

Pessarakli, M. (ed.), 2001. *Handbook of Plant and Crop Physiology*, 2nd edn, New York, Dekker

Poma, Huamán, 1978. *Letter to a King: A Picture-History of the Inca Civilisation by Huamán Poma*, arranged and edited with an introduction by Christopher Dilke, London, Allen & Unwin

Protzen, Jean-Paul, and Stella Nair, 1997. 'Who taught the Inca stonemasons their skills? A comparison of Tiahuanaco and Inca cut-stone masonry', *Journal of the Society of Architectural Historians*, vol. 56 (2), pp. 146–67

Rackham, Oliver, 1986. *The History of the Countryside*, London, Dent & Sons Ltd

Raven, Charles E., 1947. *English Naturalists from Neckam to Ray*, Cambridge, CUP

Reader, John, 1988. *Man on Earth*, London, Collins

—, 2004. *Cities*, London, William Heinemann

Rickman, Geoffrey E., 1980. *The Corn Supply of Ancient Rome*, Oxford, Clarendon Press

Royal Society, 1955. 'Salaman, Redcliffe Nathan. 1874–1955', *Biographical Memoirs of Fellows of the Royal Society*, vol. 1 (Nov. 1955), pp. 238–45

Rubies, Joan-Pau, 1991. 'Hugo Grotius's dissertation on the origin of the American peoples and the use of comparative methods', *Journal of the History of Ideas*, vol. 52 (2), pp. 221–44

Sabine, Joseph, 1822. 'On the native country of the wild potatoe', Transactions of the Horticultural Society of London, vol. 5 (1824), pp. 249–59

Sahlins, Marshall, 1968. 'Notes on the original affluent society', in Lee and DeVore (eds.), 1968, pp. 85–9

Salaman, R. N., 1911. *Journal of Genetics*, vol. 1, pp. 278–90

Salaman, Redcliffe N., 1985. *The History and Social Influence of the Potato* (rev. 1949 edn, ed. J.G. Hawkes), Cambridge, CUP

Savage, J., 1807. *Some Account of New Zealand*, London, John Murray

Scottish Crop Research Institute, 2006. *Annual Report 2004/2005*, Invergowrie, Scottish Crop Research Institute

Simmonds, N.W., 1995. 'Potatoes', in Smart and Simmonds (eds.), 1995, pp. 466–71

Smart J., and N.W. Simmonds (eds.), 1995. *Evolution of Crop Plants*, 2nd edn, Harlow, Longman Scientific and Technical

Smee, Alfred, 1846. *The Potato Plant*, London, Longmans

Smith, Adam, 1776/1853. *An Inquiry into the Nature and Causes of the Wealth of Nations, with a Life of the Author, an Introductory Discourse, Notes, and Supplemental Dissertations by J. R. McCulloch*, 4th edn, London, Longmans

Society of Friends, *Distress in Ireland 1846–47, Narrative of William Edward Forster's Visit to Ireland from the 18th to the 26th January 1847*

Spooner, D. M. and W. L. A. Hetterscheid, 2005. 'Origins, evolution, and group classification of cultivated potatoes', in T. J. Motley, N. Zerega, and H. Cross (eds.), *Darwin's Harvest: New Approaches to the Origins, Evolution, and Conservation of Crops*, pp. 285–307. New York, Columbia University Press

Spooner, David M., et al., 2005. 'A single domestication for potato based on multilocus amplified fragment length polymorphism genotyping', *Proceedings of the National Academy of Sciences*, vol. 102, no. 41, pp. 14694–14699

Stakman, E.C., 1958. 'The role of plant pathology in the scientific and social development of the world', *AIBS*, vol. 8, no. 5 (Nov. 1958)

Stirling, Stuart, 2005. *Pizarro. Conqueror of the Inca*, Stroud, Sutton Publishing

Sturtevant's Notes on Edible Plants (ed. U. P. Hedrick), 1919, New York

Super, John C., 1988. *Food, Conquest, and Colonization in Sixteenth-Century Spanish America*, Albuquerque, University of New Mexico Press

Sweeney, Del (ed.), 1995. *Agriculture in the Middle Ages*, Philadelphia, University of Pennsylvania Press

Tawney, R.H., 1912. *The Agrarian Problem in the Sixteenth Century*, London, Longmans

Thompson, Robert, 1848. 'Account of experiments made in the garden of the Horticultural Society, in 1847, with reference to the potato disease', *Journal of the Royal Horticultural Society*, vol. 3, p. 46

Trevelyan, Sir Charles, 1880. *The Irish Crisis*, London, Macmillan

Trought, K. E., 2005. 'Eminent NZ scientists in global push to decipher potato DNA code', at http://www.crop.cri.nz/home/news/releases/1133992658939.jsp

Trow-Smith, Robert, 1957. *A History of British Livestock Husbandry to 1700*, London, Routledge and Kegan Paul

Turner, Michael, 1996. *After the Famine: Irish Agriculture 1850–1914*, Cambridge, CUP

Ugent, D., T. Dillehay and C. Ramirez, 1987. 'Potato remains from a late Pleistocene settlement in south-central Chile', *Economic Botany*, vol. 41 (1), pp. 17–27

Vance, James E., Jr, 1986, *Capturing the Horizon: The Historical Geography of Transportation since the Transportation Revolution of the Sixteenth Century*, New York, Harper and Row

Vandenbroeke, Chr., 1971. 'Cultivation and consumption of the potato in the 17th and 18th century', *Acta Historica Nederlandica*, vol. 5, pp. 15–39

Vavilov, N. I., 1997. *Five Continents*, Rome, International Plant Genetic Resources Institute

Vicens Vives, Jaime, 1969. *An Economic History of Spain* (trans. Frances M. López Morillas), Princeton, Princeton University Press

Villiers-Tuthill, Kathleen, 1997. *Patient Endurance. The Great Famine in Connemara*, Dublin, Connemara Girl Publications

Von Hagen, V. W., 1952 (July). 'America's oldest roads', *Scientific American*, vol. 187, pp. 17–21

Wang, Qingbin, 2004. 'China's potato industry and potential impacts on the global markets', *American Journal of Potato Research*, vol. 81 (2), pp. 101–9

Ward, Bobby J. and Ann Lovejoy, 1999. *A Contemplation Upon Flowers: Garden Plants in Myth and Literature*. Portland, Ore., Timber Press.

Watts, Jonathan, 2005. 'The new China. A miracle and a menace', *Guardian*, 9, November, London, p. 24

Bibliography

Watts, Sheldon J., 1984. *A Social History of Western Europe 1450–1720. Tensions and Solidarities among Rural People*, London, Hutchinson

Webster, Charles (ed.), 1979. *Health, Medicine and Mortality in the Sixteenth Century*, Cambridge, CUP

Wenke, Robert J., and Deborah J. Olszewski, 2007. *Patterns in Prehistory. Humankind's First Three Million Years*, New York, OUP

Wheeler, R. M., et al., 2001. *Plant Growth and Human Life Support for Space Travel*, in Pessarakli (ed.), 2001, pp. 925–41

Wheeler, Raymond M., 2006. 'Potato and human exploration of space: some observations from NASA-sponsored controlled environment studies, *Potato Research* vol. 49, pp. 67–90

Whitaker, Arthur Preston, 1941. *The Huancavelica Mercury Mine*, Cambridge, Mass., Harvard University Press

Whittle, Tyler, 1970. *The Plant Hunters*, London, Heinemann

Wilde, William, 1851. Table of Irish Famines, 900–1500, quoted in Crawford (ed.), 1989.

Wilson, Alan, 1993. *The Story of the Potato through Illustrated Varieties*, Alan Wilson

Winterhalder, Bruce, Robert Larsen and R. Brooke Thomas, 1974. 'Dung as an essential resource in a highland Peruvian community', *Human Ecology*, vol. 2 (2), pp. 89–104

Woodham-Smith, Cecil, 1962. *The Great Hunger. Ireland 1845–9*, London, New English Library edn (1968)

World Bank, 2001. 'The costs of attaining the millennium development goals', at http://www.worldbank.org/html/extdr/mdgassessment.pdf

World Bank, 2006. Millennium Development Goals: http://web.worldbank.org/WBSITE/EXTERNAL/EXTABOUTUS/0,, contentMDK:2 0104132~menuPK:250991~pagePK:43912 ~piPK: 44037~theSitePK:29708,00.html

Wrigley, E. A., 1969. *Population and History*, London, Weidenfeld & Nicolson

www.measuringworth.com

Young, Arthur, 1892. *Tours in Ireland (1776–1779)*, ed. A. W. Hutton, 2 vols., London, George Bell & Sons

Index

Index

Index

Index